QUALITATIVE INQUIRY
AND GLOBAL CRISES

INTERNATIONAL CONGRESS OF QUALITATIVE INQUIRY

The International Congress of Qualitative Inquiry has been hosted each May since 2005 by the International Center for Qualitative Inquiry at the University of Illinois, Urbana-Champaign. This volume, as well as five preceding volumes, are products of plenary sessions from these international congresses. All of these volumes are edited by Norman K. Denzin and Michael D. Giardina and are available from Left Coast Press, Inc.

Qualitative Inquiry and Global Crises
2011, based on the 2010 Congress
ISBN 978-1-61132-021-3 hardcover 978-1-61132-022-0

Qualitative Inquiry and Human Rights
2010, based on the 2009 Congress
ISBN 978-1-59874-537-5 hardcover, 978-1-59874-538-2 paperback

Qualitative Inquiry and Social Justice
2009, based on the 2008 Congress
ISBN 978-1-59874-422-4 hardcover, 978-1-59874-423-1 paperback

Qualitative Inquiry and the Politics of Evidence
2008, based on the 2007 Congress
ISBN 978-1-59874-321-0 hardcover, 978-1-59874-322-7 paperback

Ethical Futures in Qualitative Research
2007, based on the 2006 Congress
ISBN 978-1-59874-140-7 hardcover, 978-1-59874-141-4 paperback

Qualitative Inquiry and the Conservative Challenge
2006, based on the 2005 Congress
ISBN 978-1-59874-045-5 hardcover, 978-1-59874-046-2 paperback

Another product of the congress is the quarterly refereed journal of the International Institute of Qualitative Inquiry. The *International Review Of Qualitative Research* is a peer-reviewed journal that encourages the use of critical, experimental, and traditional forms of qualitative inquiry in the interests of social justice. We seek works that are both academically sound and partisan, works that offer knowledge-based radical critiques of social settings and institutions while promoting human dignity, human rights, and just societies around the globe. Submissions to the journal are judged by the effective use of critical qualitative research methodologies and practices for understanding and advocacy in policy arenas as well as clarity of writing and willingness to experiment with new and traditional forms of presentation. Linked to the annual Congress for Qualitative Inquiry, much of the journal's content will be drawn from presentations and themes developed from these international meetings. The journal is also published by Left Coast Press, Inc.

INTERNATIONAL REVIEW OF QUALITATIVE RESEARCH
Editor: Norman K. Denzin
Quarterly in May, August, November, February
ISSN 1940-8447
For more information on these publications, or to order, go to
www.LCoastPress.com

QUALITATIVE INQUIRY AND GLOBAL CRISES

Norman K. Denzin
Michael D. Giardina

Editors

Left Coast
Press Inc.

Walnut Creek, California

Left Coast Press is committed to preserving ancient forests and natural resources. We elected to print this title on 30% post consumer recycled paper, processed chlorine free. As a result, for this printing, we have saved:

6 Trees (40' tall and 6-8" diameter)
2 Million BTUs of Total Energy
608 Pounds of Greenhouse Gases
2,927 Gallons of Wastewater
178 Pounds of Solid Waste

Left Coast Press made this paper choice because our printer, Thomson-Shore, Inc., is a member of Green Press Initiative, a nonprofit program dedicated to supporting authors, publishers, and suppliers in their efforts to reduce their use of fiber obtained from endangered forests.

For more information, visit www.greenpressinitiative.org

Environmental impact estimates were made using the Environmental Defense Paper Calculator. For more information visit: www.papercalculator.org.

Left Coast Press Inc.

LEFT COAST PRESS, INC.
1630 North Main Street, #400
Walnut Creek, CA 94596
http://www.LCoastPress.com

ISBN 978-1-61132-021-3 hardcover
ISBN 978-1-61132-022-0 paperback
ISBN 978-1-61132-023-7 electronic

Library of Congress Cataloging-in-Publication Data

Qualitative inquiry and global crises / Norman K. Denzin, Michael D. Giardina, editors.
  p. cm.
  Includes bibliographical references.
  ISBN 978-1-61132-021-3 (hardback)—ISBN 978-1-61132-022-0 (paperback)
1. Social sciences—Research—Methodology. 2. Qualitative research—Methodology. I. Denzin, Norman K. II. Giardina, Michael D., 1976-
  H62.Q343 2011
  001.4'2—dc22

                    2011006963

Printed in the United States of America

♾™ The paper used in this publication meets the minimum requirements of American National Standard for Information Sciences—Permanence of Paper for Printed Library Materials, ANSI/NISO Z39.48–1992.

CONTENTS

Acknowledgments

We thank our publisher of all publishers, Mitch Allen, for his continued support and guidance throughout the years. We also thank Carole Bernard for expert copyediting, Hannah Jennings for superb production design, and Katie Flanagan for assistance in gathering the index.

Many of the chapters contained in this book were presented as plenary or keynote addresses at the Sixth International Congress of Qualitative Inquiry, held at the University of Illinois, Urbana-Champaign, in May 2010. We thank the Institute of Communications Research, the College of Media, and the International Institute for Qualitative Inquiry for continued support of the congress as well as those campus units that contributed time, funds, and/or volunteers to the effort.

The congress, and by extension this book, would not have materialized without the tireless efforts of Katia Curbelo, Dong Hong, Melba Vélez, Koeli Goel, Li Xiong, Yiye Liu, Robin Price, and James Salvo (the glue who continues to hold the whole thing together). For information on future congresses, please visit http://www.icqi.org.

Norman K. Denzin
Michael D. Giardina
December 2010

Introduction

Qualitative Inquiry and Global Crises[1]

Norman K. Denzin and Michael D. Giardina

[W]e seemingly tolerate a rising level of violence that ignores our common humanity and our claims to civilization alike. We calmly accept newspaper reports of civilian slaughter in far off lands. We glorify killing on movie and television screens and call it entertainment. We make it easy for men of all shades of sanity to acquire weapons and ammunition they desire. Too often we honor swagger and bluster and the wielder of force; too often we excuse those who are willing to build their own lives on the shattered dreams of others.

— Robert F. Kennedy, 1968

Democracy, as well as social justice, is not a spectator sport. We cannot allow ourselves to simply sit on our couches and give passionate color commentary about what is happening in the world and how we must change it. When we do this we are playing a painful part in the continuance of the challenges we complain of. If we want the world to change it must start with us as individuals and our own actions. We can't do the same thing we did last year and expect anything in the world around us to get better this year. We have to be a part of any transformation we seek in the world.

— Cory Booker, 2011

Two glimpses of everyday life in the United States frame the collection of essays that follow: A few days after the calendar page turned forward into 2011, one of us was at our local regional airport awaiting the departure of a friend. To the right, a twenty-something U.S. Army recruit—smartly dressed in fatigues, carrying a small Nike duffel bag, soft baby-faced features betraying his nervous countenance—sat with his stoic, graying father, a solidly built man wearing weathered sneakers, faded blue jeans, a well-worn windbreaker, and a mesh army cap. For almost 30 minutes, the two sat quietly together, each clearly contemplating the forthcoming farewell and what lay beyond: a potential deployment abroad, possibly to Afghanistan—*the fact that the two might never see each other again.*

As departure time inched closer, the two made their way to the x-ray checkpoint and the now-normal theatrical performance of airport security measures. Father and son exchanged a brief handshake, which quickly evolved into a tight, warm embrace. As the father turned to leave, tears were visibly streaming down his cheeks; he hid his face in his hands, wiping them away. A middle-aged woman who witnessed the goodbye walked over and offered the man a tissue, then thanked him for his son's sacrifice to "our nation's freedom." He nodded a half-hearted smile and faded away into the crowd, lost in thought.

Not lost in the exchange is that the woman had her own tough farewell just a moment earlier, as she stood with her family trading goodbyes with her departing son of a similar age, who was heading back to college for his spring semester. Though dressed in all outward appearances of comfortable middle-classness (designer-brand labels, smartphones, high-end carry-on luggage, etc.), their topic of conversation centered on differently arrayed yet similarly striking problematics: decreasing student loan awards, low-paying part-time jobs, unexpected layoffs in the family—all-too-typical occurrences in the United States circa 2010.

The twinning of these two families and their young sons together as located within the current context of global crises is indicative of the far-reaching scope of the social, cultural, political, and economic uncertainty we currently face. A brief review of 2010 sheds further light. In January, the U.S. Supreme Court drastically altered the future of elections with its decision in *Citizens United v. Federal Election Commission*, which paved the way for unlimited corporate spending on campaign ads. In March, after a drawn-out political battle to pass the Affordable Care Act—which, when enacted, will effectively cover 95% all Americans (though not as a form of single-payer or with a public option, as progressives had hoped)—Republicans vowed to repeal the legislation because it was (to them) a form of socialism (among other things). In April, the Gulf Coast suffered yet another epic tragedy, this time caused by an accident on BP's Deepwater Horizon oil platform, which resulted in the greatest environmental disaster in U.S. history and caused untold damage to fish and wildlife as well as to the livelihoods of those living in the region. Also in April, the state of Arizona passed the controversial SB1070 bill, which implemented the harshest state-level immigration policy in the country and triggered both widespread calls for boycotts of the state as well as copy-cat legislation in several other states. Throughout the summer months, the Tea Party movement (among Republicans and some libertarians) gained momentum and ushered in a new class of reactionary if not nationalist elected officials (such as Rand Paul in Kentucky). To finish out the year, the eventual repeal of the discriminatory "Don't Ask, Don't Tell" policy related to gays and lesbians openly serving in the U.S. Armed Forces became fodder for those who continue to marginalize their fellow Americans. And through it all, the U.S.—in fact, the global—economy continued to try and right itself against a backdrop of rising unemployment and despair.

More globally, David Cameron's (shaky) Tory coalition government with Liberal Democrats in the United Kingdom came under fire for suggesting that education spending would be cut by an unthinkable 25% over the next 4 years, harsh news to a college and university system already facing £1.4 billion in cuts over the next 2 years (see Richardson, 2010); in South Africa, the spectacle of the 2010 World Cup of Soccer was hailed as a universal success, surprising news to those living in South Africa who saw global corporations sucking up the profits while the country realized only a 10% return on the £3 billion outlay of public funds used in staging the tournament (primarily used for building new stadium and updating infrastructure) (Neate, 2010); abroad in Afghanistan, the conflict raged on despite promises from the U.S. government to draw-down on schedule, with more lives lost every day; and throughout the world, the effects of global warming continued to be felt almost daily, as changing weather patterns wreaked havoc on crops, travel, and industry.

Yet, in the last analysis, it is the struggling middle class, the struggling working class, the struggling Main Streets and High Streets—but certainly not Wall Street—that bring global crises into focus: the struggling working-class soldier-to-be and the struggling middle-class student-for-now, forever intertwined in what Arundhati Roy (2004) calls a "checkbook and cruise missile" hegemony, or what Thomas Friedman (1999) somewhat differently explains as the notion that "McDonald's cannot flourish without McDonnell-Douglas." It is against such a notion that this volume is philosophically situated.

❀ ❀ ❀

The qualitative research community consists of groups of globally dispersed persons who are attempting to implement critical interpretive approaches that will help them (and others) make sense of the terrifying conditions that define daily life after the first decade of this new century. These individuals employ participatory, constructivist, critical, feminist, queer, critical race theory, and cultural studies models of interpretation. They locate themselves on the epistemological borders between postpositivism and poststructuralism. They work at the centers and the margins of intersecting disciplines, from communications to race, ethnic, religious, and women's studies, from sociology, history, anthropology, literary criticism, political science, and economics to social work, health care, and education.

As bricoleurs, they use multiple research strategies, from case study, to ethnography, phenomenology, grounded theory, biographical, historical, participatory, and clinical inquiry (Kincheloe, 2001). And, as writers and interpreters, these individuals wrestle with positivist, postpositivist, poststructural, and postmodern criteria for evaluating their written work. We are all interpretive bricoleurs stuck in the present working against the past as we move into a politically charged and challenging future.

Despite the numerous versions and traditions of qualitative inquiry,[2] the generic thread woven throughout involves a politics of the local, and a utopian politics of possibility (see Madison, 1998) that redresses social injustices and imagines a radical, progressive democracy that is not yet (Weems, 2002, p. 3). While constant breaks and ruptures define the field/s of qualitative research, there is a shifting center to the project: the avowed humanistic and social justice commitment to study the social world from the perspective of the interacting individual. From this principle flow the liberal and radical politics of action that are held by feminist, clinical, ethnic, critical, queer, critical race theory, and cultural studies researchers. Multiple interpretive communities now circulate within the field of qualitative research, but they are all united on this single point.

This volume is thus an ongoing part of the conversation we have been having for the last 5 years (see Denzin & Giardina, 2006a, 2006b, 2007, 2008, 2009, 2010; see also Denzin, 2009, 2010) concerning the moral, allegorical, and therapeutic project of qualitative research, the challenges faced by such radical inquiry, and the promise of its impact.

An Activist Project

Critical scholars are committed to showing how the practices of critical, interpretive qualitative research can help change the world in positive ways. They are committed to creating new ways of making the practices of critical qualitative inquiry central to the workings of a free democratic society. Such a commitment rests on the importance of interpretation and understanding as key features of social life. In social life there is only interpretation. That is, everyday life revolves around persons interpreting and making judgments about their own and other's behaviors and experiences—whether related to children's art (see Pineau, this volume), health care (see Flick, this volume), or the military (see Spry, this volume).

Qualitative inquiry can challenge the crises we face and contribute to social justice in the following ways[3]:

1. It can help identify different definitions of a problem and/or a situation that is being evaluated with some agreement that change is required. It can show, for example, how battered wives interpret the shelters, hotlines, and public services made available to them by social welfare agencies. Through personal experience narratives, the perspectives of women and workers can be compared and contrasted.

2. The assumptions, often belied by the experiences, that are held by various interested parties—policy makers, clients, welfare workers, or online professionals—can be located and shown to be correct or incorrect (Becker, 1967, p. 23).

3. Strategic points of intervention into social situations can be identified. Thus, the services of an agency and a program can be improved and evaluated.

4. It is possible to suggest "alternative moral points of view from which the problem, the policy, and the program can be interpreted and assessed" (see Becker, 1967, pp. 23–24). Because of its emphasis on experience and its meanings, the interpretive method suggests that programs must always be judged by and from the point of view of the person most directly affected.

5. The limits of statistics and statistical evaluations can be exposed with more qualitative, interpretive materials furnished by this approach. Its emphasis on the uniqueness of each life holds up the individual case as the measure of effectiveness of all applied programs.

Yet these are not innocent practices! First, this is a political and ethical position to take, a political and ethical project to undertake. It blends aesthetics, ethics, and epistemologies. It understands that power and knowledge are inextricably linked (Foucault, 1977). In a feminist, communitarian sense, ways of knowing are moral and ethical (Christians, 2000). They involve concepts of who the human being is (ontology), including how matters of difference are socially organized. The ways in which these relationships of difference are textually represented answer to a political and epistemological aesthetic that defines what is good, true, and beautiful to positions previously silenced or ignored.

Three interconnected criteria shape these representations of the world.[4] Interpretive sufficiency is the watchword (Christians, 2000, p. 145). Accounts should possess that amount of depth, detail, emotionality, nuance, and coherence that will permit a critical consciousness, or what Paulo Freire (1999) terms "conscientization" to be formed. Through conscientization, the oppressed gain their own voice, and collaborate in transforming their culture (Christians, 2000, p. 148).

Second, these accounts should exhibit a *representational adequacy* and be free of racial, class, or gender stereotyping (Christians, 2000, p. 145). And relatedly, texts must be *authentically adequate* in that they: (1) represent multiple voices; (2) enhance moral discernment; and (3) promote social transformation. Thus should texts empower persons, leading them to discover moral truths about themselves while generating criticism. These criticisms, in turn, should lead to efforts at social transformation (Christians, 2000, p. 147), helping persons imagine how things could be different—imagining new forms of human transformation and emancipation.

Properly conceptualized, such qualitative inquiry becomes a civic, participatory, collaborative project. It turns researchers and subjects into co-participants in a common moral project. This is a form of participatory action research, with roots in liberation theology, neo-Marxist approaches to community development, and human rights activism in Asia and elsewhere (Kemmis & McTaggart, 2000, p. 568). Such work is characterized by a shared ownership of the research project—an emancipatory, dialectical, and transformative commitment to community action (Kemmis & McTaggart, 2000, pp. 568, 598). It is a form of inquiry that "aims to help people recover, and release themselves, from the constraints embedded in the social media" (Kemmis & McTaggart, 2000, p. 598).

In this vein, as John Stanfield (2006, p. 725) argues, qualitative research should be used to bring about healing, reconciliation, and restoration between the research and the researched. This is what he calls the "restorative function of qualitative methodological techniques such as ethnography, oral history, case studies" (p. 725). Such inquiry can document or confirm social injustice, or the maltreatment of a powerless population. And it can be used as a practical methodology to transform "prolonged experiences of inter-group conflict ... into a peace-building experience" (p. 725). Such inquiry becomes a vehicle for helping persons make sense of their "newly found voices ... helping them move away from lives amputated by dehumanizing others" (p. 725). This kind of work goes beyond participatory inquiry alone, asking that researchers "realize that they are in need of healing, of recovering their humanity, while communing with the other we define as the research" (p. 726).

Additionally, and as a cultural critic, the researcher speaks from an informed moral and ethical position. He or she is anchored in a specific community of progressive moral discourse. The moral researcher-as-performer takes sides, working always on the side of those who seek a genuine grassroots democracy (Hartnett, 1998, p. 288). This business of taking sides is a complex process (Becker, 1967), involving the following steps: Researchers must make their own positions clear, including the so-called facts and ideological assumptions that they attach to these positions. Scholars must identify and analyze the values and claims to objective knowledge that organize positions that are contrary to their own. In so doing, they will show how these appeals to ideology and objective knowledge reflect a particular moral and historical standpoint, showing how this standpoint disadvantages, and disempowers, members of a specific group.

On the politics of "taking sides," Roy (2005) is worth listening to at length. She speaks for us:

> I take a position. I have a point of view. What's worse, I make it clear that I think it's right and moral to take that position and what's even worse, use everything in my power to flagrantly solicit support for that position. For a writer of the 21st century, that's considered a pretty uncool, unsophisticated thing to do. It skates uncomfortably close to the territory occupied by political party ideologues—a breed of people that the world has learned (quite rightly) to mistrust. I'm aware of this. I'm all for being circumspect. I'm all for discretion, prudence, tentativeness, subtlety, ambiguity, complexity. ... I love the unanswered question,

the unresolved story, the unclimbed mountain, the tender shard of an incomplete dream. Most of the time.

But is it mandatory for a writer to be ambiguous about everything? Isn't it true that there have been fearful episodes in human history when prudence and discretion would have just been euphemisms for pusillanimity? When caution was actually cowardice? When sophistication was disguised decadence? When circumspection was really a kind of espousal? Isn't it true, or at least theoretically possible, that there are times in the life of a people or a nation when the political climate demands that we—even the most sophisticated of us—overtly take sides? I believe that such times are upon us. And I believe that in the coming years, intellectuals and artists will be called upon to take sides. ... We will be forced to ask ourselves some very uncomfortable questions about our values and traditions, our vision for the future, our responsibilities as citizens, the legitimacy of our "democratic institutions," the role of the state, the police, the army, the judiciary and the intellectual community. (p. 12)

Related, and on the *academic* politics of Roy's point, Freire (1998) is quite clear when he asserts in *Pedagogy of Freedom* that:

My abhorrence of neoliberalism helps to explain my legitimate anger when I speak of the injustices to which the ragpickers among humanity are condemned. It also explains my total lack of interest in any pretension of impartiality. I am not impartial, or objective. ... [This] *does not prevent me from holding always a rigorously ethical position.* [p. 22; emphases added]

Consider, then, advocates of the black arts movement in the 1970s, which insisted that *art* must function *politically*.[5] Maulana Karenga ([1972] 1997), in particular argued, that black art should be political, functional, collective, and committed.[6] Politically and functionally, it would be about blacks, made by blacks for blacks, and located in local black communities, as in Du Bois's (1926, p. 134) black theater. This community art would support and "respond positively to the reality of a revolution" (Karenga [1972] 1997, p. 1973). It would not be art *qua* art; rather, it would be art for persons in the black community, art for "Sammy the shoeshine boy, T.C. the truck driver, K.P. the unwilling soldiers" (p. 1974).

As Karenga pronounced, "We do not need pictures of oranges in a bowl, or trees standing innocently in the midst of a wasteland ... or fat white women smiling lewdly... If we must paint oranges or trees, let our guerillas be eating those for strength and using those trees for cover" (p. 1974). Collectively, Karenga argued, black art comes *from* the people, and it must be returned *to the people* "in a form more beautiful and colorful than it was in real life ... art is everyday life given more form and color" (p. 1974). Such work is committed to political goals. It is democratic. It is transformative. It is restorative. It celebrates diversity as well as personal and collective freedom. And it is not elitist.

●　●　●

What we are advocating, then, as we have done so previously (see Denzin & Giardina, 2006a, p. 4), is for an *activist qualitative inquiry*, a public intellectualism on the order of the kind Noam Chomsky advanced in his 1967 article "The Responsibility of Intellectuals," in which he argued that intellectuals (i.e., *you!*) have a moral and professional obligations to speak the truth, to expose lies, and to see events in their historical perspective. Although this activist-centered project may run antithetical to the *value-neutral pursuit of knowledge* that Martyn Hammersley (2008), Peter Adler and Patricia Adler (2008), Paul Atkinson and Sara Delamont (2006), and Sally E. Thorne (2009) see for qualitative inquiry, we see such a project as *sine qua non* for challenging the scale and scope of crises we now face in our everyday lives. This volume is one step in that direction.

The Chapters

With the above in mind, *Qualitative Inquiry and Global Crises* actively inserts itself into debates concerning social justice, advocacy, and human rights. To this end, the volume is loosely organized around three parts: (I) Theory; (II) Method; and (III) Performance. Its topics: critical pedagogy, crises in humanism; consumer society; technology; mixed methods; fragmented research; splintered subjects; wartime art; broken promises; men, wars, and military machines; praise for the sacred; globalizing the rural; global economic meltdown; inquiry for justice; inquiry for peace—a collection of voices united in common purpose.

To begin Part I, Judith Preissle and Kathleen deMarrais ("Teaching Qualitative Research Responsively") advocate for what they refer to as qualitative pedagogy, or the ways of teaching and learning qualitative research that is responsive, reflexive, recursive, reflective, and contextual. Focusing primarily on responsiveness— "the interaction between researcher and research participant that generates information or data sought and where knowledge flows both ways between researcher and participant"—their chapter is a siren call for an inclusive curriculum and instruction for qualitative research design, methods, and traditions.

In Chapter 2 ("Refusing Human Being in Humanist Qualitative Inquiry"), Elizabeth Adams St. Pierre calls for the resurgence of postmodernism, a philosophically informed inquiry that will resist calls for scientifically based forms of research. In so doing, she offers a powerful postmodern critique of conventional humanistic qualitative methodology and argues that it is time for qualitative inquiry to reinvent itself, to put under erasure all that has been accomplished, so that something different can be done—a "rigorous re-imagining of a capacious science that cannot be defined in advance and is never the same again."

Working in philosophical tandem with the previous chapter, Svend Brinkmann's chapter ("Interviewing and the Production of the Conversational Self") addresses the changing formulation of interviewing within a consumer society that is a de facto interview society. Viewing all human research as conversational at its core, Brinkmann reveals not only how "our interpersonal social reality is constituted by conversations," but also the self—the "processes of our lives." Pushing back against the growing notion that interviewing is either a passive recording of opinion or an empathetic entrée into someone else's life, he turns to the notion of the epistemic interview (in the vein of Socrates) and its ethical considerations, arguing that such an approach is most useful in the current context.

Part II begins with Chapter 4 ("Qualitative Research, Technology, and Global Change"), by Judith Davidson and Silvana di Gregorio. Addressing changing conditions and practices for which qualitative data analysis software has come into increasing but still niche usage, the authors chart the trajectory of such packages and offer commentary as to its potential use value (such as dealing with "unstructured data"). They also point to a need for a greater critical discussion of such tools, especially as related to ethical standards and security.

Michelle Salazar Perez and Gaile S. Cannella follow in Chapter 5 ("Using Situational Analysis for Critical Qualitative Research Purposes"), which takes up Adele Clarke's formulation of situational analysis in arguing for perspectives and methodologies "that challenge universals, normality, and truths while avoiding oversimplification and generalizations." Specifically, they outline situational maps and show how their application can aid in determining initial research questions. To do this, they use an example of their previous research conducted in New Orleans after Hurricane Katrina. As such, they provide examples of an initial topical map, a messy situational map, and ordered situational maps as they relate to that project, and suggest further applications in critical qualitative research.

In Chapter 6 ("Mixed Methods, Mixed Causes?"), Kenneth R. Howe investigates the relationship between research methods and conceptions of causation in mixed methods research. He begins by distinguishing the *natural* conception of causation from the *intentional* conception. He then argues that both conceptions of causation have a role in social research but that the two conceptions do not map on to quantitative versus qualitative methods. Rather the relationship is crisscrossing—quantitative methods can be used to investigate intentional causation and qualitative methods can be used to investigate natural causation—within an overarching framework of *mixed methods* interpretivism in which intentional causation is primary.

Uwe Flick follows in conversation with Chapter 7 ("Mixing Methods, Triangulation and Integrated Research: Challenges for Qualitative Research in a World of Crisis"). He begins by briefly outlining a theoretical background for analyzing crisis phenomena in the field of health care in industrialized societies. He then addresses the state of the methodological discussion about using different methodological approaches for analyzing a complex problem situation. The chapter concludes by turning to some examples from his recent research to discuss how to make such a mixing of methods—or perhaps, a triangulation of different approaches—work in a sound and integrated way.

Part III opens with Charles R. Garoian's lyrical poetic chapter ("The Exquisite Corpse of Art-Based Research"), which meditates on "educational research that more closely follows the imaginary and improvisational processes and practices of artists, poets, and musicians as compared with inquiry that is commonly associated with the logical-rational approaches in the sciences and social sciences." Engaging with an "Exquisite Corpse process" (or the collective assemblage words and images) for qualitative inquiry, Garoian addresses through five artistic examples how "fragmented research and practice" can enable creative and political agency.

In Chapter 9 ("Cinderella Story: An Arts-Based and Narrative Research Project"), James Haywood Rolling, Jr., presents "arts practice both as the manifestation of a fundamental human right to represent one's lived experience, and as a catalyst for the reclamation of interpretive and reinterpretive rights neglected." Weaving childhood remembrances and narrative collages together with a keen eye toward racial and class-based issues, Rolling's chapter is a powerful "transgressive reinterpration" of (his) identity and self in the historical present.

Continuing with the engagement of arts-based inquiry, Elyse Pineau's chapter ("Intimacy, Empathy, Activism: A Performative Engagement with Children's Wartime Art") focuses on a 2003 traveling exhibit of children's drawings titled *They Still Draw Pictures: Children's Art in Wartime from the Spanish Civil War to Kosovo* and the ways in which it relates to the power of the human spirit as detailed through her use of autoethnographic performance. Responding to swatches of one particular drawing (Miguel Ercano Garcia's, drawn from an "unidentified locale" during the Spanish Civil War), Pineau's vibrant, emotionally gripping, performative renderings bear witness to the transformative potential of art as a political act.

In Chapter 11 ("Fathers, Sons, and Protest at the School of the Americas: Countering Hegemonic Narratives of Masculine

Might and Militarism"), Tami L. Spry constructs through interviews a narrative collage regarding men, masculinity, and the military. Letting the voices of her research participants sing out in raw emotion and unguarded casualness while interspersing them with critical insight, Spry's text is a stark reminder of both the challenges facing, and progressive responses to, young people who grow up embedded in an always already context of expanding militarism (especially in the present moment of ongoing wars on terror and Homeland Security initiatives).

Cynthia Dillard's chapter ("Learning to Remember the Things We've Learned to Forget: Endarkened Feminisms and the Sacred Nature of Research") follows and draws on her engagements in Ghana, West Africa, as they relate to questions of race, memory, and identity. Utilizing the idea of the praisesong ("ceremonial and social poems, recited or sung in public at celebrations such as outdoorings or anniversaries or funerals"), Dillard calls on us to consider our very conception of self as it relates to our research practices, our very location our research practices. Thus, her chapter serves as a resounding response to the challenges of living and researching within and against global crises.

Isamu Ito's chapter ("Globalizing the Rural: The Use of Qualitative Research for New Rural Problems in the Age of Globalization") brings the section, and our volume, to a close. Offering preliminary findings related to the commodification of and consumer imperatives embedded within a curious rise in interest in "simpler times" in contemporary Japan, Ito comments on interviews conducted with rural people and how they relate to this upsurge in "rurality" among the more affluent urban. At its core, Ito is concerned with the performance of rurality and competitions over the very meaning of rural life.

By Way of a Conclusion

Qualitative Inquiry and Global Crises marks the sixth[7] entry in our ongoing conversation about qualitative research in the historical present. Each of these six volumes has found its genesis in and come out of our parallel involvement organizing the International Congress of Qualitative Inquiry, held annually on the campus of the University of Illinois at Urbana-Champaign. The first, titled *Qualitative Inquiry and the Conservative Challenge: Confronting Methodological Fundamentalism* (2006b), sought to actively contest the right-wing/neoconservative political direction of regulatory policy governing scientific inquiry in the United States. Such regulatory efforts—primarily those obsessed with enforcing scientifically based, biomedical models of research—raise fundamental philosophical, epistemological, and ontological issues for scholarship and freedom of speech in the academy.

Our second volume, *Ethical Futures in Qualitative Research: Decolonizing the Politics of Knowledge* (2007), charted a radical path for a future in which ethical considerations transcend the Belmont Principles (which focus almost exclusively on the problems related to betrayal, deception, and harm), calling for a collaborative, performative social science research model that makes the researcher responsible not to a removed discipline or institution, but to those he or she co-participates in and with. In so doing, personal accountability, the value of expressiveness, the capacity for empathy, and the sharing of emotionality are stressed. Scholars were directed to take up moral projects that decolonize, honor, and reclaim (indigenous) cultural practices, where healing leads to multiple forms of transformation at the personal and social levels, and where these collective actions can help persons realize a radical politics of possibility, hope, love, care, and equality for all humanity.

In our third volume, *Qualitative Inquiry and the Politics of Evidence* (2008), our authors challenged the very ground on which evidence has been given cultural and canonical purchase: What is truth? What is evidence? What counts as evidence? How is evidence evaluated? How can evidence—or facts—be "fixed" to fit policy What kind of evidence-based research should inform this process? How is evidence to be represented? How is evidence to be discounted or judged to be unreliable, false, or incorrect?

Our fourth volume, *Qualitative Inquiry and Social Justice: Toward a Politics of Hope* (2009) continued this conversation, taking on and advocating for a more activist-minded role for scholarship and research in the academy, of making a space for critical, humane discourses that create sacred and spiritual spaces for persons and their moral communities—spaces where people can express and give meaning to the world around them.

And in our fifth volume, *Qualitative Inquiry and Human Rights* (2010), which serves as a proem of sorts to the current text, our authors addressed pressing issues related to poverty, homelessness, racial, sexual, and religious discrimination, political persecution, torture, pain, and suffering. All of which collide here in out sixth volume, charting a course forward to attend to the global crises facing our various communities.

Taken together, all six volumes work in tandem to address a fundamental question—a question we presented in our very first volume in this series: *How are we as qualitative researchers to move forward in this new paradigm?* Scholars who share the values of excellence, leadership, and advocacy need venues to engage in debate, frame public policy discourse, and disseminate research findings. We need a community that honors and celebrates paradigms and methodological diversity, and showcases scholarship from around the world—scholarship that seeks to *intervene* in rather than simply comment on the historical present. As fellow travelers, we need research agendas that advance human rights and social justice through qualitative research. If we can do this, as Egon Guba (1990) makes clear, the rewards will be "plentiful and the opportunity for professional [and societal] impact unsurpassed" (p. 387).

We have a job to do; let's get to it!

Notes

1. Portions of this chapter are drawn and reworked from Denzin, 2010.

2. Of course, much of the field still works within frameworks defined by earlier historical moments. This is how it should be. There is no one way to do interpretive, qualitative inquiry. There are multiple interpretive projects, including: the decolonizing methodological project of indigenous scholars; Marxist theories of critical pedagogy; performance [auto]ethnographies' standpoint epistemologies; critical race theory; critical, public, poetic, queer, materialist, feminist, reflexive, ethnographies; projects connected to the Frankfurt school and British cultural studies traditions; grounded theorists of several

varieties; multiple strands of ethnomethodology; and transnational cultural studies projects.

3. Adapted from Denzin, 2001, pp. 1–7.

4. We thank Clifford Christians for clarifying these principles.

5. The following paragraph is reworked from Denzin, 2003, pp. 114–116.

6. One example being Amiri Baraka's (1979) poem "Black Art."

7. Or seventh, if you count our contextually related volume *Contesting Empire/ Globalizing Dissent: Cultural Studies after 9/11* (Denzin & Giardina, 2006a).

References

Adler, P., & Adler, P. (2008). Of rhetoric and representation: The four faces of ethnography. *Sociological Quarterly, 49*, 4, 1–30.

Atkinson, P., & Delamont, S. (2006). In the roiling smoke: Qualitative inquiry and contested fields. *International Journal of Qualitative Studies in Education, 19*, 6, 747–755.

Baraka, A. (1979). *Selected poetry of Amira Baraka/Leroi Jones.* New York: William Morrow & Co.

Becker, H. (1967). Whose side are we on? *Social Problems, 14*, 2, 239–247.

Booker, C. (2011). Hypocrisy. *Huffington Post.* http://www.huffingtonpost.com/cory-booker/hypocrisy_b_803962.html (accessed January 5, 2011).

Chomsky, N. (1967, February 23). A special supplement: The responsibility of intellectuals. *The New York Review of Books.* http://www.nybooks.com/articles/archives/1967/feb/23/a-special-supplement-the-responsibility-of-intelle/ (accessed January 15, 2011).

Christians, C. (2000). Ethics and politics in qualitative research. In N. K. Denzin and Y. S. Lincoln (Eds.), *Handbook of qualitative research* (3rd ed., pp. 139–164). Thousand Oaks, CA: Sage.

Denzin, N. K. (2001). *Interpretive interactionism* (2nd edition). Thousand Oaks, CA: Sage.

Denzin, N. K. (2003). *Performance ethnography: Critical pedagogy and the politics of culture.* Thousand Oaks, CA: Sage.

Denzin, N. K. (2009). *Qualitative inquiry under fire.* Walnut Creek, CA: Left Coast.

Denzin, N. K. (2010). *The qualitative manifesto: A call to arms.* Walnut Creek, CA: Left Coast.

Denzin, N. K., & Giardina, M. D. (2006a). Introduction: Cultural Studies after 9/11/01. In N. K. Denzin and M. D. Giardina (Eds.), *Contesting empire/globalizing dissent: Cultural Studies after 9/11* (pp. 1–21). Boulder, CO: Paradigm.

Denzin, N. K, & Giardina, M. D. (Eds.). (2006b). *Qualitative inquiry and the conservative challenge: Confronting methodological fundamentalism.* Walnut Creek, CA: Left Coast.

Denzin, N K., & Giardina, M. D. (2007). Introduction: Ethical futures in qualitative research. In N. K. Denzin and M. D. Giardina (Eds.), *Ethical futures in qualitative research: Decolonizing the politics of knowledge* (pp. 9–44). Walnut Creek, CA: Left Coast.

Denzin, N. K., & Giardina, M. D. (2008). Introduction: The elephant in the living room, OR advancing the conversation about the politics of evidence. In N. K. Denzin and M. D. Giardina (Eds.), *Qualitative inquiry and the politics of evidence* (pp. 9–52). Walnut Creek, CA: Left Coast.

Denzin, N. K., & Giardina, M. D. (2009). Introduction: Qualitative inquiry and social justice: Toward a politics of hope. In N. K. Denzin and M. D. Giardina (Eds.), *Qualitative inquiry and social justice* (pp. 11–50). Walnut Creek, CA: Left Coast.

Denzin, N. K., & Giardina, M. D. (Eds.). (2010). *Qualitative inquiry and human rights.* Walnut Creek, CA: Left Coast.

Du Bois, W. E. B. (1926). Krigwa Players Little Negro Theatre: The story of a little theatre movement. *Crisis,* July, 134–136.

Foucault, M. (1977). *Discipline and punish: The birth of the prison.* New York: Random House.

Freire, P. (1998). *Pedagogy of freedom.* New York: Continuum.

Freire, P. (1999). *Pedagogy of the oppressed.* 30th anniversary edition, with an introduction by D. Macedo. New York: Continuum.

Friedman, T. (1999). *The Lexus and the olive tree: Understanding globalization.* New York: Anchor.

Guba, E. (1990). Carrying on the dialog. In E. Guba (Ed.), *The paradigm dialog* (pp. 368–378). Thousand Oaks, CA: Sage.

Hammersley, M. (2008). *Questioning qualitative research: Critical essays.* London: Sage.

Hartnett, S. (1998). "Democracy is difficult": Poetry, prison, and performative citizenship. In S. J. Dailey (Ed.), *The future of performance studies: Visions and revisions* (pp. 287–297). Washington, DC: National Communication Association.

Karenga, M. ([1972] 1997). Black art: mute matter given force and function. In H. L. Gates, Jr., and N. Y. McKay (Eds.), *The Norton Anthology of African American Literature* (pp. 1973–1977). New York: W. W. Norton.

Kemmis, S., & McTaggart, R. (2000). Participatory action research. In N. K. Denzin and Y. S. Lincoln (Eds.), *Handbook of qualitative research* (2nd ed., pp. 567–606). Thousand Oaks, CA: Sage.

Kennedy, R. F. (1968, April 5). *Remarks of Senator Robert F. Kennedy to the Cleveland City Club* (also known as "On the Mindless Menace of Violence"). Cleveland, Ohio. http://en.wikisource.org/wiki/On_the_Mindless_Menace_of_Violence (accessed January 12, 2011).

Kincheloe, J. (2001). Describing the bricolage: Conceptualizing a new rigor in qualitative research. *Qualitative Inquiry, 7,* 6, 679–692.

Madison, D. S. (1998). Performances, personal narratives, and the politics of possibility. In S. J. Dailey (Ed.), *The future of performance studies: Visions and revisions* (pp. 276–286). Annandale, VA: National Communication Association.

Neate, R. (2010). South Africa recoups just a tenth of the £3bn cost of staging World Cup 2010. *The Telegraph* (London). http://www.telegraph.co.uk/finance/newsbysector/retailandconsumer/leisure/8192484/South-Africa-recoups-just-a-tenth-of-the-3bn-cost-of-staging-World-Cup-2010.html accessed January 3, 2011).

Richardson, H. (2010, June 23). Budget: Education funding faces 25% cut. *BBC.* http://www.bbc.co.uk/news/10378384 (accessed January 3, 2011).

Roy, A. (2004). *The checkbook and the cruise missile: Conversations with Arundhati Roy.* Boston: South End Press.

Roy, A. (2005). The ladies have feelings, so. … Shall we leave it to the experts? In D. Rothenberg and W. Pryor (Eds.), *Writing the world: On globalization* (pp. 7–22). Cambridge, MA: MIT Press.

Stanfield, J. H., II. (2006). The possible restorative justice functions of qualitative research. *International Journal of Qualitative Studies in Education, 19,* 6, 723–727.

Thorne, S. E. (2009). Is the story enough? *Qualitative Health Research, 19,* 9, 1183–1185.

Weems, M. E. (2002). *I speak from the wound in my mouth.* New York: Peter Lang.

Part I: Theory

Chapter 1

Teaching Qualitative Research Responsively

Judith Preissle
Kathleen deMarrais

Learning and teaching how to inquire, to conduct research, and to enact the various traditions of qualitative research was an informal, trial-and-error, ad hoc process in the social and professional sciences until well into the latter half of the twentieth century. Scholars learned by doing, by chatting with their colleagues, and, if they were lucky, by apprenticing with their more experienced teachers. With the expansion of higher education that began midway through that century, graduate students pursuing research degrees began to outnumber their teachers and apprenticeship became an inefficient, nearly impossible model for teaching and learning research. In the early 1970s, when Judith Preissle was a doctoral student at Indiana University, qualitative research approaches were discussed toward the end of the sociological research methods course, and in the anthropological field methods course they were buried among pressing concerns for learning indigenous languages and for adapting to different diets, sanitation practices, and etiquettes.

In this chapter, we advocate curriculum and instruction for qualitative research design, methods, and traditions highlighting philosophies, theories, and practices that capture the essence of the apprenticeship and learning-by-doing experiences while providing scaffolding and supports for research in the twenty-first century. Our overall approach is called "qualitative pedagogy," a term coined by Kathleen deMarrais in the late 1990s to refer to ways of teaching and learning qualitative research generated cooperatively by the qualitative methodologists at the University of Georgia. It assumes that the *principles* guiding the *practices* of qualitative research should guide instruction in qualitative research, and it represents an overall approach to teaching qualitative research to novices and others new to qualitative traditions. Our position is that we ought to teach our research practices in ways faithful to how we practice research and scholarship. The qualitative pedagogy we advocate is responsive, reflexive, recursive, reflective, and contextual (Preissle & deMarrais, 2009). Our focus in this discussion is what we call "qualitative responsiveness."

Responsiveness is a quality characteristic of many, but not all, qualitative research traditions. It refers to an interaction between researcher and research participant that generates the information or data sought and where knowledge flows both ways between researcher and participant. Responsive research places the researcher as self, as I who acts, in the midst of a research process (Wax, 1971; Wolcott, 1994, 2002) where the participant is what Buber ([1923] 1970) calls *thou* to emphasize the relationship between humans not customarily present when humans consider, study, or interact with inanimate objects:

> The form [of another person] that confronts me I cannot experience nor describe; I can only actualize it. ... And it is an actual relation; it acts on me as I act on it. ... Such work is creation, inventing is finding. Forming is discovery. As I actualize, I uncover. (p. 61)

Responsiveness contrasts with the external position required by much experimental and survey designs that depend on removing the researcher from the world studied but requires directive positions from the outside. Scholars are acting on, intervening, manipulating, and controlling, but in these approaches they are rarely *relating*. Qualitative research traditions vary in the extent to which responsiveness is valued and has been practiced. The ideal for much early fieldwork in sociology and anthropology was that participant observers should take a fly-on-the-wall position (Preissle & Grant, 2004). Researchers should be unobstrusive and endeavor to disturb the social scenes observed as little as possible. Initial field reports were often written from an omniscient position that took the researcher out of the site altogether. However, these were sometimes followed later by more candid accounts from the same scholars, reflecting about their relationships with participants (e.g., Malinowski, 1967; Mead, 1977). Relationships with participants have become more commonly reported in recent fieldwork in sociology and anthropology (Adler & Adler, 1987), and responsiveness is central in participatory action research (Torres, 1992), in some poststructural work (Davies & Gannon, 2009), in many feminist traditions (Reinharz, [1979] 1984), and in autoethnography (Chang, 2008).

Much research of all kinds involves both responsive and directive dimensions, but the emphasis varies from one study to the next or even across phases within studies. For example, some highly directive survey studies may result from cordial relationships between survey researchers and leaders in an organization seeking current information about the membership of their group. Responsiveness itself in the conduct of most qualitative research also varies. It is arguably strongest in the highly intensive interactions of lengthy clinical interviews, but it may ebb and flow across the course of a participant observation study. It may be most subtle in scholars' use of document analysis where self-conscious consideration of reader response theory (Rosenblatt, 1978) may assist researchers in exploring how they are relating to the material they are examining.

As an attribute of human relationships, responsiveness combines cognitive and affective dimensions, operating interactively in the position or stance of researcher to research topic and research participants and in the interaction among researcher, what the researcher believes the study to be about, and whomever the researcher is studying. We consider cognitive responsiveness to be the adaptation of topic and questions to research situation, to what is studied, whereas affective responsiveness is the openness of researcher to whoever is studied. Affective responsiveness centers on the social and emotional relationship of research to participants. Being in a relationship is a central source of information and understanding.

In an early piece on classroom ethnography, for example, Erickson (1973) discussed how researchers' emotional responses in interactions with participants are clues to what may be important in a research situation:

> Really "being there" means experiencing strong relationships with whoever else is "there" (one's "informants"). Some of these relationships may feel good and others may hurt. All of them *affect me and change me* [emphasis in original]. …This is the ethnographer's tour de force: to "make sense" of "outrageous" behavior complexes … by placing the behavior complex in its socio-cultural context. To pull this off as an ethnographer one must not suppress a sense of outrage while in the field, but still stay in there, and take advantage of one's rage, using it as a barometer to indicate high salience. … The method is not that of "objectivity" but of "discipline subjectivity." (p. 15)

What Erickson does in this text is link the affective to the cognitive. The responsive researcher watches and listens to those studied, monitoring his or her own emotional variations, and changes research questions and topics according to participant interpretations and meanings. What may result, then, is primarily cognitive.

Not all scholars can tolerate the challenges of affective responsiveness and being in relationships with participants. Ethical decisions are further complicated by relationships. Priorities of knowing may conflict with the priorities of caring. When researcher identity becomes part of what must be studied, research conduct becomes more difficult and complex. Reconciling inevitable pressures for objectivity—from the researcher's expectations of her- or himself, from professional demands, from public expectations of credible research—with the realities of social and personal subjectivity requires tolerating ambiguity, uncertainty, and instability.

Finally, responsive researchers seek to generate not only rich description of who, what, where, when, how, and why (LeCompte & Preissle, 1993), but also to achieve Geertz's (1973) thick description of the participants' perspectives on these facets of social experiences. Research problems and issues integrate participant views and meanings so that what is represented is a production with many actors, although typically only one or few playwrights.

Teaching qualitative research responsively requires that qualitative methodologists position themselves as learners and researchers, more skilled and experienced than the students, but on similar journeys to understand the world. We also study our instructional practice to better understand our teaching and learning. We also must tolerate, if not celebrate, ambiguity, uncertainty, and instability. We are teachers and learners; we are researchers but also participants: We must follow our students to be able to lead them in their own research journeys.

Qualitative methodologists study students as they-as-qualitative-methodologists study research participants. Responsive qualitative instructors seek to learn the students' goals in their learning, the backgrounds they bring to learning qualitative research, the skills and talents that support that learning, and the scholarly disciplines and perspectives from which they are drawing. To an extent this is necessitated by the diversity of academic fields represented in many courses in qualitative methods, where students enroll from across the social and professional sciences. However, even within single academic areas like sociology or education, students pursue a host of different questions, lines of research, and subfields. To connect research methods to student interests and developing specialties, methods instructors must learn something about those interests and specialties.

To accomplish this, qualitative methodologists may study other responsive pedagogies such as Dewey's (1902) progressive and pragmatic approach to education, Rousseau's ([1762] 1966) premise of the natural maturation of the individual, Montessori's ([1948] 1967) assertion that learning occurs in interaction with the environment, or Du Bois's later formulations of individual uplift requiring efforts of a whole community (see Alridge, 2008). These approaches to instruction place the learner in a relationship with the teacher where what is to be learned develops in and from their interaction. Research design, methods, methodologies, and philosophies are studied and enacted within various social transactions. Instructional practices essential to a responsive qualitative pedagogy include an inclusive curriculum, multiple and varied instructional activities, and experiences in different kinds of role taking.

An inclusive curriculum in qualitative research methods and design includes scholars from around the world who represent varied identities (nationalities, genders, races, etc.); novice scholars must be able to find themselves among qualitative researchers and methodologists. They must encounter work by scholars similar to them and different from them and methodological issues and concerns familiar as well as strange. Scholarship in all areas is global, and this must be reflected in the inclusive curriculum. An inclusive curriculum also represents the variety of qualitative research traditions and topics found among the students regularly attending a course; novice scholars must be able to find their interests represented. Qualitative methodologists need not be expert in all such traditions, topics, and interests, but failure to address the breadth and depth of the area constitutes a major breech in instruction.

A responsive pedagogy depends on multiple and varied instructional activities for students. Learners should have many opportunities to define, develop, and reformulate research goals. They should engage, review, and assess goals of other scholars, including those of the instructors. They should also practice developing and sharing subjectivity statements, exploring who they are in relation to others. Such statements should be expected to be fluid, changing over time, and reflecting learners' philosophies of identity, self, and human experience. Preparing, practicing, and critiquing many data collection and analysis approaches is central to a responsive pedagogy. Our experience has been that whatever approach is most foreign and challenging to our students is the one they assess as the most illuminating. They may say that they expect to never again "do" arts-based or phenomenological, or poststructural analysis "officially," but they will incorporate these approaches into their informal explorations of their material. Finally, opportunities to lead activities, to collaborate on activities, and to follow others' leadership provides novice qualitative researchers the experience of scholarly communities: how people work together, challenge one another, quarrel civilly, and develop and advance their common scholarship.

A responsive pedagogy provides learners with experiences in different kinds of role taking: authentic and merely practice. Novices should have experiences in being the researcher and being researched by others. They should write about people they know and people who are strangers to them. They should read analyses from data they provided to others. They should be the researcher studying from inside a group or community as well as outside the particular group being examined. They should try to be a key informant for another researcher and explore what that means. Likewise, they should have opportunities to "member check" the data they provide or the analysis from such data. These different kinds of engagement in research relationships sensitize novices to ethical concerns and to issues of research integrity.

We conclude by considering the challenges that we have recognized in undertaking a responsive qualitative pedagogy. Candidly, it is neither easy nor simple to teach qualitative research methods this way. It does not lend itself to the kind of packaged methods instruction offered by many online private universities or to the overly systematized material in many introductory qualitative research textbooks. We sometimes have too many students for too few instructors. Several years ago, we were amazed as one of our colleagues at an institution elsewhere figured out how to teach responsively to classes of sixty students.

As we have already noted, our students represent so many fields of study that we are sometimes overwhelmed. Instructors who depend on their confidence of expertise would be challenged. Another issue is that, in this approach, we remain responsible for assessing students accustomed to being mentored and coached. This is not only a role conflict for the instructors, but may be experienced as betrayal by our students. And, as we have already suggested, balancing cognitive and affective facets of responsiveness (i.e., when the knowledge is compromised for the relationship) is difficult for students and instructors. What has sustained us in responsive pedagogy is what we have learned about qualitative research in participating in our students' experiences and in what they are able to contribute to their fields of study. We urge our fellow instructors in research methods and design to reflect on their own pedagogies.

References

Adler, P. A., & Adler, P. (1987) *Membership roles in field research.* Newbury Park, CA: Sage.

Alridge, D. P. (2008). *The educational thought of W.E.B. Du Bois: An intellectual history.* New York: Teachers College Press.

Buber, M. ([1923] 1970). *I and thou.* (W. Kaufmann, Trans.). New York: Charles Scribner's Sons.

Chang, H. (2008). *Autoethnography as method.* Walnut Creek, CA: Left Coast.

Davies, B., & Gannon, S. (2009). *Pedagogical encounters.* New York: Peter Lang.

Dewey, J. (1902). *The child and the curriculum.* Chicago: University of Chicago Press.

Erickson, F. (1973). What makes school ethnography "ethnographic?" *Council on Anthropology and Education Newsletter, 4,* 2, 10–19.

Geertz, C. (1973). *The interpretation of cultures.* New York: Basic Books

LeCompte, M.D., & Preissle, J. (1993). *Ethnography and qualitative design in educational research.* 2nd ed. San Diego: Academic Press.

Malinowski, B. (1967). *A diary in the strict sense of the term.* London: Routledge & Kegan Paul.

Mead, M. (1977). *Letters from the field 1925–1975.* New York: Harper & Row.

Montessori, M. ([1948] 1967). *The discovery of the child.* (M. J. Costelloe, Trans.). Mattituck, NY: Amereon House.

Preissle, J., & Grant, L. (2004) Fieldwork traditions: Ethnography and participant observation. In K. deMarrais & S. D. Lapan (Eds.), *Foundations for research: Methods of inquiry in education and the social sciences* (pp. 161–180). Mahwah, NJ: Lawrence Erlbaum.

Preissle, J., & deMarrais, K. D. (2009). Qualitative pedagogy: Thinking about teaching ethnography and other qualitative traditions. Paper presented at the Fifth International Congress of Qualitative Inquiry, Urbana-Champaign, May 20–23.

Reinharz, S. ([1979] 1984). *On becoming a social scientist: From survey research and participant observation to experiential analysis.* New Brunswick, NJ: Transaction.

Rosenblatt, L. M. (1978). *The reader, the text, the poem: The transactional theory of the literary work*. Carbondale: Southern Illinois University Press.

Rousseau, J. J. ([1762] 1966). *Émile, or on education* (B. Foxley, Trans.). New York: Dutton.

Torres, C. A. (1992). Participatory action research and popular education in Latin America. *International Journal of Qualitative Studies in Education*, 5, 1, 51–62.

Wax, R. H. (1971). *Doing fieldwork: Warnings and advice*. Chicago: University of Chicago Press.

Wolcott, H. F. (1994). *Transforming qualitative data: Description, analysis, and interpretation*. Thousand Oaks, CA, Sage.

Wolcott, H. F. (2002). *Sneaky kid and its aftermath: Ethics and intimacy in fieldwork*. Walnut Creek, CA, AltaMira.

Chapter 2

Refusing Human Being in Humanist Qualitative Inquiry

Elizabeth Adams St. Pierre

What I call "conventional humanist qualitative inquiry" is grounded in the human being of humanism—the individual, person, or self who has an identity. I have discussed that description in detail elsewhere (St. Pierre, 2000) and will not repeat it here. We generally say that the modern subject began with Descartes's ([1637] 1993) statement we remember well, "I think, therefore I am" (p. 18), and that human was elaborated differently by others, including Locke ([1690] 1924), who is generally referred to as the first of the British empiricists as well as the founder of liberalism. Locke disputed Descartes, describing a "self," an "individual," with a personal identity (sameness over time) based on consciousness whose mind is, at the beginning, a blank slate with no innate ideas.

The descriptions of human being these two Enlightenment thinkers invented, as well as variations introduced by others (e.g., Hegel's unitary, reflexive self-identical subject), pervade the social and natural sciences. In general, they assume an epistemological, knowing, rational, conscious, a priori, grammatical doer who exists ahead of the deed. That is, they believe in the truth of grammatical categories, for example, that, in Descartes's sentence there actually exists a subject "I" that precedes the verb "think." But those particular descriptions of human being and the philosophy of the subject elaborated from them have always been contested, especially in the last century, when the horrors of World War II proved humans' capacity for evil and inhumane behavior.

Post-war French thought identified the "growing instability of the subject in the writings of Koyéve, Hyppolite and Sartre" (Butler, 1987, p. 185) until proclamations declared the death of that human being who no longer seemed either self-evident or desirable. As Peters and Marshall (1993) explained, some took the radical position that that "construct is merely a philosophical and cultural mystification which sought to persuade people that they 'had' ... this unique personal identity" (p. 21). In other words, we began to realize that all those descriptions of human being we'd been led to believe were true and real were merely *descriptions*. We'd become trapped in believing in "permanence, identity, and substantiality" (Finke, 1993, p. 15), trapped in old "habits of saying 'I' and 'we'" (Rajchman, 2000, p. 97). We realized we could now think and live human being differently. Foucault ([1981] 1997a) explained as follows:

> There were two possible paths that led beyond this philosophy of the subject. The first of these was the theory of objective knowledge as an analysis of systems of meaning, as semiology. This was the path of logical positivism. The second was that of a certain school of linguistics, psychoanalysis, and anthropology—all grouped under the rubric of Structuralism. (p. 176)

I would argue that conventional humanist qualitative inquiry took up both paths Foucault identified above—logical positivism and structuralism—as well as theories and practices that emerged from the interpretive and critical turns in the social sciences. But the concept repeated with minor variation in all those social science approaches is the human being of humanism.

The Individual in Humanist Qualitative Inquiry

We generally think of qualitative inquiry as interpretive, but the logical positivism and structuralism Foucault identified are quite evident in qualitative inquiry. The stubborn persistence of positivism is evident, for example, when researchers cling to an objectivist epistemology by using terms like "bias" and "triangulation," believe that knowledge *accumulates* and has *gaps* that *findings* can fill, believe in the clarity and transparency of language, and treat data (words in interview transcripts and field notes) as *brute data* and then code them out of context. Structural tendencies are normalist and rationalist and evident when, for example: (1) Researchers cling to linearity in concepts like research "process," "development," and "systematicity"; (2) they create structured wholes with underlying systems of regularities and inner meaning (e.g., humans who have an essential, authentic, inner voice); and (3) they force what might be always already disordered, contingent, and/or arbitrary into supposedly ordered, coherent, rational structures of meaning (e.g., organizing data into *themes* and *patterns* and *linear narratives*).

But qualitative inquiry early on resisted positivist and structuralist approaches and leaned toward interpretivism with its focus on the relation among "what is studied, the means of investigation, and the ends informing the investigator" (Rabinow & Sullivan, 1979, p. 13). Researchers' aim in interpretive research is to try to understand the meaning ordinary people (the person, the individual) make of their lives, to do fieldwork in natural settings where participants live, to elicit their descriptions of everyday lived experience in their own language, and then to reproduce as accurately as possible that meaning and experience in detailed descriptions in the research report. In that work, however, meaning-making and experience too often go untroubled and are assumed to be natural, real, authentic, simply the "way it is." For that reason, interpretive social science is critiqued for too much description and not enough theoretical analysis. Nonetheless, rich, thick description (especially of the individual, of participants) is a hallmark of much qualitative inquiry, even in supposedly critical research, which one would expect to critique the naturalness of oppression in identity.

Social justice agendas popular in qualitative inquiry are also mostly grounded in an essentialist liberal humanist individual, but in this research the focus is on the intentionality, innate agency, and free will of participants. In this work, an emancipatory model of agency claims that individuals can lift themselves out of oppression and alienation—once their consciousness is raised— no matter the circumstances, though it is debatable, for example, whether it is a kindness to tell children who live on the wrong side of all the identity categories—for example, race, class, gender, sexuality—that they can be whoever they want to be. In such circumstances, free will can become a heavy burden. Such romanticized, individualist approaches to liberation—guaranteed as they are by America's founding documents, themselves inspired by Enlightenment humanism—require and restore the humanist individual in both researchers who as liberators can hear and understand stories of oppression—the enlightened, privileged saviors who can recognize and act on injustice when they see it— and in participants—the oppressed who are required to "speak for themselves," to name their oppression.

In the first instance, however, we have learned the hard lesson that those we identify as oppressed may not agree with our diagnosis and may prefer that impositional emancipators leave them alone. In the second, as Spivak (1988, 1999), for example, argued some time ago, the oppressed individual, the subaltern, cannot speak for herself—she is not "authentic" or natural but rather the product of the very ideological, cultural, historical, and hegemonic conditions that oppress her. Neither her identity nor her voice is self-evident. Her speech, her voice, is not originary, primary, fundamental, true, or brute but only speech, and the experience it describes is the normalized and regulated product of her positioning and subjection. Social justice work in qualitative inquiry grounded in the liberal individual of humanism, then, may well secure rather than upend an essentialist, oppressed identity, which seems at odds with the goal of transformation.

An example of the refusal to interrogate the essentialist, humanist individual occurs when qualitative researchers celebrate and empathize with their participants by "letting the data speak for themselves" (professing to present transparent, primary truth as if the researcher's selection of the data is not itself a mediation, an interpretation, an analysis) and/or simply "tell stories" of experience that maintain the naturalness of the oppression and do not provide needed critique. These practices, found in interpretive approaches also, assume there is a deep truth about the human that can be brought to light, expressed in language, and known. As Scott (1991) argued, however, experience (stories, narratives) doesn't exist outside naturalized, established meaning; it cannot serve as uncontestable, reliable evidence; and it cannot serve as the origin or ground of our knowing. Experience is, rather, that which we must explain. Data cannot speak for themselves, and stories can simply endlessly repeat oppression. Even though experience matters a great deal, the work of the researcher is not to revel in the swamps of experience for too long but to investigate the discursive and material conditions that constrain what can be said and lived.

The privileging of uninterpreted experience, stories, narratives, and so forth in much conventional humanist qualitative inquiry not only points to the humanist individual but also to an overreliance on the empirical (Science), as if what we sense (hear, see, etc.) can legitimate what we know—but this is a tenet of logical positivism that rejects metaphysics. It is dangerous to believe in what we hear and see without theorizing what enables us to sense as we do (Philosophy). Of course, we're aware that such reliance can be dangerous—that's why in qualitative research we use concepts like "triangulation" and "member checks" as correctives. Nonetheless, the empiricism we practice assumes a founding, sensing, meaning-making individual separate from what it senses, and that assumption enables troubling binary oppositions: subject/object, mind/body, man/nature, self/other, human/not human, and so on.

In addition, privileging and celebrating experiences, stories, and practices exhibits nostalgia for the *real*, the *true*, the *authentic*—what we imagine is a foundational, immaculate, pure origin outside being itself to which we long to return. But that truth and that real are chimeras, fictions, and *neither can ever be outside human being* but can only ever be human being—the contingent, chaotic, impoverished limit of our imaginations and practices. We do organize and reorganize human being during different historical periods in different cultures using theories and practices laden with politics, power relations, values, and desire—not necessarily evil or mistaken, but surely in need of interrogation. The point is that the description of human being we live now is not the same as past descriptions nor must it continue in the future.

In sum, a particular description of human being is at the center of what I call "conventional humanist qualitative inquiry," whether it employs positivist, interpretive, critical, or other approaches in the social sciences; and that description, that assumption, that belief, enables descriptions of other linked concepts—e.g., truth, reality, experience, freedom—that form a "grid of intelligibility" (Foucault, [1976] 1978, p. 93) that organizes and structures a certain way of understanding the world. To rethink that understanding, we must rethink and disperse that central figure, human being.

Post Human Being: Subjectivity and Agency

Our task, then, is to problematize the individual, the self, the human being of humanism rather than to perpetuate it; "to cultivate an attention to the conditions under which things become evident … and therefore seemingly fixed, necessary, and unchangeable" (Rabinow, 1997, p. xix) and to attend to the "historical constitution of various forms of the subject" (Foucault, [1984] 1997b, p. 291). We must move away from the philosophy of the subject offered by humanism and understand the modern subject as a "historical and cultural reality—which means something that can eventually change" (p. 177). It can be quite startling to realize that humanism's human is not real but only a description, to understand that we've learned to recognize human being in a particular way, and that we could, in the same way, recognize ourselves differently.

As I mentioned earlier, by the end of World War II, it seemed imperative to rethink the humanist description of human being that had come to such a terrible fruition, and various scholars in the humanities and social sciences who were later labeled "postmodern" and/or "poststructural" began to deconstruct that subject by questioning the notion that it could be centered and "present" to itself (Derrida), to track its descent and emergence using genealogical analyses (Foucault), and to question its ontological status (Deleuze and Guattari). In effect, they followed Foucault's (1982) advice that "maybe the target nowadays is not to discover what we are but *to refuse what we are*—we have to promote new forms of subjectivity through the refusal of this kind of individuality" (p. 216; emphasis added).

This refusal was evidenced, for example, by avoiding concepts linked to humanism's human being, concepts like "I," "me," "myself," "individual," and "identity." A different concept that had been in use for some time, "subject," a deliberately ambiguous term, seemed useful in that it attempts to capture the ongoing construction of human being—the always already partial, fragmented, in-process nature of human being that is, at the same time, both subject to the disciplinary and normalizing aspects of power relations, discursive formations, and practices *and* able to resist subjection. Related concepts such as "subjectivity" and "subject position" began to be used. Subject position refers to fairly well-defined and recognized culturally constructed categories within which people live, categories that assume certain attitudes, beliefs, and practices (and thus experiences) that one must take up to perform that position acceptably—mother, husband, teenager, homosexual, professor, feminist, and so on. Subject positions can conflict as, for example, when one is, at once, a son chided by an elderly parent and a university professor preparing for a doctoral seminar.

Subjectivity implies the ongoing construction of human being, human being in flux, in process—at every moment being disciplined, regulated, normalized, produced, and, at the same time, resisting, shifting, changing, producing. But the concept subjectivity is often bandied about as if it is a synonym for identity and so is often pluralized—subjectivities—which implies there are unique wholes that can indeed be pluralized. Subjectivity, however, *implies* multiplicity, which can't be located or fixed in identity. It's not that we have multiple subjectivities; *we are subjects*—that's all we need to say (and, after Deleuze and Guattari, we don't need to say *we*).

An example of confusing subjectivity with identity, especially in qualitative inquiry, is the use of a "subjectivity statement," a document the researcher is supposed to write before he begins a study in which he's expected to describe his history, his positionality, his assumptions, his values, his investments in the project, and so on—he's expected to come clean, tell all, confess, reveal his true, inner self. Before he begins fieldwork, he must identify himself: "Here I am; this is who I am, where I came from, what I think, what I believe. I am a white, middle-class, well-educated, heterosexual female who grew up in a large farming family in Iowa. I ... I ... I. ..." This work is about identification. I suspect this kind of text, the subjectivity statement, came from Peshkin's (1988) article in which, perhaps gesturing toward the poststructural, he claimed to identify several of his own "subjectivities," though I would argue he meant something like "roles," a concept from sociology, as in "the roles I play in my research project." I believe the subjectivity statement is really an identity statement grounded in the humanist description of human being.

One problem with this kind of identity work is that researchers too often assume that once they've acknowledged their commitments at the beginning of a study, they're home free. Another is "reflection,"[1] the basis of the subjectivity statement, which alerts us to at least two other problems. The first is the notion that there is, indeed, a stable, conscious identity upon which to reflect. The second is that reflection can serve as a corrective and, thus, help guarantee the validity of a study. The idea is that if we reflect enough, especially in the subjectivity statement before we begin the study, we can *know who we are* and thus know when we're being "biased" or "subjective." All this is not to say that reflection is not useful, but that it is embedded in a particular description of human being and related concepts (validity/truth, objectivity).

Importantly, in all this, we see the notion that there is a researcher who exists ahead of the research—which is out there somewhere—a self-contained individual who moves right through the process from beginning to end, whole, intact, and unencumbered, already identified and secured in the subjectivity statement.

A question that inevitably comes up when discussing subjectivity is agency, choice, free will, freedom. If we no longer believe that an individual is born with innate agency, where lies freedom? Keenan (1997) argued that freedom is possible "only when the subject is not taken for granted" (p. 66), only when the subject is *not* given in advance. Butler (1995) doubted that agency is possible for an a priori subject, when identity is secured in advance of living, because the essentialist, humanist individual "always and already knows its transcendental ground, and speaks only and always from that ground. To be so grounded is nearly to be buried: it is to refuse alterity, to reject contestation, to decline that risk of self-transformation perpetually posed by democratic life" (pp. 131–132).

Butler's point is that an essentialist individual cannot be free, cannot change or be transformed because its foundational, organizing essence must stay the same throughout time and across all occasions of living. At the core, that individual can only ever be "I." That we believe this idea to be true is illustrated by the common statement, "This is the way I am. Take it or leave it." That statement can be made only in a discursive and material formation that assumes an essentialist human being who cannot change, who is, in fact, stuck, shut down.

But Butler (1990) argued that freedom lies in our ability *not to repeat ourselves,* in the possibility of practicing "*subversive repetition*" (p. 42) or "*subversive citation*" (Butler, 1995, p. 135; emphases added). If the subject is not given in advance, then it must be constructed within everyday living, within linguistic, cultural, and material formations and practices organized within power relations, values, and so on. "To be constituted by language is to be produced within a given network of power/discourse which is open to resignification, redeployment, subversive citation from within, and interruption and inadvertent convergences with other such networks. 'Agency' is to be found precisely at such junctures where discourse is renewed" (Butler, 1995, p. 135).

Butler's point is that freedom, agency, and choice are possible even though not innate. Freedom does not exist prior to living but becomes available through cultural practices, both existing and invented, in the course of everyday living. What is important is that we can employ those practices of freedom and choose not to repeat ourselves—to be identical. But if we choose not to repeat practices that identify us to others, if we refuse what we are as Foucault advised, if we repeat ourselves differently too often, it can be disturbing for others who might say something like, "You haven't been yourself lately. What happened?," as if there's something wrong. And, of course, if we are too different, we may be labeled "abnormal," "insane," "disordered," and so on. But those who have lived long lives and know nothing about poststructuralism often acknowledge that they're not the same person they were when they were 20 or 30 or 60. In numerous relations over time and space, they have indeed produced themselves and been produced differently. They may choose to take up and inhabit subject positions (son, father) that are recognizable, often for the comfort of others, but they know they are not the same.

I believe that a different ethics comes into play with the dismantling of the essentialist human of humanism because one *can* choose not to repeat, perhaps not as much as we'd like because we are always being subjected even as we resist that subjection, but, nonetheless, we can be different. For that reason, we can no longer get off the hook by saying, "This is just the way I am." We have to learn a new responsibility both for how we produce ourselves as subjects and how, in relations, we produce others, how we subject them. It seems to me that this ethics, which is enabled by a different description of human being, was the desire of the post–World War II scholars, as well as everyday people, who were horrified by the practices of humanism's individual who could imagine and put into play the Holocaust, the atomic bomb, and the genocide and horrors that humans continue to repeat in the name of humanity.

Butler's powerful idea of agency through subversive repetition and Foucault's through the refusal of what we are (i.e., how we've been subjected and subject ourselves) are very useful in rethinking possibilities for human being. And Deleuze and Guattari ([1980] 1987) added much to that work by offering, in their normative ontology, a variety of interlocking concepts to move away from the "I," including "haecceity," "rhizome," and "assemblage." But it's not just Philosophy that enables different human being, it's also Science. Quantum physics' theory of entanglement, in my thinking, works hand-in-hand with haecceity and assemblage because both imply different conceptions of space/time in which the human and nonhuman are not simply separate entities tangled or assembled but are so imbricated that they never were and never can be separate. Barad (2007) explained entanglement in quantum theory as follows:

> To be entangled is not simply to be intertwined with another, as in the joining of separate entities, but to lack an independent, self-contained existence. Existence is not an individual affair. Individuals do not preexist their interactions; rather, individuals emerge through and as part of their entangled intra-relating. Which is not to say that emergence happens once and for all, as an event or as a process that takes place according to some external measure of space and of time, but rather that time and space, like matter and meaning, come into existence, are iteratively reconfigured through each intra-action, thereby making it impossible to differentiate in any absolute sense between creation and renewal, beginning and returning, continuity and discontinuity, here and there, past and future. (p. ix)

Quantum physics also disrupts humanism's notions of space and time in which space is a container for stable, bounded, "authentic" places where individuals live and move through the same time together (e.g., in a culture) and can be observed and studied. Space and time in modernity are separate, but in quantum physics space-time is dynamic, fractured, porous, paradoxical, and nonindividual, with sets of space-time relations existing simultaneously, rhizomatically, and overlapping, interfering with each other. When people begin to think of human being as entanglement, haecceity, assemblage, rhizome, "something happens to them that they can only get a grip on again by letting go of their ability to say 'I'" (Blanchot as cited in Deleuze & Guattari, [1980] 1987, p. 265).

Implications for Qualitative Inquiry

And there's the rub. Once the "I" fails, qualitative inquiry, dependent as it is on humanism's description of human being, fails as well. Its deeply phenenomenological approach, which "gives priority to the observing subject, which attributes a constituent role to an act, which places its own point of view at the origin of all historicity—which, in short leads to a transcendental consciousness" (Foucault, [1966] 1970, p. xiv)—no longer works. The observing subject is, of course, also the knowing, speaking, inquiring subject of qualitative inquiry. The description of the qualitative researcher is, as our texts tell us, one who collects data using interviews and observations, methods of data collection grounded in "being there" (Geertz, 1988), in *presence*, Derrida's ([1966] 1970) bane.

Qualitative researchers use those two face-to-face methods to go deep, to interview repeatedly in order to get closer and closer to the center, the core of participants' being. They are also advised to observe repeatedly for lengthy periods of time to get closer to the core, the real meaning, of practice, of experience, of life. In fact, we are taught that repeated interviewing and observation—going deeper and deeper for longer and longer—help guarantee the validity, the truth of a study.

Participants in qualitative inquiry likewise are seen as conscious individuals, receptacles of knowledge, of stories that reflect the truth of existence waiting to be revealed. In addition, they are assumed to be self-contained and self-aware individuals who not only have a real self but can also step outside it to reflect on it during an interview. And even though social constructionism, much less radical than poststructural theories, grounds much qualitative inquiry, qualitative researchers, in general, continue to view themselves and participants as doers who exist ahead of the deed. Thus, we believe that participants and researchers are separate, intact individuals who exist before the interview, not that they are products, artifacts, of the interview.

The increasing primacy of the interview in qualitative inquiry reflects the age-old and indefatigable power of Platonic phonocentrism that celebrates *voice* as the truest, most authentic data and/or evidence. Poststructuralism, however, alerts us that meaning is always deferred and that language, spoken or written, cannot be trusted to transport meaning from one individual to another as qualitative inquiry suggests. That interviewing can unearth deep, true meaning is highly doubtful. We can interview all we like, but all we can ever get from a participant is today's story, and tomorrow's will no doubt be different. The poststructuralist would claim that that has always been the case.

The point in all this is that qualitative inquiry, as presented in most standard textbooks—even though they may include an introductory chapter on theory—present qualitative methodology (Science) as divorced from epistemology (Philosophy). Note that this is especially true in texts published after the recent installation of scientifically based or evidence-based research, the phenomenon that restored positivism in social science research during the first decade of the twenty-first century (see, e.g., National Research Council, 2002).

In such texts, after an initial nod to theory, qualitative methodology is presented as just *itself*. It's a stand-alone, instrumental set of research practices that can be organized in different ways (e.g., grounded theory, case study, narrative "research designs"); that describes what counts as data (that which can be textualized in interview transcripts and field notes); that employs two chief methods of data collection (interviewing and observation); that describes what counts as data analysis (usually the quasi-statistical practice of coding of data); that relies heavily on a positivist validity (triangulation, bias, accuracy); that requires representation and a certain kind of representation at that (rich, thick description that assumes the transparency of language); and so on—you know the chapter headings. It is essentially humanist. It assumes the "I" of humanism and, more specifically, of empiricism. Many new qualitative textbooks now forget that early qualitative inquiry borrowed heavily from interpretive anthropology (see, e.g., Geertz, 1973) and set into play both interpretive and critical responses to positivist social science, which had lost its credibility.

To cement qualitative methodology as just itself, we too often teach it as process and technique in a linear sequence of courses—for example, an introductory course, then a course on data collection, and finally a course on data analysis and representation. Doing so separates Science from Philosophy because phenomenology, hermeneutics, existentialism, Marxism, critical race theory, and so on may not agree on what counts as data, as method, as analysis, and so on, and will also rely on different understandings of the humanist individual—the interpreter, the emancipator, and so on. However, we seldom teach courses in which Science and Philosophy are aligned, for example, courses in interpretive qualitative inquiry or critical qualitative inquiry or poststructural feminist qualitative inquiry or race-based qualitative inquiry and so on. Students who may have read deeply in those theories may well experience a disconnect between a theory's assumptions and those that structure conventional humanist qualitative inquiry.

Of course, poststructuralism will refuse qualitative inquiry when it assumes the humanist "I." *In this way, conventional humanist qualitative inquiry and poststructuralism are incommensurable; they cannot be thought together.* A question, then, is how might someone who was trained in conventional humanist qualitative inquiry and who has also studied and taken up poststructural theories inquire? Can one forget qualitative inquiry? Poststructuralists have been practicing the deconstructive strategy of working within/against the structure of conventional humanist qualitative inquiry for decades now, deconstructing its categories one by one—data, voice, reflexivity, validity, interview, and so on. I argue that it's time to practice another deconstructive approach, which is to overturn and leave behind the failed structure so that something else can be thought.

This is the post-qualitative inquiry (see, e.g., St. Pierre, in press) that, as Derrida suggested, is *to-come.* But it is already happening when those who have studied poststructural theories come upon humanist qualitative methodology and resist it. For example, they are leery of interviewing, refuse to "describe" participants, believe words in their literature reviews are as much data as are words in interview transcripts and field notes, refuse to code data, and refuse to write it up. We need to attend to their work, their reinvention of social science inquiry after the posts when the "I" no longer centers inquiry. Now we can rigorously imagine nonsubjective inquiry in entanglement, in assemblage, in the "AND, 'and ... and ... and. ...'" (Deleuze, [1990] 1995, p. 44) of post-inquiry. This is the lure, the work that beckons.

Note

1. See Pillow (2003) for a deconstruction of reflexivity.

References

Barad, K. (2007). *Meeting the universe halfway: Quantum physics and the entanglement of matter and meaning*. Durham, NC: Duke University Press.

Butler, J. (1987). *Subjects of desire: Hegelian reflections in twentieth-century France*. New York: Columbia University Press.

Butler, J. (1990). *Gender trouble: Feminism and the subversion of identity*. New York: Routledge.

Butler, J. (1995). For a careful reading. In S. Benhabib, J. Butler, D. Cornell & N. Fraser (Eds.). *Feminist contentions: A philosophical exchange* (pp. 127–143). New York: Routledge.

Deleuze, G. ([1990] 1995). *Negotiations: 1972–1990*. (M. Joughin, Trans.). New York: Columbia University Press.

Deleuze, G. & Guattari, F. ([1980] 1987). *A thousand plateaus: Capitalism and schizophrenia*. (B. Massumi, Trans.). Minneapolis: University of Minnesota Press.

Derrida, J. ([1966] 1970). Structure, sign and play in the discourse of the human sciences. In R. Macksey & E. Donato (Eds.), *The structuralist controversy: The languages of criticism and the sciences of man* (R. Macksey & E. Donato, Trans.) (pp. 247–272). Baltimore: The Johns Hopkins University Press.

Descartes, R. (1993). *Discourse on method and Meditations on first philosophy*. 4th ed. (D. A. Cress, Trans.). Indianapolis, IN: Hackett Publishing Company. (*Discourse on Method* first published 1637 and *Meditations on First Philosophy* first published 1641).

Finke, L. A. (1993). Knowledge as bait: Feminism, voice, and the pedagogical unconscious. *College English, 55*, 1, 7–27.

Foucault, M. ([1966] 1970). *The order of things: An archaeology of the human sciences*. (A. M. S. Smith, Trans.). New York: Vintage Books.

Foucault, M. ([1976] 1978). *The history of sexuality, Vol. 1: An introduction*. (R. Hurley, Trans.). New York: Vintage Books.

Foucault, M. ([1966] 1970). *The order of things: An archaeology of the human sciences*. (A. M. S. Smith, Trans.) New York: Vintage Books.

Foucault, M. (1982). The subject and power. *Critical Inquiry, 8*, 4, 777–795.

Foucault, M. ([1981] 1997a). Sexuality and solitude. In P. Rabinow (Ed.) *Ethics: Subjectivity and truth* (R. Hurley and others, Trans.) (pp. 175–184). New York: The New Press. (Reprinted from *London Review of Books, 3*, 9, 3, 5–6.)

Foucault, M. ([1984] 1997b). The ethics of concern of the self as a practice of freedom. (R. Fornet-Betancourt, H. Becker, & A. Gomez-Müller, Interviewers; P. Aranov & D. McGrawth, Trans.). In P. Rabinow (Ed.), *Ethics: Subjectivity and truth* (pp. 281–301). New York: The New Press.

Geertz, C. (1973). *The interpretation of cultures: Selected essays.* New York: Basic Books.

Geertz, C. (1988). Being there: Anthropology and the scene of writing. In *Works and lives: The anthropologist as author* (pp. 1–24). Stanford, CA: Stanford University Press.

Keenan, T. (1997). *Fables of responsibility: Aberrations and predicaments in ethics and politics.* Stanford, CA: Stanford University Press.

Locke, J. ([1690] 1924). *An essay concerning human understanding.* Oxford: Clarendon Press.

National Research Council. (2002). *Scientific research in education.* R. J. Shavelson & L. Towne (Eds.). Committee on Scientific Principles for Education Research. Washington, DC: National Academy Press.

Peshkin, A. (1988). In search of subjectivity—one's own. *Educational Researcher, 17,* 7, 17–22.

Peters, M. A. & Marshall, J. (1993). Beyond the philosophy of the subject: Liberalism, education, and the critique of individualism. *Educational Philosophy and Theory, 25,* 1, 19–39.

Pillow, W. S. (2003). Confession, catharsis, or cure? Rethinking the uses of reflexivity as methodological power in qualitative research. *International Journal of Qualitative Studies in Education, 16,* 2, 175–196.

Rabinow, P. (1997). Introduction: The history of systems of thought. In P. Rabinow (Ed.), *Ethics: Subjectivity and truth* (pp. xi–xlii). New York: New Press.

Rabinow, P. & Sullivan, W. M. (Eds.). (1979). *Interpretive social science: A reader.* Berkeley: University of California Press.

Rajchman, J. (2000). *The Deleuze connections.* Cambridge, MA: The MIT Press.

Scott, J. W. (1991). The evidence of experience. *Critical Inquiry, 17,* 4, 773–797.

Spivak, G. C. (1988). Can the subaltern speak? In C. Nelson & L. Grossberg (Eds.), *Marxism and the interpretation of culture* (pp. 271–313). Chicago: University of Chicago Press.

Spivak, G. C. (1999). *A critique of postcolonial reason: Toward a history of the vanishing present.* Cambridge, MA: Harvard University Press.

St. Pierre, E. A. (2000). Poststructural feminism in education: An overview. *International Journal of Qualitative Studies in Education, 13,* 5, 477–515.

St. Pierre, E. A. (in press). Post qualitative research: The coming after and the critique. In N. K. Denzin & Y. A. Lincoln (Eds.). *Handbook of qualitative research.* 4th ed. Thousand Oaks, CA: Sage.

Chapter 3

Interviewing and the Production of the Conversational Self

Svend Brinkmann

We live in a world of crises. Economic, climate, war, and poverty crises all affect our world on a global scale. Our problems are complex, but many of the world's troubles undoubtedly stem from a Western consumerist culture that seems to be out of control (Bauman, 2007). Unlike the society of producers, sometimes referred to as "industrial society," which had an economy that fundamentally worked by producing goods, the current consumer society primarily produces needs and desires in consumers. A culture that valorized stable selves is giving way to one that valorizes flexible selves that are able to change and develop in accordance with market needs. Not only are citizens increasingly seen as consumers, which threatens our political (Barber, 2007) and moral (Bauman, 2008) practices, but the exclusionist practices in the society of consumers are stricter and harsher than in the society of producers because almost all life problems and forms of failure are now seen as the outcome of individual faults (Bauman, 2007, p. 56). Consumer society is thoroughly psychologized. Furthermore, it seems that members of the society of consumers are themselves becoming consumer commodities (Bauman, 2007, p. 57), acknowledged mainly in terms of their "saleability" on the different markets (economic, romantic, etc.) (Brinkmann, 2009).

The relationships between social science, *in casu* qualitative inquiry, and the social and cultural worlds in which inquiry is practiced, are multifaceted. One legitimate reading of the current popularity of interview research in particular, however, focuses on the cultural change from industrial society with harsh objectifying means of control and power, to consumer society and its softer seductive forms of power through dialog, narrative, empathy, and intimacy (Brinkmann & Kvale, 2005). Undoubtedly, interviewing people about their lives, opinions, and experiences and allowing them freedom of expression in telling their stories is a powerful method of understanding people's life worlds (Kvale & Brinkmann, 2008). Without denying the genuine knowledge-producing potentials of interviewing, we must not remain blind to the fact that the modern consumer society is an interview society (Atkinson & Silverman, 1997). This is a society that knows itself through the conversations that circulate in the media, ranging from talk shows, radio phone-ins, and political interviews to focus group interviews for commercial purposes. However valuable interviewing may be for research purposes, as a social technique it is also part of what Denzin (1995, p. 191) has called a "pornography of the visible," or, to paraphrase in interview terms, a pornography of the *audible*. As a social technique it serves to make visible and uncover, and, like journalism, its close ally and nineteenth-century predecessor, it serves to realize "the dream of a transparent society," to borrow Foucault's words (2001, p. 190).

To stay with Foucault's analytics, it seems reasonable to think of qualitative research interviewing as a central technology of the self in a postmodern consumerist culture, where nothing is or must remain hidden, and where selves are commodified conversational products. In this chapter, I argue that we, as qualitative interview researchers, must continuously reflect on how we stage and handle interviews if this social technique is to give us something different than a simple reflection of the consumer society that is a significant cause of the world's global crisis.

Interviewing in a Conversational Reality

In a philosophical sense, all human research must be understood as conversational, since we are linguistic creatures and language is best understood in terms of the figure of conversation (Mulhall, 2007). For discourse theorists, it has long been acknowledged that "The primary human reality is persons in conversation" (Harré, 1983, p. 58). Our cultures are constantly produced, reproduced, and revised in dialogs among their members (Mannheim & Tedlock, 1995, p. 2). The same is true of the cultural investigation of cultural phenomena, or what we call social science. We should see language and culture as emergent properties of conversations rather than the other way around. Conversations—dialogs—are not several monologs that are added together, but the basic, primordial form of associated human life. In other words, "we live our daily social lives within an ambience of conversation, discussion, argumentation, negotiation, criticism and justification; much of it to do with problems of intelligibility and the legitimation of claims to truth" (Shotter, 1993, p. 29).

Not just our interpersonal social reality is constituted by conversations. It also applies to the self. Charles Taylor (1989) argues that the self exists only within what he calls "webs of interlocution" (p. 36). We are selves only in relation to certain interlocutors with whom we are in conversation and from whom we gain a language of self-understanding. In referring to Heidegger's concept of *Dasein*—or human existence—philosopher Stephen Mulhall (2007), author of the aptly entitled book *The Conversation of Humanity*, states that "Dasein is not just the locus and the precondition for the conversation of humankind; it is itself, because humankind is, a kind of enacted conversation" (p. 58). We understand ourselves as well as others only because we can speak, and "being able to speak involves being able to converse" (Mulhall, 2007, p. 26). Human reality is a conversational reality—humankind is an enacted conversation, as are particular selves.

The idea that humankind is a kind of enacted conversation gives the interview a privileged position in producing knowledge about the social world. The processes of our lives—actions, thoughts, and emotions—are nothing but physiology if considered as isolated elements outside of conversations and interpretative contexts. A life, as Paul Ricoeur (1991) has said, "is no more than a biological phenomenon as long as it has not been interpreted" (p. 28). The phenomena of our lives must be seen as interpretive *responses* to people, situations, and events. As responses they are conversational and dialogical, for, to quote Alasdair MacIntyre (1985), "conversation, understood widely enough, is the form of human transactions in general" (p. 211). When people are talking (e.g., in interviews), they are not simply putting preconceived ideas into words, but are dialogically responding to each other's expressions and trying to make sense by using the narratives and discourses that are available (Shotter, 1993, p. 1).

If conversations are the stuff that human life is made of, it becomes pertinent to study the specific qualities of our conversations and ask what kinds of persons we become through different forms of conversation. If one believes—as I do—that the conversational approach gives us a fruitful way of understanding the human predicament, we must consider the quality of our conversations, for who we are will (to some extent) depend on the conversations in which we engage, and our values and self-understandings will depend on the subject positions into which our conversations invite us. If true, it means that social scientists and others who conduct interviews are engaged in the production of human subjectivity. Below, I distinguish between different types of interviews and describe some of the subject positions that these types entail. I will argue that too many interviews today are conducted based on what I shall refer to as a spectator's stance—a voyeur's epistemology or an epistemology of the eye—which, through the analytic perspective of Foucault, seems to be part of "the disciplinary society" and its "mobile panoptic eye, an eye that could hear and see everything that was going on in the social world" (Denzin, 1995, p. 206). Against this, I will posit the need for thinking about interviewing in more active, performative, or participatory terms—based on what I have elsewhere referred to as an epistemology of the hand (Brinkmann & Tanggaard, 2010).

Interviewing and the Spectator's Stance

Based on readings of current interview studies and textbooks instructing researchers how to interview, it is my impression that qualitative interviewers today are often acting as either pollsters, who passively record people's attitudes, opinions, and experiences, or as probers who aim to enter the private worlds of the interviewees to uncover concealed aspects of their lives (for a more thorough analysis, see Brinkmann, 2007); for example, by working with what has been called "a method of friendship" (Fontana & Frey, 2005). In both cases, the practice is based on what John Dewey ([1929] 1960) criticized as the spectator theory of knowledge: The theory that true knowledge arises through passive observation of reality, which allegedly is as it is in independence of being observed (p. 23).

In the first case of the pollster, a receptive, nondirective practice is followed, where the implicit model of the interviewer resembles Carl Rogers (1945), who developed client-centered therapy and nondirective interviewing in the 1940s. In more postmodern approaches, this practice is sometimes conceptualized as polyphonic interviewing "where the voices of the respondents are recorded with minimal influence from the researcher" (Fontana & Prokos, 2007, p. 53).

In the second case of the prober, a therapeutic practice of intimacy is followed, where the probing interviewer sometimes appears in the guise of a psychoanalyst. Both of these spectator forms are, as I shall explain, doxastic (*doxa* is Greek for opinion), in being concerned with the individual's experiences, attitudes, and narratives. My argument, presented in greater detail elsewhere (Brinkmann, 2007), is that by simply recording their respondents' experiences and opinions (the *doxa*), interview researchers are often engaged in what seems like a time-consuming kind of opinion-polling, for which quantitative instruments such as questionnaires often appear to be much more efficient.

Rogers is a clear and classic example of an interviewer working with a spectator's epistemology. His early "non-directive method as a technique for social research" (Rogers, 1945) was meant to sample the respondent's attitudes toward herself: "Through the non-directive interview we have an unbiased method by which we may plumb these private thoughts and perceptions of the individual" (p. 282). In contrast to psychoanalytic practice, the respondent in client-centered therapy/research is a client rather than a patient, and the client is the expert. Although often framed in different terms, I believe that many contemporary interview researchers conceptualize the research interview in line with Rogers's humanistic, nondirective approach, valorizing the respondents' private experiences, narratives, opinions, beliefs, and attitudes, which can be captured with the concept of *doxa*.

"Empathetic interviewing" (Fontana & Frey, 2005), for example, involves taking a stance in favor of the persons being studied, not unlike the positive regard displayed by Rogerian therapists, and the approach is depicted as at once a "method of friendship" and a humanistic "method of morality because it attempts to restore the sacredness of humans before addressing any theoretical or methodological concerns" (p. 697). In line with an implicit therapeutic metaphor, the interview is turned "into a walking stick to help some people get on their feet" (p. 695). This is a laudable intention, but there seems to be significant limitations to such forms of interviewing as well, not least that it becomes difficult to interview people with whom one disagrees and does not want to help (e.g., neo-Nazis).

Attempts to include the researcher's experience in interview research (e.g., as described by Ellis and Berger [2003]), also often focus on doxastic experience, and the interviewer is presented in a therapeutic vein as someone who "listens empathically" and "identifies with participants, and shows respect for participants' emotionality" (pp. 469–470). Ellis and Berger also refer to a number of interview researchers who "emphasize the positive therapeutic benefits that can accrue to respondents and interviewers who participate in interactive interviews" (p. 470), and one experiential form of qualitative inquiry in particular, "mediated co-constructed narratives," is presented as "similar to conjoint marital therapy" (p. 477), in which a couple jointly constructs an epiphany in their relationship, with the interviewer/therapist acting as moderator. In doxastic interviews that focus on experiences, opinions, and attitudes, knowing the experiencing self is seen as presupposed in knowing as such. A key point in these forms of interviewing is that *"Understanding ourselves is part of the process of understanding others"* (Ellis & Berger, 2003, p. 486; emphasis added). This can be interpreted as analogous to therapists' own need for therapy in their professional development. As Rogers knew, the most efficient way of eliciting private doxastic elements is by engaging in a warm and accepting relationship, in line with the principles of client-centered psychotherapy (Rogers advocated what he called "unconditional positive regard").

I believe that we may read the spread of Rogers's humanistic interviews as a reflection of the contemporary consumer society where the client is always right, where his or her experiences and narratives are always interesting *because* they are some individual's experiences and narratives, and where the interviewer acts as a mirror of the respondent's feelings, attitudes, and beliefs. Consumer society is an *experience society*, to quote the German sociologist, Gerhard Schulze (1992), and the interview is a central technology for sampling and circulating experiences, not just in research contexts, but also in confessional talk shows and marketized focus groups (Kvale, 2006).

There are other and much more theoretically informed conceptualizations of the interview and the interviewee that share the psychologistic, spectator's stance. A good example comes from Wendy Hollway and Tony Jefferson (2000). In their psychoanalytic eyes, the qualitative interview researcher is always closer to the truth than the research subject (whom they call a "defended subject"), for "subjects are motivated *not* to know certain aspects of themselves and [...] they *produce* biographical accounts which avoid such knowledge" (p. 169; emphases in the original). In this perspective, the respondents can give away only *doxa*, and the researcher-therapists are in a unique position to obtain true knowledge, given their superior theoretical knowledge and psychoanalytic training. The model for the relation between interviewer and interviewee consequently becomes that of psychotherapist and patient, where the patient is cast in the experiencing, suffering position and the therapist in the seeing and (therefore) knowing position.

A critique of what I here refer to as doxastic interviews is not new. In the 1950s, David Riesman warned against the tendency to use the level of "rapport" in an interview to judge its qualities concerning knowledge. He thought it was a prejudice, "often based on psychoanalytic stereotypes, to assume the more rapport-filled and intimate the relation, the more 'truth' the respondent will vouchsafe" (Riesman & Benney, 1956, p. 10). Rapport-filled interviews often spill over with "the flow of legend and cliché" (p. 11), according to Riesman's verdict, where interviewees adapt their responses to what they take the interviewer expects from them (see Lee, 2008; and, for a related analysis that puts weight on participants' objections during the interview, see Tanggaard, 2008).

Interviewing and the Participant's Stance

What, then, are the alternatives to the spectators' doxastic interviews? To answer this question, it may be useful to look at other writings on the subject and other terminologies. Wengraf (2001), for example, does not talk about *doxa* but about "receptive interviewing" and opposes this to "assertive" styles. He also aligns the receptive practice with Rogers's model of psychotherapy, which seeks to empower the informant (p. 154), and the assertive practice with legal interrogations where the interviewer is in control and seeks to provoke and illuminate self-contradictions (p. 155). Wengraf cites Holstein and Gubrium's (1995) "active interviewing" as a form of assertive interviewing practice (but, like most researchers, he favors the receptive style). Holstein and Gubrium have long argued that interviews are unavoidably interpretively active, meaning-making practices. Interviews are not simply practices of "seeing" the other, but processes of meaning construction (i.e., of "doing" something together). The interviewer here appears as a participant rather than spectator, but active interviews are to some extent still dominated by the spectator's stance, and researchers are encouraged to experiment "with alternative representational forms that they believe can convey respondents' experience more on, if not in, their own terms" (Holstein & Gubrium, 2003, p. 20).

For some time, I have been interested in how conversations can help us produce knowledge in the sense of *episteme* (the Greek term for knowledge that has been arrived at through dialectical processes of questioning).[1] The greatest epistemic interviewer in history was no doubt Socrates, who will serve as my main inspiration for an alternative to doxastic forms of interviewing. Plato's dialogs, in which Socrates appears as "interviewer," were designed as ways of testing whether the conversation partners have knowledge (i.e., whether they are capable of adequately justifying their beliefs, and if they cannot [which is normally the case], if their beliefs are unwarranted, the dialogs unfold as dialectical processes of refining their beliefs)—their *doxa*—in light of good reasons, in order to approach *episteme*.

To illustrate more concretely what I mean by epistemic interviews, I shall give a simple and very short example from Plato's *The Republic*. It elegantly demonstrates epistemically that no moral rules are self-applying and self-interpreting but must always be understood contextually. Socrates is in a conversation with Cephalus, who believes that justice (*dikaiosune*)—here "doing right"—can be stated in universal rules, such as "tell the truth" and "return borrowed items":

> "That's fair enough, Cephalus," I [Socrates] said. "But are we really to say that doing right consists simply and solely in truthfulness and returning anything we have borrowed? Are those not actions that can be sometimes right and sometimes wrong? For instance, if one borrowed a weapon from a friend who subsequently went out of his mind and then asked for it back, surely it would be generally agreed that one ought not to return it, and that it would not be right to do so, not to consent to tell the strict truth to a madman?"
>
> "That is true," he [Cephalus] replied.
>
> "Well then," I [Socrates] said, "telling the truth and returning what we have borrowed is not the definition of doing right." (Plato, 1987, pp. 65–66)

Here, the conversation is interrupted by Polemarchus who disagrees with Socrates' preliminary conclusion, and Cephalus quickly leaves to go to a sacrifice. Then Polemarchus takes

Cephalus' position as Socrates' discussion partner and the conversation continues as if no substitution had happened.

Initially, we may notice that Socrates violates almost every standard principle of qualitative research interviewing. First, we see that he talks much more than his respondent. There is some variety across the dialogs concerning how much Socrates talks in comparison with the other participants, but the example given here, where Socrates develops an absurd conclusion from the initial belief voiced by Cephalus, is not unusual, although the balance is much more equal in other places. Second, Socrates has not asked Cephalus to "describe a situation in which he has experienced justice" or "tell a story about doing right from his own experience" or a similar concretely descriptive question, probing for "lived experience." Instead, they are talking about the definition of an important general concept. Third, Socrates contradicts and challenges his respondent's view. He is not a warm and caring conversationalist, working with "a methodology of friendship." Fourth, there is no debriefing or attempt to make sure that the interaction was a "pleasant experience" for Cephalus. Fifth, the interview is conducted in public rather than private, and the topic is not private experiences or biographical details, but justice, a theme of common human interest, at least of interest to all citizens of Athens.

Sixth, and perhaps most importantly, the interview here is radically anti-psychologistic and anti-individualist. Interestingly, it does not make much of a difference whether the conversation partner is Cephalus or Polemarchus—and the discussion continues in exactly the same way after Cephalus has left. The crux of the discussion is whether the participants are able to give good reasons for their belief in a public discussion, not whether they have this or that biographical background or defense mechanism, for example. The focus is on *what* they say—and whether it can be normatively justified—not on dubious psychological interpretations concerning *why* they say it, neither during the conversation, nor in some process of analysis after the conversation. In the words of Norwegian philosopher Hans Skjervheim (1957), the "researcher" (Socrates) is a *participant*, who takes seriously what his fellow citizen says ("what does he say?")—seriously enough to disagree with it in fact—he is not a *spectator* who objectifies the conversation partner and his arguments by ignoring the normative claims of the statements, or looks at them in terms of the causes (psychological or sociological) that may have brought the person to entertain such beliefs ("why does he say that?").

Socrates' "method" is not a method in the conventional sense, but an *elenchus*, a Greek term that means examining a person and considering his or her statements normatively (Dinkins, 2005). The Socratic conversation is a mode of understanding, rather than a method in any mechanical sense (see Gadamer, 1960). Sometimes, the conversation partners in the Platonic dialogs settle on a definition, but more often the dialog ends without any final, unarguable definition of the central concept (e.g., justice, virtue, love). This lack of resolution—*aporia* in Greek—can be interpreted as illustrating the open-ended character of our conversational reality, including the open-ended character of the discursively produced knowledge of human social and historical life generated by (what we today call) the social sciences. If humankind is a kind of enacted conversation, the goal of social science should not be to arrive at "fixed knowledge" once and for all, but to help human beings constantly improve the quality of their conversational reality, to help them know their own society and debate the goals and values that are important in their lives (Flyvbjerg, 2001).

Michel Foucault (2001) also discussed Socrates' conversational practices in some of his last writings, and the quotation below nicely brings out the normative and epistemic dimensions of Socratic interviewing. When Socrates asks people to give accounts, "what is involved is not a confessional autobiography," Foucault makes clear (p. 97). Instead:

> In Plato's or Xenophon's portrayals of him, we never see Socrates requiring an examination of conscience or a confession of sins. Here, giving an account of your life, your *bios*, is also not to give a narrative of the historical events that have taken place in your life, but rather to demonstrate whether you are able to show that there is a relation between the rational discourse, the *logos*, you are able to use, and the way that you live. Socrates is inquiring into

the way that *logos* gives form to a person's style of life. (Foucault, 2001, p. 97)

Socrates was engaged in conversational practices where people, in giving accounts of themselves, exhibited the logos by which they lived (Butler, 2005, p. 126). The conversation partners were thus positioned as responsible citizens, accountable to each other with reference to the normative order in which they acted, and the conversational topic would therefore not be the narrative of the individual's life, or his or her experiences, but rather people's epistemic practices of justification. In short, people are approached as accountable citizens rather than as consumers/clients that are always right.

Epistemic Interviews Today

It seems pertinent to ask whether this approach to interviewing is possible today, or whether it should be considered as an ancient Hellenic practice that is no longer viable. I support the former idea and believe that it is possible to point to a number of significant interview studies that have employed some version of the Socratic approach, perhaps not in a pure form, but nonetheless in a form that seeks to distance itself from doxastic interviewing.

What Bellah and coworkers (1985) referred to as "active interviews" in their classic *Habits of the Heart* correspond, for example, quite well to epistemic interviews, and they represent one worked-out alternative to the standard doxastic interviews that probe for private meanings and opinions. In the appendix to their study of North American values and character, the researchers spell out their view of social science and its methodology, summarized as "social science as public philosophy." The empirical material for their book consisted of interviews with more than 200 participants, some of whom were interviewed more than once. In contrast to the interviewer as a friend or therapist, probing deeply in the private psyche of the interviewee, Bellah and coworkers practiced active interviews, which were intended to generate public conversation about societal values and goals. Such active interviews do not necessarily aim for agreement between interviewer and interviewee, so there is no danger of instrumentalizing the researcher's feelings to obtain good rapport. The interviewer is allowed to question and challenge what the interviewee says. In this example, the interviewer, Steven Tipton, tries to discover at what point the respondent would take responsibility for another human being:

Q: So what are you responsible for?

A: I'm responsible for my acts and for what I do.

Q: Does that mean you're responsible for others, too?

A: No.

Q: Are you your sister's keeper?

A: No.

Q: Your brother's keeper?

A: No.

Q: Are you responsible for your husband?

A: I'm not. He makes his own decisions. He is his own person. He acts his own acts. I can agree with them or I can disagree with them. If I ever find them nauseous enough, I have a responsibility to leave and not deal with it any more.

Q: What about children?

A: I … I would say I have a legal responsibility for them, but in a sense I think they in turn are responsible for their own acts. (Bellah et al., 1985, p. 304)

Here, Tipton repeatedly challenges the respondent's claim of not being responsible for other human beings. With the Socratic principles in mind, we can see the interviewer pressing for a contradiction between the respondent's definition of responsibility, involving the idea that she is only responsible for herself, and her likely feeling of at least some (legal) responsibility for her children. The individualist notion of responsibility is almost used *ad absurdum*, but the definition apparently plays such a central role in the person's life that she is unwilling to give it up. I would argue that this way of interviewing, although not asking for concrete descriptions or narratives, gives us important knowledge *primarily* about the doxastic individualist beliefs of Americans in the mid-1980s, but *secondarily* about the idea of responsibility in a normative-epistemic sense. For most readers would appreciate the above sequence as implying the argument that the respondent is wrong—she *is* responsible for other people, most clearly her children. At the very least, the reader is invited into an epistemic discussion not just about beliefs, but also about citizenship, virtue, responsibility, and ethics. The authors of *Habits of the Heart* conclude that unlike "poll data" generated by fixed questions that "sum up the *private* opinions," active (epistemic) interviews "create the possibility of *public* conversation and argument" (Bellah et al., 1985, p. 305). We are far away from the pollster and the traditional doxastic view of social science interviews, portraying these as ways of understanding what people privately think, feel, and want.

Concluding Ethico-Political Thoughts

The project of developing the epistemic potentials of interviewing is allied, I believe, with other recent explorations of alternative interview forms, for example Denzin's (2001) idea of performance interviews in the "cinematic-interview society." Denzin formulates "a utopian project," searching for a new form of the interview, which he calls "the reflexive, dialogic, or performative interview" (p. 24). The utopian project of epistemic interviewing outlined above, however, has a more explicit emphasis on civic responsibility. Qualitative researchers are increasingly becoming aware that interviewing, as Charles Briggs (2003, p. 497) has argued, is "a 'technology' that invents both notions of individual subjectivities and collective social and political patterns." Different conversational practices, including research interviews, produce and activate different forms of subjectivity and social life. Thus, ethico-political issues are always internal to practices of interviewing. Epistemic interviews position respondents as accountable, responsible citizens, which I have presented as an alternative to experience-focused, psychologized interviews that position respondents as clients or patients. And epistemic interviews position interviewers as participants rather than spectators.

According to the view of social science that goes back to Plato and Aristotle (1976), the social sciences are *practical* sciences that should ideally enable the creation of a knowledgeable citizenry capable of discussing matters of communal value (this was also Dewey's view; see Brinkmann, 2004). Social science should serve the political community in the sense of engaging this community in conversations about ethical, political, and other normative issues. Qualitative social science, according to this view, should not just serve to bring forth privatized narratives or other intimate aspects of people's lives. It should also serve the *Res Publica* (i.e., the ethical and political relations between human beings that are not constituted by intimacy) (Sennett, 1977).

In *The Fall of Public Man*, Richard Sennett warned against seeing society as a grand, psychological system (Sennett, 1977, p. 4), where the question "Who am I?" is constantly pursued, and where psychological categories invade and destroy public life, making us forget that political questions cannot be dealt with alone through trust, empathy, warmth, and a disclosure of private opinions (p. xvii). Under the conditions Sennett describes as "the tyranny of intimacy," public, social, civic, and political phenomena are transformed into questions of personality, biography and individual narratives (p. 219). As an antidote, Sennett calls for more "impersonal" forms of action in public arenas (p. 340).

My worry is that some of the social science interviews, which I have referred to as doxastic, can be said to uncritically reproduce and reinforce the view of social life as reducible to psychology in the form of people's experiences and opinions. Here, the researcher is a spectator, a voyeur, who observes, sees, and hears the intimate details of the respondents. What Sennett said of contemporary life in general also applies to much interview research: "Each person's self has become his principle burden; to know oneself has become an end, instead of a means through which one knows the world" (Sennett, 1977, p. 4). Current doxastic interviews are often about getting to know people's selves, which is often portrayed as an end in itself in the contemporary "interview society" (Atkinson & Silverman, 1997), and I would echo Sennett's claim that we need a forum "in which it becomes meaningful to join with other persons without the compulsion to know them as persons" (Sennett, 1977, p. 340)—also in the contexts of qualitative inquiry. No doubt, we also often need to know others "as persons," and here doxastic interviews have been very efficient, but if we genuinely want to examine ethical and political issues for the sake of the public good, one way could be to add epistemic interviews to the repertoire of qualitative inquiry to a larger extent.

Still, we may ask, if the practice of Socratic interviews involves challenging respondents and confronting them with the task of giving reasons and normative accounts, isn't this ethically problematic? I would counter this by arguing that epistemic interviews have the potentials for at least as great a transparency of its power relations as doxastic interviews and do not commodify or instrumentalize human feeling, friendship, and empathy (Brinkmann & Kvale, 2005). Certainly, like all other human practices, epistemic interviews come with certain ethical challenges that should be taken into consideration. Nevertheless, I believe that the active and assertive style in epistemic interviews in many ways enable researchers to proceed ethically in qualitative knowledge production. As shown in the epistemic interviews above, the interviewers do not try to suck as much private information out of the respondents as possible without themselves engaging in the conversation with all the risks that are involved in this. Interviewers become participants in, rather than spectators of, the production of social life.

In conclusion, I want to make clear that the purpose of this chapter has definitely not been to invalidate the use of phenomenological or narrative interviews that focus on experiences and opinions—the *doxa*. Rather, my aim has been to argue that other kinds of human conversations can also be practiced with the goal of reaching knowledge, as classically illustrated by Socrates in the role of epistemic interviewer. Socrates is never content to hear what people believe or how they experience the world. He is always interested in examining whether people's beliefs and experiences can be justified, and his dialectical method (his *elenchus*) was developed to bring human beings from a state of being opinionated to a state of knowing. In what I have called epistemic interviews, the analysis is in principle carried out *in* the conversation, together with the accountable respondents involved, since the analysis mainly consists of testing, questioning, and justifying what people say. Such interviews involve a co-construction of conversational reality *in situ*. In Plato's dialogs, we do not hear about Socrates continuing his analyses in solitude after the public meetings. In conventional research interviews, on the other hand, the analysis is typically carried out after the interview has taken place, often informed by the researcher's theoretical preferences that may be totally alien to the participants. I believe that researchers ought to experiment more with testing their own and their respondents' statements in public discussion in the course of the interview, rather than just seeing this as something to be carried out behind closed doors. I believe that this could often improve the analyses and perhaps also create more interesting interviews. Often, the use of challenging and confronting questions in epistemic interviews generates more readable interview reports compared with the long monologs that sometimes result from phenomenological and narrative approaches.

The epistemic interviewer is not a spectator, gazing at a research subject and consuming his stories, but a participant in the creation of our conversational reality. His "intrusion" into the conversation is not thought of as a source of error, or as something unnatural. On the contrary, if knowledge and subjectivity are produced in conversations, it is an epistemic virtue to become visible as a questioner in the interview.

Note

1. The ensuing discussion reworks parts of Brinkmann, 2007.

References

Aristotle. (1976). *Nichomachean ethics*. London: Penguin.

Atkinson, P. & Silverman, D. (1997). Kundera's immortality: The interview society and the invention of the self. *Qualitative Inquiry, 3*, 3, 304–325.

Barber, B. (2007). *Consumed: How markets corrupt children, infantilize adults, and swallow citizens whole*. New York: W.W. Norton & Co.

Bauman, Z. (2007). *Consuming life*. Cambridge: Polity Press.

Bauman, Z. (2008). *Does ethics have a chance in a world of consumers?* Cambridge, MA: Harvard University Press.

Bellah, R. N., Madsen, R., Sullivan, W. M., Swidler, A., & Tipton, S. M. (1985). *Habits of the heart: Individualism and commitment in American life.* Berkeley: University of California Press.

Briggs, C. L. (2003). Interviewing, power/knowledge, and social inequality. In J. A. Holstein & J. F. Gubrium (Eds.), *Inside interviewing: New lenses, new concerns* (pp. 495–506). Thousand Oaks, CA: Sage.

Brinkmann, S. (2004). Psychology as a moral science: Aspects of John Dewey's psychology. *History of the Human Sciences, 17*, 1, 1–28.

Brinkmann, S. (2007). Could interviews be epistemic? An alternative to qualitative opinion-polling. *Qualitative Inquiry, 13*, 8, 1116–1138.

Brinkmann, S. (2009). Literature as qualitative inquiry: The novelist as researcher. *Qualitative Inquiry, 15*, 8, 1376–1394.

Brinkmann, S., & Kvale, S. (2005). Confronting the ethics of qualitative research. *Journal of Constructivist Psychology, 18*, 2, 157–181.

Brinkmann, S., & Tanggaard, L. (2010). Toward an epistemology of the hand. *Studies in Philosophy and Education, 29*, 3, 243–257.

Butler, J. (2005). *Giving an account of oneself.* New York: Fordham University Press.

Denzin, N. K. (1995). *The cinematic society: The voyeur's gaze.* Thousand Oaks, CA: Sage.

Denzin, N. K. (2001). The reflexive interview and a performative social science. *Qualitative Research, 1*, 1, 23–46.

Dewey, J. ([1929] 1960). *The quest for certainty.* New York: Capricorn Books.

Dinkins, C. S. (2005). Shared inquiry: Socratic-hermeneutic interpre-viewing. In P. Ironside (Ed.), *Beyond Method: Philosophical conversations in healthcare research and scholarship* (pp. 111–147). Madison: University of Wisconsin Press.

Ellis, C., & Berger, L. (2003). Their story/my story/our story: Including the researcher's experience in interview research. In J. A. Holstein & J. F. Gubrium (Eds.), *Inside Interviewing: New lenses, new concerns* (pp. 467–493). Thousand Oaks, CA: Sage.

Flyvbjerg, B. (2001). *Making social science matter—Why social inquiry fails and how it can succeed again.* Cambridge: Cambridge University Press.

Fontana, A., & Frey, J. H. (2005). The interview: From neutral stance to political involvement. In N. K. Denzin & Y. S. Lincoln (Eds.) *The Sage handbook of qualitative research* (3rd ed., pp. 695–727). Thousand Oaks, CA: Sage.

Fontana, A., & Prokos, A. H. (2007). *The interview: From formal to postmodern.* Walnut Creek, CA: Left Coast.

Foucault, M. (2001). *Fearless speech*. (J. Pearson, Ed.). New York: Semiotext(e).

Gadamer, H. G. (1960). *Truth and method*. (2nd revised edition, 2000). New York: Continuum.

Harré, R. (1983). *Personal being*. Oxford: Basil Blackwell.

Hollway, W., & Jefferson, T. (2000). Biography, anxiety and the experience of locality. In P. Chamberlayne, J. Bornat, & T. Wengraf (Eds.), *The turn to biographical methods in social science* (pp. 167–180). London: Routledge.

Holstein, J. A., & Gubrium, J. F. (1995). *The active interview*. London: Sage.

Holstein, J. A., & Gubrium, J. F. (2003). Inside interviewing: New lenses, new concerns. In J. A. Holstein & J. F. Gubrium (Eds.), *Inside interviewing: New lenses, new concerns* (pp. 3–30). Thousand Oaks, CA: Sage.

Kvale, S. (2006). Dominance through interviews and dialogues. *Qualitative Inquiry, 12,* 3, 480–500.

Kvale, S., & Brinkmann, S. (2008). *InterViews: Learning the craft of qualitative research interviewing*. Thousand Oaks, CA: Sage.

Lee, R. M. (2008). David Riesman and the sociology of the interview. *The Sociological Quarterly, 49,* 2, 285–307.

MacIntyre, A. (1985). *After virtue*. (2nd ed., with postscript). London: Duckworth.

Mannheim, B., & Tedlock, B. (1995). Introduction. In D. Tedlock & B. Mannheim (Eds.), *The dialogic emergence of culture* (pp. 1–32). Urbana: University of Illinois Press.

Mulhall, S. (2007). *The conversation of humanity*. Richmond: University of Virginia Press.

Plato (1987). *The republic*. London: Penguin.

Ricoeur, P. (1991). Life in quest of narrative. In D. Wood (Ed.), *On Paul Ricoeur: Narrative and interpretation* (pp. 20–33). London: Routledge.

Riesman, D., & Benney, M. (1956). The sociology of the interview. *Midwestern Sociologist, 18,* 1, 3–15.

Rogers, C. (1945). The non-directive method as a technique for social research. *The American Journal of Sociology, 50,* 2, 279–283.

Schulze, G. (1992). *Die Erlebnisgesellschaft: Kultursoziologie Der Gegenwart* [The experience society: A cultural sociology of the present]. Frankfurt: Campus.

Sennett, R. ([1977] 2003). *The fall of public man*. London: Penguin.

Shotter, J. (1993). *Conversational realities: Constructing life through language*. London: Sage.

Skjervheim, H. (1957). *Deltaker og tilskodar* [Participant and spectator]. Oslo: Oslo University Press.

Tanggaard, L. (2008). Objections in research interviewing. *International Journal of Qualitative Methods*, 7, 1, 15–29.

Taylor, C. (1989). *Sources of the self.* Cambridge: Cambridge University Press

Wengraf, T. (2001). *Qualitative research interviewing.* Thousand Oaks, CA: Sage.

Part II: Method

Chapter 4

Qualitative Research, Technology, and Global Change

Judith Davidson
Silvana di Gregorio

Over the last century and a half, qualitative research, with its emphasis on unstructured or nonnumerical data, has played a vibrant role in the social sciences. Qualitative researchers, skilled in the use of unstructured data, have contributed to the development of classical sociology and anthropology and to postmodern movements in reflexive perspectives that bring attention to concerns for global justice.

This same period has also been characterized by dramatic changes in globalization of technology and the subsequent data deluge as we went from the industrial age to the computer age and now stand on the brink of the information age, dominated by the Internet and the World Wide Web (Anderson, 2007). Strikingly, however, mainstream qualitative research has elected to participate on the margins of this technological revolution. This is surprising, as one of the key features of the most recent technological changes we are facing is the enormous need to understand how to make use of huge amounts of unstructured data—a qualitative research specialty.

Mainstream qualitative researchers have been active in making changes to ontological and epistemological approaches to research and tools for data collection and representation

(Denzin & Lincoln, 2000, 2003). They have not, however, been as active in thinking about tools for analysis or the digital challenges to the discipline. Despite the silence from the majority in these areas, a minority of qualitative researchers has been working on the fringes of analysis and qualitative research technologies. In tandem with the development of personal computers, beginning in the 1980s these innovators developed stand-alone software programs Qualitative Data Analysis Software (QDAS) that have become comprehensive all-in-one packages that offer qualitative researchers:

1) a convenient digital location in which to organize all materials related to one study:

2) a suite of linked digital tools that could be applied to those materials, including the ability to store and organize data; fragment, juxtapose, interpret, and recompose that same material;

3) easy portability; and

4) a remarkable new form of transparency that allowed the researcher, and others the opportunity to view and reflect upon the materials. (di Gregorio & Davidson, 2008, 2010).

As described by Lewins and Silver (2007), these tools are distinctive for their capacities to aid qualitative researchers in organizing, reflecting, exploring, and integrating data. Originally developed by sociologists, the tools are now used in diverse disciplinary areas.

Thirty years after the initial development of QDAS, qualitative researchers now stand on the brink of a global technological revolution in the form of the Internet and the World Wide Web. In this new age, people from every continent and walk of life are connected through new technologies. Stand-alone computer work is being pushed aside for the benefits of computing in the cloud, the term used to describe networked storage resources. New user communities spring up every minute for every conceivable purpose, and their members are eager to find good tools to keep track of the information they glean in their new communities. Libraries and Boolean searching are giving way to twitter, crowdsourcing, and folksonomies—an-ask-and-see-who-knows approach (di Gregorio, 2008, 2009, 2010; Vander Wal, 2007). Every individual now trails vast clouds of unstructured data produced by the activities of communicating in this new world (Thorpe, 2010). These clouds of data are now referred to by many as "big data" (*The Economist*, 2010).

Where qualitative researchers were once the queen bees of unstructured data and their tools, today there are many individuals and groups who are eager to work with these kinds of data. These new users, however, want quick, easy, intuitive, inexpensive tools for organizing these data and making sense of them. They would be hard-put to deal with the sharp learning curve of the comprehensive QDAS packages created for social scientists (di Gregorio, 2009, 2010).

These global developments place qualitative researchers and QDAS developers in a novel place. We are both expert in the new, big thing, yet our expertise is relatively obscure to the new publics who are concerned with the new, big thing. In this chapter, we explore the dilemmas facing qualitative researchers as we struggle to come to grips with this new dynamic. We begin with a quick historical look at the development of QDAS and consideration of the shift from QDAS to what we have termed QDAS 2.0 (QDAS in a Web 2.0 environment). We conclude with speculation on what will be the next set of developments—Cloud QDA.

Caveat: In this chapter, we focus on digital technologies for the organization and analysis of unstructured data. We are purposely avoiding issues related to the use of technology for presentation or technologies as sites for qualitative research study.

QDAS to QDAS 2.0

QDAS: Stand Alone Computer Software

In Denzin and Lincoln's framework of the Eight Moments of Qualitative Research (2000, 2003), the first two moments (Traditional and Modernist periods from the early 1900s to post–World War II) could also be dubbed the "precomputer era of qualitative research." As the foundations of this methodological approach were under construction, researchers used notebooks, typewriters, carbon paper, and note cards. Not surprisingly, these are also the tools of the offices of the industrial age, where transportation, communications, manufacturing, and financing underwent rapid development, laying the groundwork for today's tightly interconnected global environment (Kelly, 2010).

The next quarter century of qualitative research history (1970–2008) represents five moments in Denzin and Lincoln's framework, during which qualitative researchers struggled with issues of representation, social justice, and reflexivity. In technological terms, this is the era of QDAS. QDAS, too, passed through a number of critical developmental stages, from the early isolated experiments and the first commercially marketed packages to increasing knowledge of cross-package features, the increased capacity for using multi-modal data, and specialization among tools.

Earliest packages were the Ethnograph, NUD*IST, and AQUAD. Both Mac and PC packages were common until the 1990s, when three major commercial packages came to the fore— ATLAS.ti, MaxQDA, and NVivo. Not surprisingly, it was during this period of software consolidation that QDAS aficionados placed particular emphasis on metaperspectives to QDAS (di Gregorio & Davidson, 2008; Lewins & Silver, 2007).

From the development of QDAS to the present, the mainstream of qualitative research has followed a separate path from the world of QDAS interest and development. Qualitative researchers in the mainstream looked toward the humanities for ways of approaching social questions and for insight on new data collection techniques that were not digital. QDAS adherents, on the other hand, focused on qualitative research analysis techniques as facilitated by digital analysis tools. For this reason, one finds rich discussions in mainstream qualitative research about epistemology, ontology, data collection, and representation, but limited discussion about the specifics of data analysis. In contrast, QDAS discussions are highly focused on data analysis techniques to the exclusion of topics of greater interest to the mainstream of the field.

In speculating why some qualitative researchers have developed an antipathy to new technological developments, we turned to the historical roots of our field in anthropology and sociology. Early anthropologists were dedicated to describing the lives of native peoples whose livelihoods and cultures were threatened by industrialization, often symbolized by new forms of technology. Likewise, early sociologists were dedicated to describing and fighting for the rights of laborers and other marginalized groups who were at the mercy of the effects of industrialization, here too symbolized by new forms of technology. Also connected to this symbolic dichotomy between industrialization and technology were the research methods of quantitative (like industrialization and technology) and nonquantitative or qualitative research methods (not like industrialization and technology). Many qualitative researchers (methodologists at the merger between sociology and anthropology), whether consciously or unconsciously, depicted themselves as nonindustrial, nonnumerical, and nontechnological. As the opposite, they are humanists, who honor the personal touch and decry the juggernaut of industrial progress (Davidson, 2010b).

In an interesting twist, two important affordances of QDAS—portability and transparency—may have also been off-putting to potential new users. Portability and transparency allow for visibility and scrutiny of data analysis approaches. Although mainstream qualitative researchers speak eloquently about the importance of reflexivity, transparency, and parity between researcher and researchee, their older technological approaches make in-depth scrutiny of project organization and decisions difficult. Threatened by the unknowns QDAS raised, technophobia allowed some qualitative researchers to avoid these threats, at least temporarily, and maintain the status quo (and power and resources). By keeping a shroud over issues of the techniques of data analysis through resisting the use of QDAS, which would support greater transparency, senior researchers were, in a way, ensuring their position as the dispensers of the special knowledge of qualitative research, something akin to being a shaman in the field (di Gregorio & Davidson, 2008, 2010).

An important aspect of the technophobia that grew up among mainstream qualitative researchers toward QDAS centered around the mistaken belief that each QDAS package was developed to support a certain, restricted methodological approach within qualitative research. Under this mistaken belief, one had to match one's methodology to specific QDAS programs or risk contamination and, worse, death by QDAS! In particular, many qualitative researchers came to believe QDAS was designed with grounded theory in mind, so researchers working with other approaches should not attempt to use it (Fielding, 2008; Fielding & Lee, 2007). As Tesch (1990) demonstrated, QDAS are designed to meet the generic needs of qualitative researchers and can be used by researchers working within the broad range of qualitative research approaches. This information, however, did not make its way to the broader world of qualitative researchers.

By 2005, the QDAS model was well entrenched. Each of the various packages could be depended on to provide tools to allow researchers to reflect, explore, organize, and integrate their data. No matter what the brand, there was always a component for the storage of documents or sources, organizational tools for indexing or coding the materials, and analysis tools for searching, linking, and visualizing.

Web 2.0 to QDAS 2.0

Within the last decade, the globe has been swept by a tidal wave of technological change, often referred to as Web 2.0. Web 2.0 represents the second and more interactive stage of the development of the World Wide Web. The development of the web and its evolution into Web 2.0 has had massive effects on every facet of life, from the ways we communicate and learn to how we shop and bank. Despite the reluctance of many qualitative researchers, raised in earlier eras, to actively engage with new technologies, the force of these new tools cannot be ignored. For qualitative researchers being raised in the new era, not using available digital tools is not an option (Case, 2010; Wesch, 2010).

Web 2.0 is a global phenomenon. People from every location on Earth are now able to connect digitally—reading, listening, writing, and watching—in a rich stew of interactions made possible by the presence of the Internet, the vast electronic network that spans the continents. Web 2.0 has geographically decoupled us from our physical coordinates on Earth, allowing us to enter a world in which we often feel as close to those on the other side of the globe as we do to the neighbors in the house next door. This uncoupled world takes place "in the cloud," meaning the digital world of the web. No longer are we tethered to our stand-alone computers; instead we are tethered to the web, needing a connection to access or work with our materials or to communicate with others (Kelly, 2010). Indeed, the things themselves are becoming increasingly interconnected in a process referred to as "the network of things" (IBM Social Media, 2010).

Globalization, as brought to us by Web 2.0, presents profound challenges for qualitative research and QDAS as we try to make sense of vast amounts of unstructured data, shifting markets, and a new understanding of the meaning of indigenous (Berners-Lee, 2009; Wang, 2006). The task for QDAS in the world of Web 2.0 was to transition from the stand-alone software of the proceeding era to a web-based capacity. We have dubbed this development QDAS 2.0.

Development

The beginning stages of QDAS 2.0 have been halting and inconsistent, as makes sense in the early experimental period of using a new technology. There is a major divide between the earlier QDAS developers, who are locked into technologies originally devised in a stand-alone computer era, and those developers who are starting from web-based programming.

QDAS developers have been working to transform their products from stand-alone to web-based platforms. For example, NVivo 9 Server (released in October 2010) allows for simultaneous collaboration for research teams sharing a project on a server. However, NVivo has not made the transition to cloud computing, as the server is limited to an institutional one and does not meet the needs of trans-institutional collaboration.

Web-based tools, on the other hand, have emerged rapidly, often offering one component of a research tool, requiring a combination of tools to the same thing one QDAS package could accomplish. DiRT is a web resource where you can find links to many of these tools. Examples of specific tools include the brands

Evernotes, Delicious, and Zotero. (See the references section for more information.)

Corollary developments to web-based tools are in mobile technologies. Examples of mobile technologies with implications for qualitative research include such tools as Everyday Lives, Ecove, Quickvoice, Mindject, and Ustream. (See the references section for more information.)

As QDAS developed, the major challenges to the use of technologies were internal, that is, related to the issues put forward by qualitative researchers in multiple disciplinary areas. And, as we move into the new age of Web 2.0, in addition to internal challenges, external challenges to the use of new technologies arise for qualitative researchers. Some of these challenges come with the new capacities of the technology and some arise because of the social demands that accompany Internet use by multiple communities.

In particular, many kinds of users have a desire to organize and interpret unstructured data, and developers far beyond the boundaries of qualitative research are working to meet their needs. As a result, new tools are emerging that do many of the things qualitative researchers would like in a tool, but they are not developed by those within the qualitative research field. Examples of these kinds of new tools are A.nnotate, Many Eyes, and Sand. (See the references section for more information.)

Comparison

As Web 2.0 tools have come into existence, it has been possible to match and compare them to the components of QDAS tools (see Table 4.1). As described above, both QDAS and Web 2.0 tools provide options for the critical processes in qualitative analysis— organizing, reflecting, exploring, and integrating. QDAS packages, however, are comprehensive, all-in-one forms. The user does not have to go outside to find other aids. When using Web 2.0 for the same functions, however, the user is often in the position of mashing together several different kinds of tools from different developers to get the same comprehensive results.

Both QDAS and Web 2.0 have advantages and disadvantages. QDAS has an advantage in that it is able to provide a relatively

Table 4.1: Comparison of QDAS and Web 2.0 tools

	QDAS	Web 2.0
Organizing Tools	Coding	Tagging
	Sets, families	Grouping
	Hyperlinking	Hyperlinking
Reflective tools	Memoing	Blogging
	Annotating	Annotating
	Mapping	Mapping
Exploring tools	Model, map, network	Visualizing
	Text search, coding search	Searching
Integrating tools	Memoing with hyperlinks	Blogging with hyperlinks
	Merging projects	Collaborating through wikis

(Davidson & di Gregorio, 2010; di Gregorio, 2010)

seamless container in which data and analysis functions are used, whereas until recently it was more difficult in Web 2.0 to work across tools. Another issue is that QDAS, with its stand-alone base, is much more private than Web 2.0, which is located in the cloud, as techies would say. However, the comprehensiveness of QDAS tools has resulted in a high learning curve. In contrast, most Web 2.0 tools are distinguished by their low learning curve. It remains to be seen which aspects of the old and the new will be combined to create the next versions of QDAS tools.

Fulfilling the Promise of QDAS 2.0

In speculating on the future development of QDAS 2.0, we hypothesized the QDAS packages of the future would be grounded in Web 2.0 and:

- possess an intuitive and visually attractive interface;
- be easily accessible;
- have powerful, intuitive, and contextualized search tools;
- be easily combined to create new user-specialized tools;
- provide opportunities for visualization and spatialization;
- offer ease of integration with quantification tools; and
- offer strong functionality for collaborative work. (di Gregorio & Davidson, 2010)

Such a tool emerged in July 2010 under the name of Dedoose, a fully web-based comprehensive QDAS package that meets the bulk of the criteria above. Interestingly, although the developer had initially created a stand-alone QDAS package (Ethno-notes), he jumped out of the stand-alone mode to work from a web-based platform rather than transform the earlier work. Knowledgeable about the comprehensive needs of QDAS packages, he was able to move more efficiently into the new environment. The results are worthy of review as this is the first QDAS package to truly shake off the chains of the stand-alone computer age.

Dedoose has an intuitive and visually attractive interface. There are limited menus, and the icons used are clear and quickly discernible. The program is web based and, thus, easily accessible, if one has Internet access. Users pay a monthly fee for access. It possesses a range of visualization tools, similar to other QDAS tools. Dedoose provides ease of collaboration, and multiple team members can work on the project. Dedoose has made strong efforts to provide robust security for users.

It is important to note that Dedoose, although a web-based tool, is in the traditional QDAS model. It is structured in a similar way to other QDAS tools, with sources/documents. memos, codes/nodes, search, and visualization tools, similar to what the major stand-alone QDAS packages are offering. Being web based, however, Dedoose is able to be nimble in its response to changes, patches, and developments in ways that the stand-alone software developers, who must wait for the release of a new version, cannot be.

Dedoose seeks to brand itself as a tool for mixed methods, emphasizing the quantitative tools it makes available (i.e., identification of demographics or variables) and the ability to run searches by single, double, or multi-variables and view the results with various visualization tools. In this capacity, Dedoose is no different than the stand-alone QDAS packages, but they have not chosen to describe themselves as mixed methods, fearing, perhaps, that this designation would scare off some qualitative researchers.

The arrival of Dedoose is cause for celebration; it is a hybrid form that serves as a bridge between the traditional stand-alone PC CAQDAS and a cloud-computing application.

Web 2.0 to Cloud QDA

We have dubbed what is beyond QDAS 2.0 as Cloud QDA. In Cloud QDA, we anticipate that the early experimental Web 2.0 developments will consolidate. Moreover the new global, collaborative, and virtual-time ways of working will gain greater foothold for scholarly work. Tim Berners-Lee, the recognized founder of the web, identifies Web 3.0 (the era following Web 2.0) as a world of data, and Cloud QDA can be seen as a response to these circumstances (Berners-Lee, 2009).

As we did once with QDAS 2.0 (di Gregorio & Davidson, 2010), we are now speculating about the ways Cloud QDA will develop. Our speculations are grounded, this time, in our increasing knowledge about the global impact of the new Internet technologies and the ways it has affected higher education and research communities.

We believe Cloud QDA will break from the QDAS model that first emerged in the 1980s. We anticipate there will be significant changes in design and capacities.

A first step in Cloud QDA is DiscoverText (www.discovertext.com). It is dissimilar from traditional QDAS products in that it focuses on analyzing large amounts of textual material—particularly web-generated text such as tweets, emails, Facebook news feeds, etc. It also differs in that it uses algorithms, as well as human coding, to trawl through textual data. It is a cloud application as your data reside in the web. What is unique is that it hopes to emulate social networking sites in creating a network of analysis peers. Users create a profile on the site with their interests and qualifications. Users can search the peer database for people they may want to work on a project—for example, to find coders—or they may invite others not registered yet with DiscoverText to join them as peers. The site is targeting a range of users from academics, government agencies, market researchers, and law firms as well as ordinary consumers and citizens.

It will be essential for global partnerships to emerge between qualitative researchers in academia and those in other realms (business, government, etc.). This is necessary if we are to have access to adequate intellectual and financial resources to pursue development of robust Cloud QDA tools. For instance, IBM's social networking team is developing many kinds of software with vast implications for qualitative research. It is conceivable that they could benefit from access to qualitative researchers' perspectives.

Development of Cloud QDA will need to turn to the online global community. No longer can we rely solely on one organizational or institutional base. It is critical that we work in an environment where we can flexibly integrate resources to develop this next set of tools. Examples of two organizations that are models in their forwarding-looking approach to these issues are the Joint Information Systems Committee in the United Kingdom and the Office of Digital Humanities of the National Endowment for the Humanities in the United States. (See the references section for more information.)

The tensions related to collaboration in these new formats must be addressed for Cloud QDA development to thrive. The tensions come from many directions. Previously in academic circles, collaborative work was often not rewarded. There was also tension for academics in collaborating with nonacademic partners. In collaborating across institutional barriers, major differences in culture, style, and expectations must be considered.

In Cloud QDA, we anticipate that research will increasingly include more extensive and more equitable involvement with participants. Thus, crowd sourcing and folksonomies will be important to future qualitative researchers. Participants will be able to actively engage with researchers in data collection, analysis, and the representation of the findings. All aspects of a collaborative study will be available to both parties. The distance between expert and participant will be diminished by the key qualities of QDAS and its subsequent iterations—portability and transparency. For instance, Ushahidi (http://www.ushahidi.com/) is an open source crowd sourcing tool that brings together information collection, visualization, and interactive mapping tools to support information sharing during times of crisis. This tool was developed in Africa and is now widely used in other parts of the world where individuals on the scene can serve as participants and researchers as they report on conditions in emergency situations.

The logic and methods of search are also changing rapidly. For example, the semantic web is a search mechanism that shoots us far beyond the Boolean logic of the past. What has come to be called the" Internet of Things," objects connected by sensors, will also come to play an increasingly important role in the logic and methods of search (IBM Social Media, 2010).

The trend toward development of applications for web-based and mobile computing will continue in the era of Cloud QDA, and qualitative researchers will not be immune to the lure of widgets and add-ons for data collection and analysis. The iPad and cell phones have both demonstrated important possibilities for the support of qualitative research activities (Johnson, 2010; Raento et al, 2009).

Text-to-voice transcription, voice-to-text transcription, and all other forms of moving audio and visual to textual will continue to advance. This will greatly ease the burden of transcription for qualitative researchers and increase the amount of analyzable material available to researchers on specific projects.

An area that has been begging for attention in the realm of QDAS are issues related to chronological or longitudinal analysis of project materials. Currently within QDAS, we lack significant timeline tools. We anticipate that Cloud QDA will bring many innovations in the realm of tracking project material in this area. Dedoose, with its new timeline tools, offers the first hints of this development.

Some of the data in the world of web data are structured and some are unstructured. Qualitative researchers are, by nature, gluttons for unstructured or nonnumerical data, but increasingly they will have the opportunity to cross the barriers seamlessly with tools that connect qualitative and quantitative perspectives easily. This is a trend in QDAS 2.0 and will only increase in importance in Cloud QDA.

In the early twenty-first century, will the QDAS emphasis on data analysis continue or will it be subsumed by the humanities concerns of mainstream qualitative research? Is something new in the development? Will the transparency of the new tools cause analysis to transition to a completely new set of expectations and standards? Many scholars have attempted to create a merger between QDAS and qualitative research's aesthetic concerns. Their work points to new directions for the field (Battacharya, 2009; Battacharya & McCullough, 2008; Davidson, 2009, 2010a; Davidson et al, 2009; Hundley, 2009a, 2009b).

Finally, the opportunities of Web 3.0 bring with them an equal set of dangers. In particular, how will the increasing openness of the web-based world be countered by the continuing need to protect the safety of participants in any qualitative research study and ensure the security of the materials—words, pictures, and artifacts—that they share? In each era, developers have had to create new solutions to these problems. Web-based researchers and developers have created solutions with which to meet required ethical standards, but there will have to be continued vigilance to these concerns (Bassett & O'Riordan, 2002; Buchanan et al., 2010; di Gregorio & Davidson, 2009; Raento et al, 2009).

Conclusions

When we began our foray into the uses of QDAS, we could not have anticipated the vast changes that would occur over the last decade. Nor could we have anticipated the speed at which the development of the web would proceed and all the changes this entails.

Our journey with QDAS has been a global one, collaborating ourselves across two continents and with colleagues from multiple nations. What seemed like a fairly narrow interest area—qualitative research technologies—has, with the development of Web 2.0 and the corresponding deluge of unstructured data, become an issue of global significance.

If qualitative researchers are to meet the challenges of global contexts, they must have digital tools that provide support for this new, challenging, and complex environment. Moreover, they must have the will to engage with the tools and the foresight to demand a place at the table where conversation about needed tools takes place. In today's world, QDAS development has expanded rapidly beyond a handful of academic locations to include diverse public and private entities. New partnerships and creative collaborations undertaken in new global circumstances will be at the heart of future developments in qualitative research and its technologies.

References

Anderson, P. (2007). What is Web 2.0? Ideas, technologies and implications for education. *JISC Technology and Standards Watch*. www.jisc.ac.uk/media/documents/techwatch/tsw0701b.pdf (accessed January 15, 2011,).

Bassett, E., & O'Riordan, K. (2002). Ethics of internet research: Contesting the human subjects research model. *Ethics and Information Technology, 4*, 3, 233–247.

Battacharya, K. (2009). Portal to three wiki spaces developed by K. Battacharya's qualitative research classes. http://kakali.org/memphiswebsite/kakaliorg1/community.html (accessed August 21, 2009).

Battacharya, K., & McCullough, A. (2008). *De/colonizing democratic digital learning environments: Carving a space for wiki-ology in qualitative inquiry.* Paper presented at a pre-conference day of the Fourth International Congress on Qualitative Inquiry, University of Illinois, Urbana-Champaign, Urbana, May 14–17.

Berners-Lee, T. (2009). The next web of open, linked data. http://www.youtube.com/watch?v=OM6XIICm_qo (accessed August 11, 2009).

Buchanan, E., Delap, A., & Mason, R. (2010). Ethical research and design in cyberspace. Paper presented at the 43rd Hawaii International Conference on Systems Science, Kauai, January 5–8.

Case, A. (2010). Cyborg anthropology: A short introduction. http://www.you-tube.com/watch?v=rCvMWZePS8E (accessed October 17, 2010).

Davidson, J. (2009). Autoethnography/self-study/arts-based research/qualitative data analysis software: mixing, shaking, and recombining qualitative research tools in the act of recreating oneself as qualitative researcher, instructor, and learner. Paper presented at the Fifth International Congress on Qualitative Inquiry. University of Illinois, Champaign-Urbana, May 20–23.

Davidson, J. (2010a). The journal project. Presentation to the Associates Group of the Center for Women and Work, University of Massachusetts-Lowell, October 12.

Davidson, J. (2010b). Technology, aesthetics, and qualitative research: Reshaping the agenda of our methodological future. Invited paper delivered at a conference to honor the work of scholar Bertram Bruce, University of Illinois, September 16.

Davidson, J., Donohoe, K., Tello, S. Christensen, L., Steingisser, G., & Varoudakis, C. (2009). Initiating qualitative inquiry: Report on an experiment with a cluster of powerful tools-autoethnography, arts-based research, and qualitative data analysis software. Poster session presented at the Fifth International Congress on Qualitative Inquiry, University of Illinois, Champaign-Urbana, May 20–23.

Denzin, N. K., & Lincoln, Y. S. (2002). Introduction: The discipline and practice of qualitative research. In N. K. Denzin & Y. S. Lincoln (Eds.), *The landscape of qualitative research* (2nd ed., pp. 1–53). Thousand Oaks, CA: Sage.

Denzin, N. K., & Lincoln, Y. S. (2003). Introduction: The discipline and practice of qualitative research. In N. K. Denzin & Y. S. Lincoln (Eds.), *The landscape of qualitative research* (2nd ed., pp. 1–45). Thousand Oaks, CA: Sage.

di Gregorio, S. (2008b). Folksonomies and delicious. http://folksonomiesand-delicious.pbworks.com/ (accessed August 12, 2009).

di Gregorio, S. (2009). Qualitative analysis and Web 2.0. Paper presented at the 2nd International Workshop on Computer-Aided Qualitative Research, Utrecht, The Netherlands, June 4–5.

di Gregorio, S. (2010). *Using Web 2.0 tools for qualitative analysis: An exploration.* Proceedings of the 43rd Annual Hawaii International Conference on System Sciences (CD-ROM), January 5–8. Washington, DC: Computer Society Press.

di Gregorio, S., & Davidson, J. (2008). *Qualitative research design for software users.* London: Open University Press/McGraw-Hill.

diGregorio, S., & Davidson, J. (2009). *Research design and ethical issues when working within an E-Project.* Paper presented at the 5th International

Congress of Qualitative Inquiry at the University of Illinois, Champaign-Urbana, May 20–23.

di Gregorio, S., & Davidson, J. (2010). Qualitative data analysis software development and future trends in qualitative research. Presented at the 3nd International Workshop on Computer-Aided Qualitative Research, Lisbon, Portugal, October 7–8. http://prezi.com/82arnt4a5pyb/qdas-development-and-future-trends/ (accessed January 15, 2011).

Economist, The. (2010). New rules for big data. February 25. http://www.economist.com/node/15557487 (accessed January 15, 2011).

Fielding, N. (2008). The role of computer-assisted qualitative data analysis: Impact on emergent methods in qualitative research. In S. Hesse-Biber & P. Leavy (Eds.), *Handbook of emergent methods* (pp. 675–695). New York: Guildford Press.

Fielding, N., & Lee, R. (2007). Honouring the past, scoping the future. Plenary paper presented at CAQDAS 07: Advances in Qualitative Computing Conference, Royal Holloway, University of London, April 18–20.

Hundley, M. (2009a). *Data as event.* Paper presented at the Fifth International Congress on Qualitative Inquiry, University of Illinois, Champaign-Urbana, May 20–23.

Hundley, M. (2009b). Gilding the lily: Creating the bard on the digital porch. Paper presented at the Fifth International Congress on Qualitative Inquiry, University of Illinois, Champaign-Urbana, May 20–23.

IBM Social Media. 2010. The Internet of things. http://www.youtube.com/watch?v=sfEbMV295Kk (accessed November 21, 2010).

Johnson, F. (2010). Ten ways the iPad will radically change market research. Blog on qualitative marketing research. Posted: September 21. http://www.researcharts.com/2010/09/ten-ways-the-ipad-will-radically-change-market-research/ (accessed October 17, 2010).

Kelley, K. (2010). *What technology wants.* New York: Viking Press.

Lewins, A., & Silver, C. (2007). *Using software in qualitative research: A step-by-step guide.* Thousand Oaks, CA: Sage.

Lieber, E. 2009. Mixing qualitative and quantitative methods: Insights into design and analysis issues. *Journal of Ethnographic and Qualitative Research*, *3*, 2, 218–227.

Raento, M., Oulasvirta, A., & Eagle, N. (2009). Smartphones: An emerging tool for social scientists. *Sociological Methods and Research*, 37, 426.

Tesch, R. (1990). *Qualitative research: Analysis types and software tools.* Basingstoke, UK: Falmer.

Thorpe, J. (2010). Hacking the newsroom. Presentation at the IBM Center for Social Software Speaker Series, Cambridge, Massachusetts, June 6.

Vander Wal, T. (2007). "Folksonomy coinage and definition" (static permanent web document). http://www.vanderwal.net/folksonomy.html (accessed December 12, 2008).

Wang, H. (2006). Globalization and curriculum studies: Tensions, challenges and possibilities. *Journal of the American Association for the Advancement of Curriculum Studies*, 2, February, 1–17. http://www2.uwstout.edu/content/jaaacs/vol2/wang.htm (accessed August 25, 2008).

Wesch, M. (2010). University of Kansas Digital Ethnography Project. http:mediatedcultures.net (accessed November 21, 2010).

Agencies

JISC; Joint Information Systems Committee. http://www.jisc.ac.uk/ (accessed November 21, 2010).

Office of Digital Humanities, National Endownment for the Humanities. http://www.neh.gov/whoweare/divisions/DigitalHumanities/DHSUGprojects.html (accessed November 21, 2010).

Qualitative Data Analysis Software

ATLAS.ti . *ATLAS.ti Home Page.* http://www.atlasti.com/ (accessed July 31, 2009).

MAXQDA. http://www.maxqda.com/ (accessed August 21, 2009).

NVIVO. A product of QSR International. http://www.qsrinternational.com (accessed August 21, 2009).

Other Tools

A.nnotate. http://a.nnotate.com/about.html (accessed August 13, 2009).

Dedoose. www.Dedoose.net (accessed November 21, 2010).

Delicious. www.delicious.com (accessed November 21, 2010).

DiRT. Digital Research Tools Wiki. http://digitalresearchtools.pbworks.com/ (accessed July 31, 2009).

DiscoverText. http://www.discovertext.com (accessed November 21, 2010).

Evernote. http://www.evernote.com (accessed November 21, 2010).

Everyday Lives. www.everydaylives.com (accessed December 30, 2009).

Many Eyes. http://www-958.ibm.com/software/data/cognos/manyeyes/ (accessed November 21, 2010).

Sand. http://www.research.ibm.com/social/projects_sand.html (accessed November 21, 2010).

Ushahidi. http://www.ushahidi.com (accessed November 26, 2010).

Zotero. www.zotero.com (accessed November 21, 2010).

Chapter 5

Using Situational Analysis for Critical Qualitative Research Purposes

Michelle Salazar Perez
Gaile S. Cannella

In our contemporary condition of global neoliberal hypercapitalism in which new forms of imperialism are constituted in the name of democracy, education, and even social justice, conceptualizations and practices of critical qualitative social science are a necessity. Research perspectives and methodologies are required that challenge universals, normality, and truths while avoiding oversimplifications and generalizations. Power is complex, intersecting, and always/already everywhere. We have come to realize that we may need to eliminate beliefs about research that have labeled individuals and groups and resulted in power/control/ intervention by one group over others. Our research will most likely require partnering with traditionally marginalized and silenced communities as well as recognizing systemic, institutionalized power structures that dominate society(ies). To construct a critical social science that would reconceptualize what we think we can know and how we take actions in solidarity with/for those who have been traditionally marginalized, research methodologies are needed that do not require restricted boundaries. Rather methods are called for that are emergent, reflexive, and malleable in order to mirror the complexity of the issue, structure and/or system being studied. Situational Analysis (SA), developed by Adele Clarke (2005), offers great potential as such a method.

Introduction to Situational Analysis

Emerging from the field of medicine, SA is a feminist, postmodern research method rooted in conceptualizations of grounded theory. Social phenomena are studied employing qualitative methodologies like inductive coding and categorizing techniques (Clarke, 2005). Although phenomenological research typically attempts to produce data from interviews and/or ethnographic practice to study human action, SA makes possible a more complete construction of the full situation, including the discourses that both legitimated and are created by the situation. Without being bounded by a particular set of rules, SA offers a way in which to organize and frame a study focusing on discourse (or what Clarke describes as already produced data) with the flexibility necessary to address the unanticipated issues that may surface. The assumptions and processes involved in SA include: (1) valuing and legitimating multiple knowledges; (2) reflexivity (e.g., the researcher as instrument, as subjective, and producer of knowledge); (3) the use of the narrative, visual, and historical as revealing social life; (4) the use of cartography or mapmaking as an *analytical tool* throughout an emergent research process; and (5) the provision of a thick analysis to address complexity, differences, contradictions, and heterogeneity rather than attempting to develop formal theory.

SA allows for qualitative inquiry to focus on the way in which discourses: (1) are negotiated in social relationships and interactions; (2) manufacture "identities and subjectivities" (Clarke, 2005, p. 155); and (3) construct "power/knowledge, ideologies, and control" (Clarke, 2005, p. 155). Maps are used as tools to examine these three ways of understanding discourse by inductively analyzing the content found in the data while using supplementary qualitative research approaches to facilitate a hybridity of methods. The content used to construct maps is found in the discourses that directly address the situation, those related to the situation, and the positions explicitly expressed or absent (Clarke, 2005).

Because the construction of situational maps is a postmodern analytical method, the process requires reflexivity and multiple readings of discourses from various sources to continually develop and revise research focus and design. Clarke instructed three types of maps in the initial construction of SA: situational, social spheres/power arenas, and positional. Situational maps allow the researcher to articulate the elements associated with a particular issue. Social spheres/power arenas maps illustrate analyses of how people organize relationships within structured conditions.[1] Positional maps represent the range of locations found in discourse practices, including exclusions and erasures of individuals, groups, concepts, knowledges, and perspectives. The method does not require that all types of maps be used, and the maps chosen or analytical processes may be modified. Further, a researcher engaged with/in a particular investigation may create new maps as needed.

The purpose of this chapter is to explain the use of SA for both initial research questions/design and as a data construction and analysis process tool. We describe the process as it was used to construct and implement a research study of early childhood public education in post-Katrina New Orleans.

Situational Analysis and Initial Research Design

To begin any form of qualitative research that can be considered trustworthy and credible (Lincoln & Guba, 1985), the researcher must immerse her- or himself within the context. Exposure to the discourse practices that are constructing and being constructed by the circumstance facilitate decisions regarding both research questions and the types of data that should be used to address those questions. Media awareness, personnel community engagement, and informational meetings are examples of the forms of engagement that contribute to the construction of a plan for research.

Using Situational Maps to Determine Initial Research Questions

Situational maps allow the researcher to broadly articulate the elements (both human and nonhuman) emerging from the context that are associated with a particular issue (Clarke, 2005). The initial focus of our New Orleans study was developed by creating three types of situational maps: a topic map, a messy map, and an ordered map. Although there are two types of situational maps described by Clarke (the messy map and the ordered map), as we began to explore initial research questions, a more basic foundation for analysis seemed to be needed. Therefore, we first developed what we called a "*topic* situational map." We used this type of map to focus our attentions toward the extremely broad environmental context. A *messy* map then identified the broader discourses related to the situation and the key individuals, groups, organizations, and/or institutions that participate in, are a part of, make invisible, or produce constructions of the issues that emerge (Clarke, 2005). A messy situational map includes "all the analytically pertinent human and nonhuman, material, and symbolic/discursive elements of a particular situation *as framed by those in it and by the analyst*" (Clarke, 2005, p. 87; emphasis in the original). Once the initial messy map had been created, an ordered situational map was used to organize the ideas in a more systematic fashion and provide additional, more specific examples of individuals, groups, and issues to present a better picture of the discourses related to the situation.

Map 1: Topic Map

Topics for this map (Figure 5.1) were selected based on brainstorming from broad personal experiences with issues impacting education for young children related to disaster in New Orleans as we lived there after Hurricane Katrina. Volunteering, attending public community meetings, having conversations with families and former teachers, and conducting general readings of discourses found in the media are examples of these experiences.

An example of the way in which key issues were chosen to be part of the initial topic map can be illustrated with one of our volunteer experiences that occurred in a fourth-grade classroom in a New Orleans public school. One morning, an administrator required that the teacher give a survey to her students, which the teacher then asked me to administer to the class as a whole. The content of the survey was extremely personal and intrusive as it inquired about the children's experiences during and after

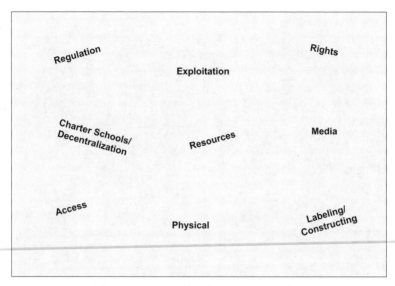

Figure 5.1. Initial topic map: Public discourses and lived experiences, specifically relating public education, disaster, and young children. Adapted from "Messy Situational Map: Nurses' Work under Managed Care," by A. E. Clarke, 2005, *Situational Analysis: Grounded Theory after the Postmodern Turn,* p. 95. Copyright 2005 by Sage Publications, Inc

hurricane Katrina. Once it was complete, the children were asked to resume with a Louisiana Educational Assessment Program test preparation activity. In reflecting on this experience, it seems that requiring students to fill out a survey for an undisclosed research purpose with little privacy given and no anonymity can be viewed as exploitative. Therefore, this situation provides a rationale for choosing "exploitation" as one of the overall issues impacting young children in New Orleans, and, as a result, was chosen to be part of the initial topic map. Additional issues on the map were chosen on a similar basis. A reflexive reading/analysis of the issues chosen to be placed on the initial topic map led to the development of the specific purpose for the study: How are discourses created that influence access to an equitable public education for all young children following disaster? This specific purpose is the focus of the second messy situational map.

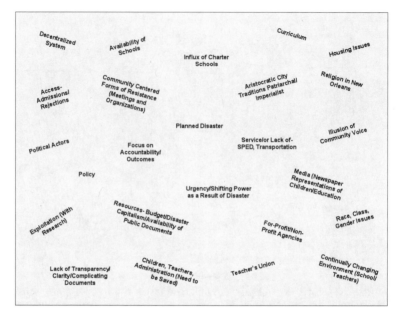

Figure 5.2. Messy situational map: Discourses created that influence access to an equitable public education for all young children following disaster. Adapted from "Messy Situational Map: Nurses' Work Under Managed Care," by A.E. Clarke, 2005, *Situational Analysis: Grounded Theory After the Postmodern Turn*, p.95. Copyright 2005 by Sage Publications, Inc.

Map 2: Messy Situational Map

Our second situational map (Figure 5.2), labeled a "messy situational map" by Clarke, includes specific situations related to the purpose of the study. The content of this map was determined from a reflexive rereading/analysis of the initial topic map and the discourses associated with additional volunteer experiences, attending public community meetings, and further rereadings of the discourses found in the media. Although every topic listed on this messy situational map was not addressed in detail during the course of the study (which would be the case in most studies), each topic was chosen because it represented part of the overall situation impacting young children and public education in New Orleans during the time period being considered.

For one year, we attempted to immerse ourselves in the everyday culture of New Orleans by attending community meetings and events. This was especially true for the first author related to community organizations. One organization was a group called Concern, Community, and Compassion (C3), a grassroots group that meets regularly and advocates for the right to fair public housing in New Orleans. C3 also mobilizes resistance for other causes relating to social justice such as protecting homeless civil rights and fighting against civic repression (an issue that has intensified since Hurricane Katrina with a heightened police presence, especially in low-income neighborhoods and communities of color). Accounts witnessed during this involvement with C3 influenced the decision to consider housing as an issue directly related to equity for young children and is therefore included in the messy map. Other issues selected to be part of this map were determined by similar experiences or with general readings of discourses found in public documents.

Map 3: Ordered Situational Map

The ordered situational map frames and organizes the issues addressed in the messy map. The organization process for developing the ordered map is in itself a form of analysis. A series of headings is suggested in order to group the issues from the messy map. These include: individual human elements/actors, collective human elements/actors, discursive constructions of individual and/or collective human actors, political/economic elements, temporal elements, major issues/debates, other kinds of elements, nonhuman elements/actants, implicated/salient actors/actants, discursive construction of nonhuman actants, sociocultural/symbolic elements, spatial elements, and related discourses (Clarke, 2005). However, the phrasing/meaning of the headings may be modified (and are not all required) so that the map can appropriately fit the context of a study. As the issues from the messy map are revisited to create the ordered map, some may become more specific in description (as depicted in Figure 5.3A and Figure 5.3B in the highlighted elements). Additionally, developing and revising the ordered map: (1) Frames issues/actors/actants impacting young children and

Individual Human Elements/Actors- *Key individuals and significant (unorganized) people in the situation*

Governor Kathleen Babineaux Blanco*   Teachers   Members of school boards*

Administrators   Political actors   Parents*   Students

Collective Human Elements/Actors- *Particular groups; specific organizations*

Cowen Education Institute*   Teacher's Union

Conservative Think Tanks (Thomas B. Fordham Foundation/Heritage Foundation)*

Charter Schools/School choice groups*   Business Leaders*

Community centered forms of resistance (meeting s and organizations)

Discursive Constructions of Individual and/or collective human actors-*As found in the situation*

Social world constructions of young children and communities of color (needing to be saved)*

Illusion of community voice

Political/Economic Elements- *The state; particular industry/ies; local/regional/global orders;*

political parties; politicized issues

Resources- Budget/disaster capitalism   Decentralized System   For profit/non-profit agencies

General Policy*   Lack of transparency/clarity/ complicating documents

Specific Policy Agenda (e.g. federal funding for charter schools)

Temporal Elements: US National Historical Frame- *Historical, seasonal, crisis, and/or trajectory aspects*

Planned Disaster   Capitalism*   Neoliberalism*

School Choice/Charter School movement in the US*

Major Issues/Debates (Usually Contested) *-As found in the situation; and see positional map*

Influx of charter schools (privatization of public schools)   Services (or lack of- SPED/transportation)

Access- admissions/rejections   Focus on Accountability/Outcomes

Figure 5.3A Part one of ordered situational map: Discourses that influence access to an equitable public education for all young children following disaster. Adapted from "Ordered Situational Map: Nurses' Work Under Managed Care," by A.E. Clarke, 2005, *Situational Analysis: Grounded Theory After the Postmodern Turn*, p.97. Copyright 2005 by Sage Publications, Inc.

public education in New Orleans as related to disaster; (2) assists in examining the social relationships and interactions found in the discourses; and (3) begins the process of identifying possible constructs of "power/knowledge, ideologies, and control" (Clarke, 2005, p. 15).

Examining the content of the ordered map created during the initial design of the study then assisted us in developing the specific research questions:

• How are young children being discussed/represented in the charter school discourse surrounding public education in post-Katrina New Orleans?

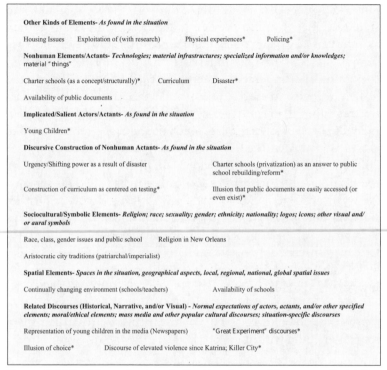

Figure 5.3B Part two of ordered situational map: Discourses that influence access to an equitable public education for all young children following disaster. Adapted from "Ordered Situational Map: Nurses' Work Under Managed Care," by A.E. Clarke, 2005, *Situational Analysis: Grounded Theory After the Postmodern Turn,* p.97. Copyright 2005 by Sage Publications, Inc.

A. What and who is included?

B. What and who is excluded (being left out)?

• What are specific lived experiences that illustrate social justice/injustice and/or increased/decreased opportunities related to this discourse for young children and disaster?

• How are these situations related to the way in which young children are constructed publically?

The ordered map also helped determine the major and supplementary sources that would be used to collect, construct, and analyze data specifically to answer the research questions.

One would expect that additional public gatherings, media, and state documents would provide a depth of information as well as interviews related to personal experience. However, because of our concern with the imperialist practices embedded within the notion of ethnographic interviews that claims to "know" the "other," we chose to use documents and public conversations as data sources rather than constructing new information gathering from individual persons. The sources included: major data sources like the *Times Picayune* (the local newspaper) articles since August 29, 2005 (the day the hurricane made landfall as a Category 3 storm), the Louisiana Department of Education website and documents, New Orleans Public School and New Orleans Recovery District websites and policy documents; supplemental data sources (as illustrations of issues generated from the major sources) like New Orleans Charter School websites, New Orleans Parent Guide, and a range of additional public meetings. Our decision not to interview individuals is/was independent of the use of situational mapping. Although SA does require a variety of data sources to capture the complexity of the context, decisions regarding these sources are fluid within the method.

Data Collection, Construction, and Constant Analysis

SA requires that all data sources, both major and supplementary, be utilized simultaneously to address each specific question developed for the study as all are related and impact the overall understanding of the situation. As new maps are fashioned and data emerge, research design and procedures are/can be revised. As data are collected, situational, social spheres/power arenas, and positional maps are created resulting in new constructions of data (as the body of maps) and continued analysis and revision. Further, the method is fluid, allowing for new visions of map components and even conceptualizations of new types of maps.

Situational Maps

Messy Maps

Since SA allows for and facilitates the continual revisiting and revisioning of maps throughout the research project, data collection and analysis can begin with maps created during initial design of the research questions, like the situational maps that we constructed to provide focus to our research questions for the New Orleans early childhood study. The development of additional situational maps, as well as the revision of initial maps, is then shaped by the data retrieved from major and supplementary sources and the researcher's engagement with that data.

We also suggest that the researcher determine an organizational method to facilitate rereading, tracking, and location of bits of data (in our study, e.g., example personal stories, circumstances in a particular school, quotes from public officials). SA involves a large amount of information that cannot all be specifically shown on maps that tend to represent the "whole" of a particular circumstance. Therefore, we chose to use "constant comparison" (Lincoln & Guba, 1985, p. 335) to facilitate map construction. First, we describe the detailed process (including constant comparison as a method for organizing data) used to create situational maps throughout the study. The two additional types of maps suggested by Clarke, social spheres/power arenas and positional, were also used during constant analysis. However, as the process for constructing these two types of maps is often dependent on analysis of situational maps, these types of maps are described in more general terms.

The following is a description of how a messy map was constructed and information from the map coded for analysis using one component of the New Orleans study; articles from the *Times Picayune* determined using "charter school" as the search term.

- The researcher first immersed herself in the content of the articles retrieved, beginning with articles immediately following Hurricane Katrina.
- Emerging discourse themes were placed in an informal fashion on the messy map. The map was given a label, Messy Map 1-A. The 1 symbolizes the first group of maps

Messy Map 1-A, TP, CS,
10-12-05a, 12-08-06c

Element/Discourse from Messy Map: **Equity**

Equity is talked about in terms of distribution of funding and access to safe and functional facilitates.

Figure 5.4. Example note card for a messy map. Illustrates the way in which an index card that corresponds to a messy map might be fashioned.

(in various studies, there could be additional groupings as the discourses are analyzed) and the A represents the first map in the series of a group.

- Note cards were then created for each item listed on the messy map. An example of the way in which an individual card was coded is Map 1-A (e.g., the corresponding map), TP (the source, *Times Picayune*), CS (the search term, *Charter School*), and all dates of the articles that correspond to the item on the map. When there were multiple articles from the same newspaper with the same date, the articles were coded as 10-12-05a, 10-12-05b, and so on. Also, if a particular theme emerged in multiple articles, the multiple dates were recorded on the card. Therefore, a particular card representing a discourse theme listed on a messy map may have the code Map1-A, TP, CS, 10-12-05a, 12-08-06c. See Figure 5.4 for an example of a note card that corresponds to a particular messy map.

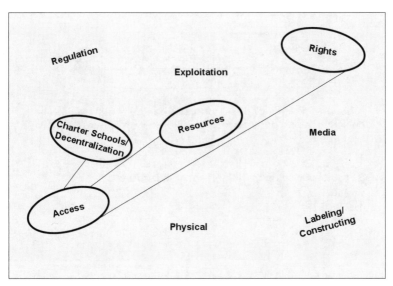

Figure 5.5. Relational analysis map. Illustrates the relationship between access, charter schools/decentralization and rights. Adapted from "Relational Analysis Using Situational Map: Focus on Nurses' Emotion Work," by A.E. Clarke, 2005, *Situational Analysis: Grounded Theory After the Postmodern Turn,* p.105. Copyright 2005 by Sage Publications, Inc.

- After making note cards for each element listed on the initial messy map, a memo, or narrative, is provided on each card to explain the rationale for choosing the particular discourse for the map along with any other information pertinent to that term/issue (e.g., multiple representations of the term in the discourse, links to a specific group).
- After rereading a particular set of data used to create an initial messy map and a revisiting of the information on the corresponding note cards, the data were analyzed by revising the messy map to show possible shifts in the focus of the discourses relating to the text.

Analysis has been "saturated" (Clark, 2005, p. 108) when all possibilities for composure of the situational messy map and multiple readings of major and supplementary sources have taken place.

Relational Analysis with Messy Map 1-A
Focal Word "Access"
Relationship: Access and Charter Schools/
Decentralization

A general reading of the discourses has shown that some charter schools deny access to children with admission requirements.

Specific examples of this relationship is found in:

TP, CS, 10-05-06a
TP, CS, 04-12-07c

Figure 5.6. Example note card for relational analysis map. Illustrates the way in which an index card that corresponds to a relational map might be fashioned.

Relational Analysis with Messy Maps

Clarke (2005) also describes relational analysis as a tool for analyzing relationships among discourses listed on a messy map. Although this type of analysis may be used for some portions of a study, the method may not be employed for every messy map developed. To conduct relational analysis, one must first have a general understanding of all the discourses associated with an initial/revised messy map. Then, each term on the messy map will be used as a focal point to determine the relationships that exist (or may not exist) among the issues. Lines can be drawn from the chosen focal point to the related elements on the map. Using the content of the topic map originally created as part of initial design in the New Orleans study, Figure 5.5 is an example of a relational analysis messy map; the focal point of "access" is related to "charter schools/decentralization," "resources," and "rights."

Three note cards were created in this example to describe the relationship that exists between the focal point access and each of the related terms chosen. The note cards denote the corresponding relational map with similar memo and coding as described previously (see Figure 5.6).

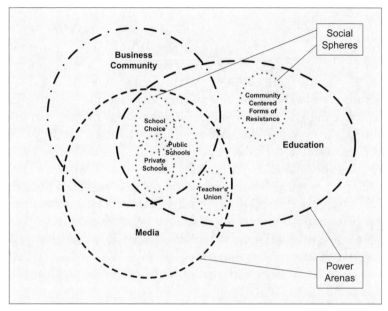

Figure 5.7. Example social spheres/power arenas map. Illustrates the way in which power arenas like education, the business community, and the media interact with social spheres like school choice, private schools, public schools, the teacher's union, and community centered forms of resistance. Adapted from "Social Worlds/Arenas Map: RU486 Discourse Project," by A.E. Clarke, 2005, *Situational Analysis: Grounded Theory After the Postmodern Turn,* p. 195. Copyright 2005 by Sage Publications, Inc.

Once all elements on the map have been placed at the center of analysis and note cards have been made, additional messy and relational maps are fashioned to uncover further issues and relationships among them. Eventually, this process will facilitate decisions concerning which "stories" (Clarke, 2005, p. 102) to pursue based on connections (or lack of connections) made between elements listed on each map.

Ordered Situational Map

The ordered map serves as a tool to organize, structure, and provide further detail of the content from the messy maps. (Again, see Figure 5.1 and Figure 5.2 for ordered maps created for the initial design of our New Orleans study.) Although categories have been developed by Clarke (2005) to assist in creating the ordered map (e.g., *Sociocultural/Symbolic Elements* and *Political/Economic Elements*), these can be used as suggested or modified to fit a particular set of data and/or messy map focus. As the elements from messy maps are revisited to generate the ordered map, some descriptions of the issues may become more specific (for instance by including names of organizations or political figures that are part of the overall understanding of a situation but that have not been included in the messy maps). The process of developing and revising the ordered map in itself is a form of analysis as it assists in: (1) framing the issues/actors/actants impacting the situation; (2) examining the social relationships and interactions found in the discourses; and (3) beginning the process of identifying possible constructs of "power/knowledge, ideologies, and control" (Clarke, 2005, p. 155). The number of ordered maps constructed for constant SA varies with the study and cannot be preplanned.

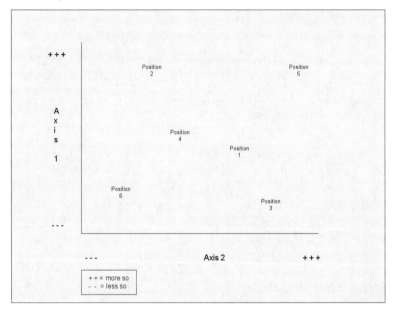

Figure 5.8. Example template of a positional map. From "Abstract Positional Map," by A. E. Clarke, 2005, *Situational Analysis: Grounded Theory after the Postmodern Turn,* p. 129. Copyright 2005 by Sage Publications, Inc.

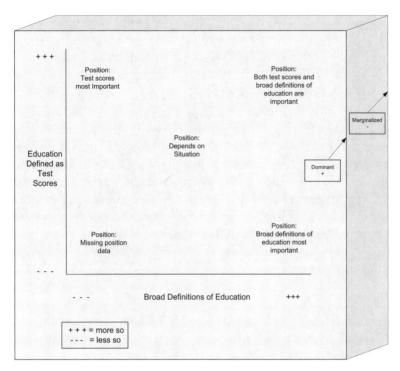

Figure 5.9. Fabricated example of a positional map. Illustrates the differing positions on education defined as test scores and broad definitions of education. Dominant and marginalized positions are also represented in abstract form. Adapted from "Positional Map: Clinical Efficiency and Emotion Work in Nursing Care," by A. E. Clarke, 2005, *Situational Analysis: Grounded Theory after the Postmodern Turn*, p. 130. Copyright 2005 by Sage Publications, Inc.

Social Spheres/Power Arenas Maps

Social spheres/power arenas maps (see Figure 5.7) are "cartographies of collective commitments, relations, and sites of action" (Clarke, 2005, p. 86). These types of maps illuminate power and the way in which people organize (whether voluntarily or involuntarily) in relation to larger structural situations by "acting [out], producing, and responding to discourses" (Clarke, 2005, p. 109). Clarke explains:

> Discourses per se are not explicitly represented on social worlds/ arenas maps. This is not because they are not present in worlds

and arenas but because social worlds *are* universes of discourse (Strauss, 1978) in arenas constituted and maintained *through* discourses. Instead, the focus of social worlds/arenas maps is on *collective social action*. (p. 114)

This type of map depicts social spheres and power arenas that interact with each other, overlap, and include the individuals/groups seemingly absent from discourses to give a broader picture of the situation. Again, we chose to combine map construction with unitized constant comparison creating memos on note cards to describe the discourses that make up each major social sphere/power arena, Multiple revisions were made as discourses were analyzed through map construction, ultimately changing the focus and appearance of the social spheres/power arenas map and helping to determine which "stories to tell" (Clarke, 2005, p. 111) or to give focus.

Positional Maps

Positional maps (see Figures 5.8 and 5. 9) are used to represent the range of positions found in discourses (including issues, absence where one might expect presence and contradictions). Clarke (2005) emphasizes that these maps are *not* symbolic of (or meant to analyze) a specific person, group, or institution's position, but rather "represent the heterogeneity of positions" (p. 126) found within discourses. The elements placed on the axes of the map and the positions (or lack of positions) charted are determined based on the examination of discourses already illuminated by situational maps and/or social spheres/power arenas maps. Figure 5.8 provides a template for a positional map, and Figure 5.9 is a fabricated example of a positional map that illustrates the differing positions on the "definition of education" (as testing or as understood more broadly). Additionally, Figure 5.9 takes on a three-dimensional shape to highlight dominant and marginalized understandings of education (e.g., silenced knowledges, erased people, disqualified skills).

Attending to Research Questions

Once all data sources and maps are fully analyzed both individually and comprehensively (through the process of constructing maps, creating note cards/memos, and reflexive revisions), the discourses found to be related to each specific question, along with additional situations/issues that may emerge, can be part of the overall findings, contingencies, and discussion of the study. Additionally, specific kinds of data may emerge as addressing particular questions more thoroughly; serving as the "research instrument," we suggest that the investigator purposely and reflexively focus on the research questions through both journaling and directed rereadings. To illustrate, in our example study in New Orleans, the 151 articles from the "charter school" search resulted in three initial messy situational maps constructed from a focus on the discourses found in: (1) the titles of the articles; (2) the major points of each article that include/exclude young children; and (3) the issues that seem to be left out of the content of each article. The initial messy maps developed for each of these three categories specifically address the first question related to the ways that "young children are represented," "included," and/or "excluded." Further mapping was conducted to assist in allowing for a more in-depth understanding of the discourses and to assist in determining illustrative experiences that would be chosen from supplementary resources. Research questions can be addressed specifically, as in situational interaction with each other, and reflexively throughout the study.

Critical Qualitative Research and Using SA in Times of Global Crisis

SA is a reflexive, fluid, and open research methodology that offers avenues for critical qualitative research that can unveil the complexities of societal systems and inequities, whether related to public policy, institutional structures, or other societal constructs that constitute hegemonic conditions. Although micro situations can undoubtedly be explored using this form of phenomenological analysis, the contemporary global circumstances that have resulted in complex networks of power, disaster capitalism, and neoliberal intrusions into every aspect of life require a range of research methodologies that can be used to reveal the complexities of power. SA can certainly provide one such lens.

Note

1. As critical scholars, we chose to insert the "power" construct. Clarke's initial work uses social spheres/arenas without the necessary concern for power).

References

Clarke, A. E. (2005). *Situational analysis: Grounded theory after the postmodern turn.* Thousand Oaks, CA: Sage.

Lincoln, Y. S., & Guba, E. G. (1985). *Naturalistic inquiry.* Newbury Park, CA: Sage.

Additional References Using Situational Analysis

Clarke, A. (2003). Situational analysis: Grounded theory mapping after the postmodern turn. *Symbolic Interaction, 26,* 4, 553–576.

Clarke, A. (2006). Feminisms, grounded theory, and situational analysis. In S. Hesse-Biber (Ed.), *The handbook of feminist research: Theory and praxis* (pp. 345–370). Thousand Oaks, CA: Sage.

Clarke, A. (2007). Grounded theory: Conflicts, debates and situational analysis. In W. Outhwaite & S. P. Turner (Eds.), *Handbook of social science and technology studies* (pp. 838–885). Cambridge, MA: MIT Press.

Clarke, A., & Star, S. L. (2007). The social worlds/arenas/discourse framework as a theory-methods package. In E. Hackett, O. Amsterdamska, M. Lynch, & J. Wacjman (Eds.), *Handbook of science and technology studies* (pp. 113–137). Cambridge, MA: MIT Press.

Clarke, A., & Friese, C. (2007). Situational analysis: Going beyond traditional grounded theory. In K. Charmaz & A. Bryant (Eds.), *Handbook of grounded theory* (pp. 363–397). London: Sage.

Gagnon, M., Jacob, J. D., & Holmes, D. (2010). Governing through (in)security: A critical analysis of a fear-based public health campaign. *Critical Public Health, 20,* 2, 245–256.

Mills, J., Chapman, Y., Bonner, A., & Francis, K. (2007). Grounded theory: A methodological spiral from positivism to postmodernism. *Journal of Advanced* Nursing, *58*, 1, 72–79.

Mills, J., Francis, K., & Bonner, A. (2008). Getting to know a stranger—rural nurses' experiences of mentoring: A grounded theory. *International Journal of Nursing Studies, 45*, 4, 599–607.

Chapter 6

Mixed Methods, Mixed Causes?

Kenneth R. Howe

The general idea of mixed methods social research is no longer under significant challenge. But the degree to which it can be accomplished and the proper role to be played by different methods are, particularly regarding causal explanation. This chapter is a nascent attempt to clear up these issues.

Causation, Methods, and Epistemological Paradigms

Two general conceptions of causal explanation underpin social and educational research: the *natural* conception (*N-explanation*) and the *intentional conception* (*I-explanation*). N-explanation incorporates an associated natural conception of causation (*N-causation*) that construes causal explanation as establishing and accounting for ordered patterns of human behavior on the model of the natural sciences. N-explanation is typically associated with experimental quantitative research methods. By contrast, I-explanation incorporates an associated intentional conception of causation (*I-causation*) that construes causal explanation as establishing and accounting for ordered patterns of human behavior in terms of norm-governed institutions and practices. I-causation is typically associated with interpretative qualitative research methods.

At the level of epistemological paradigms, N-causation is often identified with positivism, which does embrace a particular version, namely, the regularity (or Humean) conception. In this conception, causation applies to temporally ordered regularities among observations. But this is not the only conception of N-causation. The realist conception of N-causation applies to underlying mechanisms and powers often not manifest solely in terms of temporally ordered regularities among observations (e.g., House 1991; Maxwell, 2004). Whether the regularity or realist conception provides the best characterization of N-causation is an important philosophical question, but doesn't need to be answered to make the central contrast I make here between N-causation and I-causation. In a related vein, it is not only positivist epistemology that is problematic vis-à-vis its conception of causation in social research, it is any epistemology that embraces some version of the *unity of science* such that N-causation is the only permissible conception of causation. In this regard, causal explanation in social science is to be modeled exclusively on causal explanation in natural science so that explaining the behavior of human beings is like explaining the behavior of machines. Or at least the difference is only one of the degree of "noise" and the "error limits" (National Research Council, 2002) involved are such that explaining the behavior of humans is like explaining the behavior of somewhat unreliable machines.

The Interpretive Paradigm and I-Explanation

There is an alternative way to conceive of the explanation of human behavior that sharply distinguishes it from the naturalistic form of explanation that applies to the behavior of machines. The general idea of such an alternative has a long history, important elements of which can be traced as far back as to Aristotle's conception of *phronesis* (e.g., Flyvbjerg, 2001). With the emergence of the social sciences in the nineteenth century, Wilhelm Dilthey brought to prominence the distinction between *Giesteswissenshaften* (social science) and *Naturwissenshaften* (natural science), which, in turn, is associated with the distinction between understanding and explanation. More recent postpositivist philosophy of social science exemplifying the "interpretive turn" (Rabinow & Sullivan, 1987) has replaced *understanding* with *interpretation* and has merged interpretation into its conception of explanation rather than drawing a line between the two. Against the principle of the unity of science, it retains Dilthey's boundary between the social and natural sciences by replacing or augmenting N-explanation with I-explanation.

In philosophical work, the idea of "intentionality" includes intentions to act but also encompasses a much broader domain of mental concepts that have the characteristic of "aboutness." Beliefs, doubts, and knowledge, for example, are always about something, and fears and worries usually are. Intentional concepts are of particular interest because they go into descriptions of the actions people perform, as distinct from the mere movements of physical bodies. And often closely related to this, intentional concepts are involved in explaining why people act as they do. Consider the description, "Derek's hand went up." If this were the result of some sort of tic, it would be a movement, not explicable in terms of intentionality—beliefs, desires, intentions, and the like. Now, consider the following description in the context of the classroom activities of a typical American school, "Derek raised his hand in response to Ms. Williams's question." This describes Derek as performing an action because it attributes to him an intention to be recognized by the teacher along with a belief that raising one's hand is a way to accomplish this. And if we were to unpack things in this way for someone unfamiliar with the practice of hand raising in American classrooms, it would provide her with an I-explanation of Derek's behavior.

In general, I-explanations involve unpacking the role of intentionality in social behavior. This becomes quite complicated when we move away from simple straightforward examples to a comprehensive framework of causal explanation in the social sciences. This is a task that philosopher John Searle has taken on (1984, 1995) with quite fruitful results.

Searle's framework incorporates a complex array of concepts, but three are of particular importance: "collective intentionality," "social facts," and the "Background" (Searle, 1995). After describing each of these concepts and how they are interwoven to create a comprehensive framework of I-explanation, I will illustrate the framework with several examples.

When beings cooperate in the pursuit of goals they exhibit collective intentionality, and it is not only human beings that do this. Many animals exhibit collective intentionality as well, for example, as in a pride of lions hunting impala. Humans are unique among animals, however, in that via collective intentionality, humans construct a special class of social facts that, unlike the brute facts of the physical world, wouldn't exist but for the activities of human beings.

Searle's (1995) favored illustration is money. That money is a human construction that has no existence as a brute fact should be all the more apparent by its decoupling from physical tokens such as gold and silver, and, more recently, by our ability to store and exchange it in cyberspace. Its value and function have nothing to do with the brute fact physical form it takes, but are found in our collective acceptance of, and behavior in accord with, the rules of monetary exchange.

Money is an institutional fact, a special kind of social fact, in which status functions are explicitly codified by the formula "X counts as Y in C." For example, "A five dollar bill (X) counts as [has the status of] money (Y) in the United States (C)." Status functions also apply to institutional roles: for example, "A person possessing a valid Colorado teacher's license and otherwise in good standing (X) is a qualified public school teacher (Y) in the state of Colorado (C)," and "A person legally enrolled in Colorado public school (X) counts as a pupil (Y) in the state of Colorado (C)." Along with the roles of teacher and pupil go certain kinds of powers and responsibilities, which are created by the assignment of the status functions.

Less formalized social facts, like the roles associated with being a member of the Kiwanis Club, for example, function in similar ways to institutional facts in assigning status functions, powers, and responsibilities. According to Searle, no bright line can be drawn between these more informal social facts and institutional facts, and their status relative to practices can change. He suggests it is a matter of the degree of discretion that agents should be afforded while engaging in given practices that determines whether such practices should be institutionalized through the formal codification of rules. An example of dismantling a certain codification of rules and thus increasing individuals' discretion is illustrated by the elimination of formal institutional status functions associated with being a man versus a woman in marriage law in certain jurisdictions. Moving in the other direction, the powers and responsibilities of teachers are in the process of being further codified via legislated testing and accountability regimens.

That social and institutional facts are underlain by collective intentionality entails that they are human *constructions* in the sense that they wouldn't exist but for the activities of human beings. But, and this is crucial: *Collective intentionality does not entail that agents always or even usually consciously follow the rules governing status functions or even know that such things exist.* Consider pupils raising their hands to be recognized in class (Y=pupil) or buying milk in the school cafeteria (Y=money).

In some cases, the idea of following rules applies to learning certain activities, such as balancing a bicycle or reading, but only to the early stages of learning such that once a certain level of skill is reached, following rules is no longer necessary and can actually become an impediment to performance. In other cases, such as speaking grammatically, agents often just "catch on" to the rules without at any point consciously appealing to them, using criteria such as what "sounds right." In each of these cases, we might say that rather the following the rules (consciously or unconsciously), agents are tracking them.

Searle introduces the Background to help account for the phenomenon that I've just described as tracking the rules. He describes the Background as "the set of nonintentional or preintentional capacities that enable intentional states to function" (1995, p. 129). These capacities include abilities, dispositions, and know-how, and among the things they do is to enable linguistic and perceptual interpretation, structure motivation, and dispose persons to certain kinds of behavior. It is worth quoting Searle at length on this point:

> One develops skills and abilities that are, so to speak, functionally equivalent to the system of rules, without actually containing any representations or internalizations of those rules. ...
>
> There is a parallelism between the functional structure of the Background and the intentional structure of the social phenomena to which the Background capacities relate. That strict parallelism gives the illusion that the person who is able to deal with money, cope with society, and speak a language must be [consciously or] unconsciously following rules. (1995, p. 142)

In many situations, Searle says, "we just know what to do," and it's an unwarranted stretch to say we're following rules, either consciously or unconsciously (whatever that might mean). Of course, we do consciously follow rules in many situations—civil law, institutional by-laws, and so forth—but the applicable rules are never self-interpreting and never exhaustive. So, even when consciously following rules, we have to exercise the kind of interpretive and creative capacities associated with the Background.

Searle thus unpacks the definition of I-explanation provided at the outset—establishing and accounting for ordered patterns of human behavior in terms of rule-governed institutions and practices—by: (1) Identifying the social (including institutional) facts assigned by status functions by a given social group; and (2) explicating how members of that group (a) follow or (b) track the associated rules.

Before I turn to the promised illustrative examples of Searle's framework, a potential problem should be acknowledged and addressed. In particular, under Searle's account, humans typically have little or no say in what the social facts and rules are, for they are *thrown* into the social life circumscribed by these facts and rules where they (often unreflectively) learn to how to act and develop their identities. This is potentially a problem for the idea of intentional causation because if humans are shaped by external forces and not by their own intentions, and are thus products of causes beyond their control, I-explanation, or at least much of it, seems to be subsumable under N-explanation.

There are two kinds of responses to this challenge. First, humans do sometimes play an active role in shaping their lives. This varies significantly, of course, for the degree to which individuals have the opportunity to shape their own lives depends on the kind of political regime they inhabit, their social position, and the dispositions and skills they develop, including dispositions and skills produced by their formal educations. Second, the social shaping of individuals from outside forces is not a species of the mechanical shaping that characterizes how the wind, rain and snow shape a mountainside. Mechanical accounts of how nature shapes things are non-normative and must be revised if their predictions are not borne out. For example, a mountainside doesn't behave wrongly or inappropriately or incompetently if it doesn't erode as predicted. And the geologic formulas, measurements, and so on that led to the inaccurate prediction of how much erosion would occur would have to be revised. By contrast, social shaping is normative and its rules do not have to be revised when violated. An individual who runs a red light, for example, behaves wrongly, but the occurrence of such an event does not invalidate the rule that one must stop for red lights. The rule remains in place, subject to enforcement by moral criticism, fines, and the like.

Illustrative Examples

Consider the following two contrasting examples, beginning with Thomas Kuhn's account in the *Structure of Scientific Revolutions* (1962) of the behavior of members of communities of natural scientists. Much of what natural scientists qua natural scientists do is conscious intentional behavior, circumscribed by rules. However, they rarely behave in terms of following explicit rules versus tracking them in terms of their capacity to "know what to do." Similar to Searle's account of the codification of social rules, in Kuhn's account of scientific communities, the focus on codifying (methodological-epistemological) rules is associated with "pre-paradigmatic" and "revolutionary" science, where agreement—collective intentionality—on the fundamental givens has not yet formed or has broken down. Furthermore, although scientists choose to be members of scientific communities rather than being thrown into them, scientists nonetheless catch on to, rather than evaluate and choose, the fundamental givens and associated practices shared by members of the community.

The general point I want to make by referring to Kuhn's account of scientific communities is that while I-explanation is fundamental to investigating the domain of human behavior, for which N-explanation is inadequate, the particular conception of it I have provided is clearly not committed to the idea that all or even much human behavior is to be explained in terms of conscious rational intent. Kuhn's account of scientific communities shows that even the paragon of conscious-intentional-rational activity—science—involves much of what I have been calling "social shaping" as well as "tracking" the rules. Social shaping does not qualify as conscious, rational, and intended. Tracking the rules sometimes counts as all three, but typically not in the sense of following the (explicit) rules.

Now consider the genealogical account of the modern "disciplinary society" in Michel Foucault's *Discipline and Punish* (1970). This, too, fits the general I-explanation conception, though there is little danger in Foucault's case of overemphasizing the role of conscious rational intent. Indeed, because Foucault's account seems to leave so little "elbow room" (Dennett, 1984) for people to choose how to live their lives, the form of explanation he employs might be construed as N-explanation. But this would be a mistake. Central to Foucault's analysis are norms that place people on scales from good to bad that are associated with various rules of behavior and that are backed by means of shaping individuals' identities and capacities. However this might unfold—and it does so in a markedly sinister way as conceived by Foucault, in terms of pervasive surveillance and "swarming" disciplinary technologies—it is contingent on collective intentionality on which discourse and power relations depend. Unlike N-explanation, it is normative through-and-through and violations of the rules typically call not for their abandonment but enforcement. Where they are abandoned, it is not because they have failed to adequately provide explanations or be borne out by predictions, but because they have been adjudged outmoded, oppressive, inefficient, and so on.

Implications for Causal Explanation in Mixed Methods Research

In a previous article (Howe, 2004), I coined the term "mixed-methods experimentalism" to refer to the view embraced by the "new methodological orthodoxy" (National Research Council, 2002) that advocates the use of both experimental-quantitative and interpretative-qualitative methods but reserves causal investigations into "what works"—the central question of scientific research—for the former. Qualitative-interpretive methods are relegated to the auxiliary roles of description and exploration. The alternative that I advocated is "mixed methods interpretivism." This view reverses the epistemological ordering of methods such that interpretivist-qualitative methods are central, and experimental-quantitative methods play the auxiliary role of identifying black box patterns of association that require further investigation by qualitative-interpretive methods to obtain a deeper understanding of causation. I will take this as my point of departure and now refine and more fully flesh out mixed methods interpretivism regarding causal explanation.

Although quantitative methods are often associated with N-causation, the relationship is not one of entailment, for quantitative methods can be used to investigate I-causation. Consistent with my previous characterization of mixed methods interpretivism, quantitative methods can often be construed as establishing black box associations marking underlying I-causation, for example, as in how the relationship between concentrated poverty and poor educational performance marks the lack of role models and social capital that socially shape the character of the "truly disadvantaged" (Wilson, 1987). But quantitative methods can also be used to directly investigate I-causation, for example, as in using a survey to ascertain the reasons people give for voting for or against given policies with the underlying assumption that the beliefs reflected in the responses are I-causally related to their votes (Moses et al., 2010).

On the flipside, qualitative methods can be used to investigate N-causation. For example, physicians interview patients to zero in on an underlying biological process of disease. On a larger scale, public health officials interview persons infected with disease to determine such things as whether disease causing agents are transmitted through the air, saliva, by insects, or sewage.

So, the question of whether and investigation is of N-causation or I-causation does not track the question of whether quantitative or qualitative methods are indicated, for the relationship is crisscrossing. The question of which kind of explanation to pursue has to do, rather, with whether the phenomena to be investigated are natural, as in the shaping of a mountain by the elements and the mechanism of transmission of disease agents, or intentional, as in the shaping of human identities and capacities and the performance of actions in accordance with norm-governed practices.

The further question is whether and, if so, how, these two kinds of causal explanation might be integrated within social research. This is too complicated a question to which to provide an elaborate response here. Instead, I'll confine myself to just a few suggestive examples of what this might involve.

Example 1

Consider the discovery that certain inner-city children were ingesting lead from eating paint that had chipped off the walls of the tenements in which they lived. There is an established relationship between the ingestion of lead and impaired cognitive performance so that lead-poisoned children tend to perform relatively poorly in school. In this case, then, the underlying natural process of the interaction between lead and neural tissue (N-causation) serves as the explanation of the low academic performance of these children, academic performance being the manifestation of a set of intentional processes.

Example 2

Humans possess submerged psychological associations that unconsciously trigger responses to certain situations, which, although not natural processes in the way lead poisoning is, seem to better fit N-causation than I-causation. For example, unbeknownst to them, people tend to behave more kindly when the smell of fresh-baked pastry is wafting through the air (described in Appiah, 2008). Although they may explain their own behavior *post hoc* in terms of their general disposition to be kind, it turns out that they may simply be unaware of the *quasi-natural* springs of their behavior in this situation.

Example 3

In a related vein, people's behavior can be controlled or coerced by phobias, as they might be by a natural process associated with a paranoia-inducing drug. Claustrophobia seems to be a relatively pure form that affects behavior in a way similar to a chemical imbalance in the brain might, for it appears to have little or nothing to do with following or tracking norms and practices competently or, in this case, incompetently. (Of course, its classification as a disorder derives from interpreting it against a background of norms and practices.) How to think about a phenomenon such as musophobia (fear of mice) is less clear. It is gender linked and thus related to Searle's status functions, which do figure directly into I-causation. Related to phobias are various kinds of performance anxieties. For example, stage fright parallels claustrophobia in being relatively pure; stereotype threat parallels musophobia in being linked to race.

Each of these examples can be interpreted in terms of Searle's pre- or nonintentional Background component of his comprehensive framework of I-explanation. Combining this observation with the previous observation regarding how quantitative and qualitative methods map on to and N- and I-causation, or fail to, yields a more nuanced and layered version of mixed methods interpretivism. That is, *mixed methods crisscross with mixed causes in various and complex ways that are anchored in an overarching I-explanatory framework*. Indeed, this goes considerably beyond conflicts with the original conception that limits N-causation and quantitative-experimental methods to the auxiliary role of revealing black boxes that must then be examined by qualitative-interpretive methods for I-causation.

Conclusion

Mixed methods, mixed causes? Yes, but not for the reason that different methods neatly map onto different kinds of causal investigations. To be sure, there is a relatively close association between quantitative methods and N-causation, on one hand, and qualitative methods and I-causation, on the other. But as I illustrated with several examples, these associations do not always hold.

However, there is the prior question of whether the idea of mixed causes per se is plausible. And it is not plausible if the idea of intentional causation is not plausible, which is by no means an uncommon charge. A standard objection to the idea of intentional causation is that it is muddled because the alleged causes and effects are logically related. For example, the effect "Mary bought a book" cannot have as its cause "Mary intended to buy a book," because the description "Mary bought a book" logically assumes that "Mary intended to buy a book." But one can respond that this explanation, though causal, is trivial, and that more complicated intentional explanations grounded in following or tracking norms against a Background in the ways described above are quite informative and don't merely tell us what we already knew.

There is another source of the challenge to intentional causation that is associated more closely with the epistemology of social and educational research. Ludwig Wittgenstein identifies an impulse in the context of epistemological analysis to "sublime" concepts deemed central (1958, section 38). In the same vein, Ian Hacking refers to "elevator" concepts (1999). Truth and objectivity provide paradigm cases of what Wittgenstein and Hacking have in mind. Their "natural homes" are historically contingent "language games," where people typically don't have much trouble operating with them, as in "It's true that the Earth moves" and "It's an objective fact that Thomas Jefferson owned slaves." But in epistemological analysis, they are removed from the context of the language games and sublimed or elevated to such lofty heights that we must conclude that there is no truth and there is no objectivity. And from these heights, we can no longer assert, "It's true that the Earth moves" or "It's an objective fact that Thomas Jefferson owned slaves."

Something similar has characterized the analysis of causation. In our day-to-day activities, we often don't have all that much trouble with claims like some people switch to light beer because it's less fattening or many conservatives oppose tax hikes because they think it'll keep them in office. In the context of social science, we can claim with some confidence that English working-class "lads" often perform poorly in school be*cause* they participate in a *culture of resistance* (Willis, 1977) and that academically talented college women often abandon their career aspirations be*cause* of getting caught up in the *culture of romance* (Holland & Eisenhart, 1990). But such claims do not measure up to the strict demands so often placed on causation, demands that led Bertrand Russell (1912) to suggest, "the word 'cause' is so inextricably bound up with misleading associations as to make its complete extrusion from the philosophical vocabulary desirable" (p. 1). As *there is no causation*, Russell also suggested that science could do without the notion of cause and, indeed, did: "the reason why physics has ceased to look for causes is that, in fact, there are no such things" (p. 1).

In social and educational research, the predominant view is not that of Russell. More like what prompts Russell's skepticism, the predominant view is that establishing causation is exceedingly fraught with uncertainty. And this encourages conflating making a causal inference per se with making a causal inference with a high degree of certainty. This, in turn, helps explain the exclusive reliance on precise measurement, randomization, and powerful quantitative analysis procedures in inferring causation, as in the mixed methods experimentalism. It also helps explain why more than a few qualitative researchers who themselves accept this conception of causal inference disavow having any interest in it.

Causal inferences are, indeed, uncertain, and inferring I-causation is typically more uncertain than inferring N-causation. But the fixation on precision and certainty is a bad reason to force human behavior into a causal framework that doesn't fit. As Aristotle famously remarked: "Our treatment will be adequate if we make it as precise as the subject matter allows. The same degree of accuracy should not be demanded in all inquiries any more than in all the products of craftsman" (1963, p. 287).

References

Appiah, A. (2008). *Experiments in ethics.* Cambridge, MA: Harvard University Press.

Aristotle. (1963). Ethics. Book I. In Bambrough, R. (Ed.), *The philosophy of Aristotle* (pp. 313–334). New York: The New American Library.

Dennett, D. (1984). *Elbow room: The varieties of free will worth wanting.* Cambridge, MA: The MIT Press.

Flyvbjerg, B. (2001). *Making social science matter: Why social inquiry fails and how it can succeed again.* Cambridge: Cambridge University Press.

Foucault, M. (1970). *Discipline and punish: The birth of the prison.* New York: Vintage Books.

Hacking, I. (1999). *The social construction of what?* Cambridge, MA: Harvard University Press.

Holland, D., & Eisenhart, M. (1990). *Educated in romance: Women, achievement and college culture.* Chicago: University of Chicago Press.

House, E. (1991). Realism in research. *Educational Researcher, 20,* 6, 2–25.

Howe, K. R. (2004). A critique of experimentalism. *Qualitative Inquiry, 10,* 4, 42–61.

Kuhn, T. (1962). *The structure of scientific revolutions.* Chicago: University of Chicago Press.

Maxwell, J. (2004). Causal explanation, qualitative research, and scientific inquiry. *Education Educational Researcher, 33,* 2, 3–11.

Moses, M., Farley, A., Gaertner, M., Paguyo, C., Jackson, D., & Howe, K. R. (2010). *Investigating the defeat of Colorado's Amendment 46.* New York: Public Interest Projects.

National Research Council. (2002). *Scientific research in education.* Washington, DC: National Academy Press.

Rabinow, P., & Sullivan, W. (1987). The interpretive turn: A second look. In P. Rabinow & W. Sullivan (Eds.), *Interpretive social science: A second look* (pp. 1–32). Los Angeles: University of California Press.

Russell, B. (1912). On the notion of cause. *Proceedings of the Aristotelian society, 13,* 1,1–26.

Searle, J. (1984). *Minds, brains and science.* Cambridge, MA: Harvard University Press.

Searle, J. (1995). *The construction of social reality.* New York: The Free Press.

Willis, P. (1977). *Learning to labor: How working class kids get working class jobs.* New York: Columbia University Press.

Wilson, W. (1987). *The truly disadvantaged: The inner city, the underclass, and public policy.* Chicago: University of Chicago Press.

Wittgenstein, L. (1958). *Philosophical investigations.* Oxford, UK: Blackwell.

Chapter 7

Mixing Methods, Triangulation, and Integrated Research

Challenges for Qualitative Research in a World of Crisis

Uwe Flick

Health Care in a World of Crisis

A world of crisis can become an issue for social research on different levels. We may focus on the far-reaching phenomena of global crises like the fiscal crashes of banks or countries' economies and their impacts on public and private lives. This may require a comprehensive and representative approach if we want to grasp the complexity of the phenomena and their consequences.

We can also focus on the continuing crises in poorer countries and try to find empirical answers for the most urgent problems characterizing their situation and that of the people living under these circumstances. Again, this may require a more general approach.

A third approach is to take a more limited but focused approach to phenomena that may be indicators that the normality of biographies in our own societies has been put into question. Then we can start to explore the situation of people concerned with such a fragmentation of life histories and analyze how they ended up in these circumstances and how they deal with them.

Finally, we can look at our institutions that support people in such circumstances and study how they deal with these issues and how they work in such a situation. Then we will quickly see these issues as indicators of a more general crisis of our health (or social) care systems. If we want to consider situations of problems and crisis on the one hand and institutional realities and ways of processing people and problems on the other, we may need to use different methods in the same study. Again, this loss of normality and fragmentation of life histories can be seen as symptoms of a more global crisis.

In this chapter, I will first outline a theoretical background for analyzing crisis phenomena in the field of health care in our own industrialized societies. Then I will address the state of the methodological discussion about using different methodological approaches for analyzing a complex problem situation. In the last step, I will turn to some examples from my recent research to discuss how to make such a mixing of methods—or better: triangulation of different approaches—work in a sound and integrated way. I will draw on two examples of the loss of normality in the life course: The first can be seen in the wider context of adolescence and the crisis experience may be the result of a lack of perspectives. It will focus on the health and illness of homeless adolescents and their experiences in seeking help for their health problems (Flick, 2010). The second example focuses on end-of-life perspectives and the issue of living in a nursing home (Flick et al., 2010). In particular, it addresses how issues like residents' sleeping problems are handled by the staff.

Although both examples may not have much in common at first sight, they are quite similar from an interactionist perspective: Individuals in a vulnerable situation become a special social group characterized by specific needs and restrictions. Problems are experienced and (should) become the issue of professional reactions. These reactions contribute to (re-)defining the problem and to processing the people in a specific way as the redefinition of the problem has some unintended new problems as a consequence. This makes both situations an issue for analysis from a perspective that goes back to the approach of "social problems work" (Holstein and Miller, 1993).

Social Problems Work in a World of Crisis

What happens if, for example, homeless adolescents with a chronic illness start to ask for help (Flick, 2010)? What are the institutional patterns of reaction if a resident has sleeping problems in a nursing home? If we take up the perspective of "social problems work," the following process is initiated: "Social problems work involves procedures for expressing and applying … culturally shared categories to candidate circumstances. … For example, labeling persons 'mentally ill' or 'homeless' requires the availability of the categories plus the interpretive activity through which a category is articulated with a case" (Holstein & Miller, 1993, p. 153).

In their description of the social problems work approach, Holstein and Miller link two sociological theoretical traditions: a ethnomethodologically informed version of the social constructivism in the tradition of Garfinkel (1967) and the approach of collective representations in the tradition of Durkheim, mainly according to Douglas (1986):

> a more ethnomethodological concern for the interpretative practices by which everyday realities are locally accomplished, managed, and sustained urges constructionism to broaden its focus to include those practices that link public interpretative structures to aspects of everyday reality, producing recognizable instances of social problems. We refer to such practices as social problems work. … The approach combines ethnomethodologial impulses with concerns for collective representations. (Holstein & Miller, 1993, p. 152)

Durkheim's distinction of individual representation as an issue of psychology and collective representations as an issue of sociology includes the poles individual versus society and instability versus stability at the same time. This triple polarity becomes more concrete in Durkheim's study about suicide ([1897] 1951) in the thesis of anomy as a loss of the stability a collective representation may provide for the individual. Durkheim's ideal concept of a collective representation was Catholicism before reformation (Moscovici, 1984, p. 950). The characteristics of such a collective representation are that: First, it is shared by all members of a society; second, there is a high degree of stability across several generations; and third, it is static (Moscovici 1988, p. 218). Anthropologist Mary Douglas (1986, p. 91) uses this Durkheimian concept as a background for discussing in some detail, "how institutions think" and what impact this has on the thinking of its members: "When the institutions make classifications for us, we seem to lose some independence that we might conceivably have otherwise had."

Durkheim's concept of collective representations was picked up in the 1950s by French social psychologist Serge Moscovici and further spelled out in Moscovici's concept of "social representations" (see Moscovici, [1961] 2008, and Flick, 1998). Compared to collective representations, social representations are more socially differentiated. This means that several versions, forms, and types of social representations coexist. If we take up Durkheim's example, we have now several religions side by side and competing even in the framework of Christianity. This means that the stabilizing influence of the single religion on society as a whole gets lost and is limited for the individuals at least: Now they are confronted with the question, whether to believe at all and—facing alternative belief systems—what to believe.

Once we add Moscovici's idea of social representations to Holstein and Miller's perspective of social problems work, we separate the latter from the idea of a collective representation what homelessness or chronic disease or sleep disorder means. Instead, it becomes more open to the idea that there are different concepts of these phenomena. These concepts again are influenced by social conditions like the professional, institutional, or biographical background of their bearers. These concepts and backgrounds influence what is recognized as a social problem and—above all—how this is perceived. At this point, the idea of institutional thinking as suggested by Douglas becomes relevant again, even if not in such a schematic way as Douglas formulated it referring to Durkheim.

Studying Social Problems Work

The agenda of the research about social problems that Holstein and Miller (1993) formulated becomes relevant and up to date again in a new way: "The task of social problems theorists ... is to reconstruct members' ways ... of constituting social problems as moral objects ... by focusing on the "condition-categories" that are applied and used in practical circumstances to produce meaningful descriptions and evaluations of social reality" (p. 151).

This agenda can be put to work for the two social problems I use as examples in this chapter—chronic illness in homeless youth and sleeping problems in nursing homes—in two ways. First, we could consider concrete interactions that occur when a homeless adolescent asks for professional help for a health problem or when residents complain about their sleeping problems in a nursing home. Then the starting point would be to analyze such interactions on the conversation level between a health professional and the adolescent or between a nurse and the resident—similar to the examples Holstein and Miller (1993, pp. 155–159) give. Second, we can look on the other side of the potential relations to find out why these relations do not materialize. With the homeless adolescents, we might determine what experiences they have had in such situations and which they may refer to when asked about why they no longer immediately ask for help if they have a health problem (Flick, 2010).

Looking at the situation from a different perspective, it might be interesting to know which assumptions the professionals in institutions hold and which professionals the adolescents could have turned to. Such assumptions could refer to the problem situation and help-seeking behavior of potential clients. They can also refer to interpretive patterns about the relevance and ways of addressing a social problem like sleep disturbances in institutions. If we want to understand how social problems work is done and what its context looks like, both problems considered here as examples of crisis phenomena ask for more than one empirical approach.

Next, I discuss alternatives of combining research methods— or more generally research approaches—before I return to the examples in the last part of this chapter.

Combining Research Methods

Combining research methods has a long tradition in social research. However, much of the attention to this approach has focused on a specific type of combination in the last 20 years: the combination of qualitative and quantitative methods. Several key-words have been used in this regard: Mixed methods research is the most prominent (e.g., Morse, 2009; Tashakkori and Teddlie, 2010). The discussion about mixed methods has been developed in distinction from approaches like triangulation and defines a rather limited role for the latter. Bryman (1992, pp. 59–61) identifies eleven ways of integrating quantitative and qualitative research. Among these ways, the logic of triangulation (1) means for him to check for example qualitative against quantitative results. Qualitative research can support quantitative research (2) and vice versa (3); both are combined in or to provide a more general picture of the issue under study (4), etc.

In a similar way, we find five justifications of such combinations in Bryman (2006) and Greene et al. (1989): Triangulation again is limited to looking for convergence of results. Complementarity refers to elaborating, enhancing results. Development uses results from one method to inform the other method, for example to develop a survey after doing an interview study. Initiation focuses on the discovery of paradox and contradictions in the results coming from using two methods. And expansion extends the breadth and range of enquiry.

In such programmatic suggestions, triangulation is given a rather limited relevance. At the same time, far-reaching claims are made for combinations of qualitative and quantitative research in general. Implicitly, at least, they include that the strongly differentiated range of methods in both areas should be used and combined.

Qualitative and Quantitative Research: What Is Combined?

After more than 10 years of emphatic discussion concerning the use of mixed methods approaches, there are now a number of rather critical stocktaking studies about the research practice that has resulted from these discussions. These were not presented by critics of the approach but by some of its main protagonists.

Mixed Methods in Research Practice

Bryman (2006) has analyzed 232 articles published between 1994 and 2003. His criterion for selecting the papers was that the authors used the following keywords for their publications: qualitative and quantitative, multimethod, mixed method, or triangulation. Bryman found that the following methods were used in these studies: In eighty-two of the articles, 4% used a survey (questionnaire, structured interview) as the quantitative method. In seventy-one of them, 1% of the articles refer to using interviews (open, semistructured) as the qualitative method. In sixty-two, 9% of the studies are based on cross-sectional designs both in the qualitative and in the quantitative part. And in forty-one, 8% of the works used a combination of survey, interview, and cross-sectional designs in both parts. From this analysis, we may conclude with Bryman that the range of social science research methodology is exhausted and used in mixed methods research in a rather limited way.

Open Questions in Mixed Methods Discussions

In an editorial for the *Journal of Mixed methods Research*, Greene (2008, p. 17) reviewed the development of the field and identified a number of issues. First, Greene sees that only little conceptual work on how to choose particular methods for a given inquiry purpose has been provided. Second, the central question still is not sufficiently addressed: Around what does the mixing happen? And finally, it is unclear what a methodology of mixed methods should look like (Greene, 2008, p. 17). From this review, we may conclude that the methodological basis of mixed methods research still is rather underdeveloped and that there is little clarification about which methods are or should be combined for which purpose.

Maps and Lacks in Mixed Methods Research

Creswell (2009), in an editorial for the same journal, has marked the territory mixed methods research ("maps") and compared it with the discussions of the mixed methods conference in Cambridge 2008. His conclusion is:

> I was surprised to not find any papers at the conference on theoretical lens and *mixed methods* research, such as ethnic, racial, disability, sexual orientation and feminist topics as used in *mixed methods* studies ..., that no papers were taking on the issue of validity ... to learn that the conference papers did not continue to probe a definition of *mixed methods*. (Creswell, 2009, pp. 97–98; emphases added)

On the one hand, here again are some impressions of a methodological limitation of the mixed methods discussion ("lacks"). On the other hand, these reviews underline that the mixed methods research fall behind the claims its protagonists have made (also as distinguished from triangulation—see Tashakkori & Teddlie, 2010). Mixed methods research is still a pragmatic combination of methods rather than a methodologically sound enterprise of integrated research approaches. It is characterized by a juxtaposition of different paradigms, which means the blocks of qualitative and quantitative research are seen as closed entities and not as open perspectives knit together in a reflexive way. And this causes neglect of theoretical backgrounds and differences in the approaches rather than taking them into account.

Triangulation—Weak and Strong Program

If we compare this characterization with the discussions about triangulation in general (Denzin [1970] 1989; Flick, 1992, 2008), we rather find a theoretically justified combination of methods. Instead of paradigms, which are juxtaposed, we see research perspectives that are combined. Another feature is the emphasis on the sovereignty of the approaches in the application. This more general discussion and development can be condensed into three questions: (1) How can we avoid qualitative research being pragmatically absorbed in mixed methods research? (2) How is possible to maintain that the theoretical and methodological reflection in mixed methods research is equal to what is "standard" in qualitative research? (3) What justifies limiting method combinations more or less to combinations of qualitative with quantitative research?

These discussions could be a starting point for returning to triangulation as a relevant concept in the context of combining qualitative and quantitative research. Then we may conclude: Triangulation can be used as a criterion in qualitative research (as Lincoln & Guba [1985] suggested). We can employ triangulation as a strategy of assessment when we use other methods and the results we obtained with them for critically evaluating the results we obtained with a first method (as suggested in the list of Bryman [1992] as a major task for triangulation). And we can use the label of triangulation and then apply a rather pragmatic mix of methods. This is what I would like to call "a weak program of triangulation," as opposed to a strong one. In the latter, triangulation first becomes relevant as a source of extra knowledge about the issue under study and not just a confirmation of what we know from our first approach. Also, triangulation is seen as an extension of our research program, which also includes a systematic selection of the different methods and the systematic combination research perspectives (see Flick, 1992). In this context, it should also be underlined again that triangulation always has been and still is more than just a combination of methods.

Norman Denzin ([1970] 1989) has already suggested several levels of triangulation: Besides methodological triangulation, which is differentiated in "within-method" (e.g., the use of different subscales within a questionnaire) and "between-method" triangulation, which will allow the triangulation of data, he suggested triangulation of several investigators and of various theories. Triangulation of various methods can be applied by combining qualitative methods (e.g., interviews and participant observation), quantitative methods (e.g., questionnaires and tests), or qualitative and quantitative methods. Within-methods triangulation can be realized in approaches like the episodic interview (Flick 2000, 2008), which combines question-answer parts with invitations to recount relevant situations in a narrative.

Thus, triangulation requires that researchers take different perspectives on an issue under study or more general in answering research questions. These perspectives can be substantiated by using several methods and/or in several theoretical approaches. Both are or should be linked. Triangulation also refers to combining different sorts of data on the background of the theoretical perspectives, which are applied to the data. As far as possible, these perspectives should be treated and applied on an equal footing and in an equally consequent way. At the same time, triangulation (of different methods or data sorts) should allow a principal surplus of knowledge. For example, triangulation should produce knowledge on different levels, which means they go beyond the knowledge made possible by one approach and thus contribute to promoting quality in research (see Flick, 2008, p. 41). Finally, if we take the different forms of triangulation Denzin suggested into account, triangulation becomes a basis for integrated social research. This strong program of triangulation will be illustrated for research examples addressing the crisis phenomena mentioned in the beginning of this chapter.

Triangulation in the Context of Qualitative Research

In qualitative research, methodological approaches on different levels are available that can be combined in studying a complex phenomenon related to experiences in crisis situations. Here, we can think of an approach to personal experiences people in a critical situation have and can report. Or we can think of an approach focusing on practices related to specific aspects in this situation. And we can focus on the professional side of dealing with claims and needs of people in such a situation.

Example I: Lack of Perspectives—Health and Illness of Homeless Adolescents

In this example, the crisis experiences are linked to a lack of perspectives in adolescents that is linked to living in the context of homelessness (see Flick, 2010, for more details). Although homelessness per se is a situation of crisis, it is intensified if the adolescents have to cope with one or more chronic diseases.

In the study I did with Gundula Röhnsch,[1] we took three approaches to explore the health and illness situation, the help-seeking behavior, and the institutional perception of homeless adolescents in Berlin. The first approach was to do participant observation at spots where these adolescents hang out, panhandle pedestrians for money, meet service people, etc. Our observations became more and more focused on health-related practices and interactions among the adolescents or with social workers who contacted them in the context of street work. The second approach was based on episodic interviews with the adolescents, stressing their health concepts and experiences with service providers. We wanted to find out what health meant under these circumstances, what relevance it is given, and what happens when adolescents in this situation seek professional help. The third approach was based on expert interviews with general practitioners, social workers, nurses, medical specialists, and special service providers for homeless people in general. These interviews with experts were aimed at understanding the perception of homeless adolescents by professionals and their views of available health care. The interviews with the adolescents focused on a number of areas to reveal the complexity of their current situation and how they came to be in it:

- subjective definitions of health;
- situation of living (housing, financial problems, eating);
- consequences for health;
- dealing with health risks (drugs, alcohol, sexuality) and health problems; and
- experiences with illness and services.

We paid special attention to how adolescents coped with chronic illness. Analyzing what they said in interviews, we noted some general tendencies: Adolescents tend to ignore their chronic illnesses, mostly because of general resignation. They turn to alcohol and drugs as a strategy of problem solving. Their network of street youth is experienced at taking advantage of their chronic illness and is not very empathetic about the adolescents' specific situation. A major part of the adolescents' statements referred to negative experiences, mainly with physicians who prevented them from further utilizing professional help. The experts, on their part, emphasize that the adolescents' ways of coping with chronic illness fails in general and that they are not ready to deal with their disease and its challenges. Alcohol and drugs are seen as preventing the adolescents from solving their problems. The network of street youth stabilizes street life and prevents the adolescents from leaving this situation. The "internal" help (i.e., informal support by peers in the group) leads to new dependencies. In general, the adolescents are perceived as being stressed by illness and street life. They develop very particular needs for help, but there may not be institutions that are ready to help them adequately. Finally, the observations reveal the adolescents' problems in acting according to what they said in the interview concerning their health practices and problems.

Thus, the results of the three approaches represent different levels of insights about the issue under study: A social interactionist perspective on practices and interactions about the issue (observation), an internal perspective from the point of view of the adolescents (interviews), and an external perspective from a professional point of view on this situation (expert interviews). The results complement each other and the different aspects they reveal justify the extra effort of planning and collecting data on three levels. Each level provides a different form of insights into the health crisis for this specific group resulting from the combination of homelessness and chronic illness. In this example, we also see the different perspectives of institutional providers (experts) and potential users of institutional support, which, in the end, contribute to patterns of nonutilization on the part of the potential users even when their crisis becomes more dramatic.

Challenges for Qualitative Research

If we return to the more general methodological focus of this chapter, we can identify two major challenges for qualitative research here: The first is how to maintain and develop a program of using multiple methods in qualitative research beyond mixed methods research. As this example revealed, there is a need to combine methods also in the field of qualitative research, which is not covered by the current mixed methods rhetoric with its focus on combining qualitative and quantitative methods. The second challenge is how to make this program theoretically and methodologically sound beyond just using several methods in one study. In the example discussed here, Röhnsch and I (2007) took three theoretical perspectives for analyzing the social problems work in this case and these perspectives were broken down to three different methods.

Triangulation in the Context of Integrated Social Research

Methodological Framework

Coming back to the combination of qualitative and quantitative approaches discussed above, let's look at another example applying a concept of "integrated social research" (see Flick, 2011, chap. 10). First, we should check how developed the knowledge is about the issue under study and which empirical approaches to it make sense, are necessary, and should be combined. This also includes taking account of the theoretical approaches and differences in conceptualization of the concrete methodological procedures. For planning such a study, the various designs presented by Miles and Huberman (1994, p. 41) can give an orientation. According to these suggestions, qualitative and quantitative methods can either be linked in parallel or one after the other in various sequences—depending on the research question and the point of departure. Data collection and analysis then are based on methodological and data triangulation according to Denzin ([1970] 1989). The presentation of results takes the characteristics of the linked approaches into account: case studies or histories and displays of overviews in tables and charts.

Example II: Sleeping Problems in Nursing Homes

Triangulation is currently applied in an ongoing project focusing on sleeping problems in nursing homes.[2] The lack of alternative ways of living and support at the end of life causes many older people to live in nursing homes, a more or less closed institution.

Frailty and multi-morbidity are present in most cases. The crisis here can be intensified when additional problems (e.g., sleeping disorders) develop and are more or less adequately managed by the professionals in these institutions. For studying this situation, I and my coauthors (Flick et al., 2010) triangulate two approaches. In one, assessment data of 10% of the nursing-home residents in Berlin (*n*=2,577) are reanalyzed. These assessments include several variables about sleep, sleep quality, and disturbances (nonrestful sleep, insomnia, short sleep duration). At the same time, we held interviews with thirty-two nurses at different qualification levels and with physicians and residents' relatives. The interviews focus on knowledge and problem awareness concerning sleeping problems of residents in nursing homes.

The assessment data show that 62.6% of the residents have sleep disorders; 37% suffer from severe problems like insomnia; and 5.4% have these problems every night. Another 29.6% suffer from nonrestful sleep, which means they are tired in the morning after a night of nonrestful sleep. The assessment data also show that 5.4% of the residents were awake less than one-third of the day, spending more than two-thirds of the day dozing, sleeping,

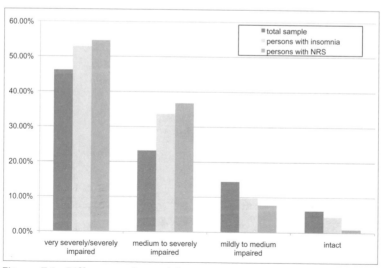

Figure 7.1. Differences in social engagement (ISE-scores) between persons with and without sleep disorders (%).

taking a nap, etc. These data show the extent of the problem, which is often neglected in research and nursing practices. They also show the impact of sleep problems on multi-morbidity (see Garms-Homolovà et al., 2010) and specific diseases. These data also show that people with sleeping problems participate in social activities in the institution much less than residents without these problems. Figure 7.1 shows the differences in the social engagement for the residents in general, for those with nonrestful sleep and those with insomnia.

The data show that sleeping problems at night have a lot to do with lack of activity during the day. Thus, sleeping problems are not only somatic problems, they may also be the result of specific forms of dealing with them during the day or the lack of interventions preventing them from occurring. Finally, these data show that the management of these problems could be part of the professional activities of nurses in these institutions. The more activities they offer residents during the day to prevent them from dozing and daytime sleepiness, the better the residents' sleep quality is at night. In the episodic interviews, questions and comments referring to this were, for example: "What are the sleeping habits of your residents? What happens when you have to help them going to bed? Can you describe such a situation?" "What can you do to prevent sleep problems of your residents? What is done here in your institution for this purpose? Please describe such a typical situation to make it clear to me."

In the interviews with the nurses, we could identify three interpretive patterns about the relations between sleeping problems and activation during the day and more generally about possible influences of their own work:

- intervention: The interviewees know that offering daytime activity improves residents' sleep quality. They apply this knowledge in active structuring of daytime activities and motivating residents to take part (*professional concept*).

- missed opportunity: Although the interviewees know about the relation of sleep quality and activities, residents are not motivated to participating in activities (*semi-professional concept*).

• ignorance: Issues of sleep disorders are not relevant for the interviewees in their daily work (*lay concept*).

These interpretive patterns show the differences in the states of knowledge about the relations (between activation and sleep), which became evident in the first approach (Flick et al., 2010). These discrepancies can be taken as a starting point for further education programs addressing these relations.

This study permits analysis on two levels: the reality of care and the professional perception of the problem under study. For this purpose, it combines two methodological perspectives: a quantitative secondary analysis of routine data (assessments) and a qualitative primary collection and analysis of interviews. The quantitative approach shows the prevalence of the problem under study in the context of the research and its links to more general issues like diseases and multi-morbidity. The qualitative approach shows how much the staff in the institutions are aware of the problem and how they deal with it or don't. Thus, it shows the general situation of crisis.

On the methodological level, a triangulation of different approaches is applied. It is an approach of integrated social research because not only are the results of qualitative and quantitative analyses interlinked, but both approaches were involved in a comprehensive design right from the beginning.

Possible Results and Their Consequences

If we leave aside the rather limited understanding in mixed methods discussions that triangulation should provide convergence in multi-methods research, what can we expect from triangulation and what are the consequences? There are three options.

One: Seen rather generally (i.e., independent from the exact research question and the specific methods used in the single research), results can, of course, converge. This means they correspond completely, in general, in tendency, or in parts. The use of several methods leads to a confirmation of what one method has demonstrated with the results of its application. However, as should have become evident, correspondence here can have several facets. Do we always need complete correspondence, which degree of correspondence is necessary, if we only have partial correspondence? More generally: If results correspond, if we just have more of the same, does this justify the extra efforts necessary to receive these extended results? What is the extra insight we can draw from such a confirmation?

Two: Although this seems to be what to expect from triangulation if we agree with mixed methods authors, this will be the least exciting outcome of triangulation in the end. Its use becomes more interesting when results complement each other. Then the two methods offer insights, which make up a fuller picture and are located on different levels or focus on different aspects of the issue. Then the extra effort of using two or more methods can lead to extra benefits in levels of outcomes of research. This extra outcome may, for example, be that interviews provide deepening, detailing, explaining, or extending results compared to the analysis of questionnaire used in parallel.

Three: Finally, results may diverge (i.e., in the interviews, statements are made that reveal views that are completely, generally, in tendency, or partly different from what the questionnaire data have shown). That would be the starting point for further theoretical or empirical clarification of the differences and their reasons (see also Kelle & Erzberger, 2004).

For each of the three options—convergence, compromise, divergence—we are confronted with the same questions or problems: How is the specific theoretical background of the two empirical approaches in collecting and analyzing data taken into account? Do divergences not already result from the differences in understanding reality and the issue in qualitative and quantitative research? Should too much convergence not be a starting point for skepticism rather than a simple confirmation of one result by the other? How far are both approaches and the results obtained with them seen as equally relevant and substantive so that using triangulation is justified in this concrete case? How far has one or the other approach been limited to a subordinated role of for example only testing the plausibility of the results coming from the other approach?

Comprehensive Triangulation

For making triangulation a solid basis for combining several methodological approaches in qualitative research or including quantitative approaches in an integrated approach, we can now take up the original suggestions by Denzin ([1970] 1989) again. However, we will no longer see them as alternative ways of doing triangulation but in a more comprehensive way as steps building on each other.

If the issue under study calls for several approaches, it may be necessary to include more than one researcher (investigator triangulation) who should bring different conceptual perspectives into the study (theory triangulation). This should be the background and lead to applying different methodological approaches (methodological triangulation) either one within-method or by using different independent methods (between-methods). The result of this will be data on different levels and with different qualities (data triangulation). This makes sense, if we take care that really different perspectives are pursued in the approaches. Such a systematic triangulation of perspectives (Flick, 1992) should include the use of different methods, which are given the same weight in the study and are systematically used. This means that the integration and reflection of theoretical backgrounds of different methods is considered in the methodological planning of the study.

The additional effort of carrying out a project with more than one methodological approach will be justified if it allows approaching different levels or dimensions, as in the examples above. Such different dimension can include one method addressing the subjective meaning of an issue and the dimension of social structure in this context or focus on the process (of dealing with the issue) and the state (of knowledge about it at a moment). Another possible distinction here is to focus on knowledge and practices related to the issue. This is different from what Bryman (2006) found for the ongoing mixed methods research and the dominance of interview plus survey combinations, which basically remain in the same dimension (knowledge and attitudes concerning an issue). This leads to the last feature of a systematic triangulation of perspectives: The choice and use of methods should be purposeful and reflected and finally based in the issue under study.

Multiple Methods in Qualitative Research in a World of Crisis

In this chapter, I addressed crisis on two levels—the more general one that consists of living on the street or in an institution more or less purposely and the more concrete one that is intensified by chronic illness in the first case or sleeping problems in the second. A social problems work perspective includes addressing the variety of problem understandings in the field, which influence and sometimes obstruct ways of dealing with these problems. If we want to fully understand this process and how institutions manage such phenomena of crisis, and how professionals in these institutions represent or misrepresent the crisis and the problems, we mostly need more than one empirical approach. The methodological focus in this chapter was on alternative ways of combining multiple methods for such a research. A comprehensive approach of triangulation was discussed as an alternative to a more pragmatist mixed methods rhetoric. It includes the combination of several qualitative methods as well. For combinations of qualitative and quantitative research, a model of integrated research was discussed that goes beyond a simple combination of methods.

Notes

1. This study was funded by the German Research Council (DFG)-FL245/ 10-1-2; G. Röhnsch was a co-researcher (see also Flick and Röhnsch, 2007).
2. This study was funded by the German Ministry of Research (01ET0707). The research was done with V. Garms-Homolovà, G. Röhnsch, and J. Kuck (see also Flick et al., 2010, and Garms-Homolovà et al., 2010).

References

Bryman, A. (1992). Quantitative and qualitative research: Further reflections on their integration. In J. Brannen (Ed.), *Mixing methods: Quantitative and qualitative research*, pp. 57–80. Aldershot, UK: Avebury.

Bryman, A. (2006). Integrating quantitative and qualitative research: How is it done? *Qualitative Research, 6*, 1, 97–113.

Creswell, J. W. (2009). Editorial: Mapping the field of mixed methods research. *Journal of Mixed Methods Research, 3*, 2, 95–108.

Denzin, N. K. ([1970] 1989). *The research act* (3ʳᵈ ed). Englewood Cliffs, NJ: Prentice Hall.

Douglas, M. (1986). *How institutions think.* Syracuse, NY: Syracuse University Press.

Durkheim, E. ([1897] 1951). *Le suicide* (*Suicide: A study in sociology*). New York: The Free Press).

Flick, U. (1992). Triangulation revisited—Strategy of or alternative to validation of qualitative data. *Journal for the Theory of Social Behavior, 35*, 2, 175–197.

Flick, U. (Ed.) (1998). *Psychology of the social: Representations in knowledge and language.* Cambridge: Cambridge University Press.

Flick, U. (2000). Episodic interviewing. In M. Bauer & G. Gaskell (Eds.), *Qualitative researching with text, image and sound: A practical handbook*, pp. 75–92. London: Sage.

Flick, U. (2008). *Managing quality in qualitative research.* London, Sage.

Flick, U. (2010). Triangulation of micro-perspectives on juvenile homelessness, health and human rights. In N. K. Denzin & M. D. Giardina (Eds.), *Qualitative inquiry and human rights*, pp. 186–204. Walnut Creek, CA: Left Coast.

Flick, U. (2011). *Introducing research methodology—A beginner's guide to doing a research project.* London: Sage.

Flick, U., Garms-Homolová, V., & Röhnsch, G. (2010). "When they sleep, they sleep"—Daytime activities and sleep disorders in nursing homes. *Journal of Health Psychology, 15*, 5, 755–764.

Flick, U., & Röhnsch, G. (2007). Idealization and neglect—Health concepts of homeless adolescents. *Journal of Health Psychology, 12*, 5, 737–750.

Garfinkel, H. (1967). *Studies in ethnomethodology.* Englewood Cliffs, NJ: Prentice Hall.

Garms-Homolová, V., Flick, U., & Röhnsch, G. (2010). Sleep disorders and activities in long term care facilities—A vicious cycle? *Journal of Health Psychology, 15*, 5, 744–754.

Greene, J. C. (2008). Is mixed methods social inquiry a distinctive methodology? *Journal of Mixed Methods Research, 2*, 1, 7–22.

Greene, J. C., Caracelli, V. J., & Graham, W.F. (1989). Toward a conceptual framework for mixed-method evaluation design. *Educational Evaluation and Policy Analysis, 11*, 3, 255–274.

Holstein, J. A., & Miller, G. (1993). Social constructionism and social problems work. In G. Miller & J. A. Holstein (Eds.), *Reconsidering social constructionism: Social problems and social issues*, pp. 131–152. Chicago: Aldine.

Kelle, U., & Erzberger, C. (2004). Quantitative and qualitative methods: No confrontation. In U. Flick, E. v. Kardorff, & I. Steinke (Eds.), *A companion to qualitative research*, pp. 172–177. London: Sage.

Lincoln, Y. S., & Guba, E. G. (1985). *Naturalistic inquiry*. London: Sage.

Miles, M. B., & Huberman, A. M. (1994). *Qualitative data analysis: A sourcebook of new methods* (2nd ed.). Newbury Park, CA: Sage.

Morse, J. (2009). *Mixed method design: Principles and procedures*. Walnut Creek, CA: Left Coast.

Moscovici, S. ([1961] 2008). *La psychanalyse, son image et son public* (*Psychoanalysis—Its image and its public*). Paris: Presse Universitaire Française.

Moscovici, S. (1984). The myth of the lonely paradigm: A rejoinder. *Social Research, 51*, 4, 939–968.

Moscovici, S. (1988). Notes towards a description of social representation. *European Journal of Social Psychology, 10*, 2, 211–250.

Tashakkori, A., & Teddlie, C. (Eds). (2010). *Handbook of mixed methods in social & behavioral research* (2nd ed). Thousand Oaks, CA: Sage.

Part III: Performance

Chapter 8

The Exquisite Corpse of Art-Based Research

Charles R. Garoian

[T]here was a lot of multi versions of all kinds of things, we were always pulling things apart, I had like a big junk yard of stuff, as the year went by, if something wasn't complete, I just pulled out the parts I liked, it was like pullin' the parts you need from one car, put 'em in the other car so that car runs[1]

— Bruce Springsteen (2010) on writing
"Darkness on the Edge of Town"

twenty, twenty acres, empty land, twenty acres of empty land, nothing, absolutely nothing could grow on it, nothing but sand, tumble weeds and Johnson grass that is ... gopher holes everywhere, jack rabbits all over the place, but otherwise empty God-forsaken land where Chester Alexanian[2] lived, collected, and installed rusted, broken, cannibalized tractor parts, worn out farm implements, some animal powered, others powered by machines ... corroded cultivators, plows, thrashers, buggy parts, dilapidated cars, junked pick ups, delivery trucks, forklifts, tractors, you name it, he had it, spread across that barren twenty acres of land, a veritable outdoor museum of agricultural implements, historical artifacts, material culture from the late nineteenth century to the present, he had one of everything it seemed ... others' throw-aways, he was collector, curator, conservator, and docent, all in one, Chester's eccentricity was conspicuous, not a hoarder, but close to it.

... I didn't relate even though I was studying to become an artist, I didn't understand the logic of his eclectic impulse even though I was amassing my own load, I didn't get it even though, even though my stuff was being exhibited in galleries and museums ... it was only afterwards, after Chester constructed his rickety forklift that my burden of assumptions lifted ... the forklift that he composed from parts, fragments of a rundown '32 Ford Model A, '52 Chevy flatbed, and a '55 Yale forklift, all of which were appropriated from his junk heap, the anthology that he had archived on that empty patch of land, the twenty acres where he stockpiled his stuff ... where he was played by play, the tinkering play that anthropologist Victor Turner[3] refers to as the "supreme bricoleur of frail transient constructions," ... Z-Z-Z-Z-Z-Zuht, Z-Z-Z-Z-Z-Z-Z-Z-Zuht, Z-Z-Z-Z-Z-Z-Z-Z-Z-Z-Z-Zuht, Chester cut here and there, then he welded there and here (see Figure 8.1), Z-Z-Z-Z-Z-Zhut, he cut and welded, welded and cut and welded again to assemble an elaborate Frankenstein algo-rhythm, Z-Z-Z-Z-Z-Z-Z-Z-Z-Zhut, a monstrous forklift with its linkages and sutures readily apparent like the folds of Exquisite Corpse... cannibalized Ford, Chevy, and Yale body parts whose differences were easily discernable, there was no attempt, none at all to conceal the radical juxtaposition of junk, rusted yellow contours adjoining a dented black frame adjoining scarred yellow-orange forks, Chevy, Ford, Yale, all three absent yet present, their surfaces and parts grimy and pitted from years of use and oxidation, their three-in-one differences and particularities exposed, yet, yet like those incongruous constructions of the Dadaists and Surrealists, the crazy thing actually worked on many levels, visually, conceptually, materially, but most of all mechanically ... notwithstanding its raw aesthetic, what pleased him most about his resurrected Corpse was its ability to do the heavy lifting, the hard work of hauling fresh and dried fruit, and wine grapes to the market, Chester's objective was always steadfastly modest ... it was only then, then, after my assumptions had blurred, that I associated and understood his assemblage work and those that I was ironically constructing in my studio by affixing cultural fragments and detritus to my canvas ... was mine fine art and his simply junk? There was a beauty in the way his forklift monstrosity looked and worked, while lacking pretension its differential forms and functions overwhelmed, restored and renewed my way of seeing and understanding the world.

Figure 8.1: Z-Z-Z-Z-Z-Z-Z-Z-Zuht. Photograph courtesy Charles Garoian.

I offer the story that you have just read as a prelude to my exploration and characterization of the "Exquisite Corpse of Art-Based Research," the topic of this chapter. My objective in complicating its narrative is to draw attention to *what* my story is about, the precarious construction of Chester's forklift, and *how* my collaged, stammering prose is constructed to expose in-between spaces where you, as readers, can linger on its juxtapositions, and fold your own stories among its contiguous, disjunctive associations, correspondences and complementarities. About such lingering philosopher John Dewey (1938) writes: "The crucial educational problem is that of procuring the *postponement of immediate action* upon desire until observation and judgment have intervened" (pp. 64, 69; emphasis added). Such postponement affords the contemplation, seeing, and transformational becoming of subjectivity through art research and practice.

Indeed, in exposing the *how* of my writing about Chester's forklift, I am responding to the call of arts-based researchers and educators like Graeme Sullivan (2005), Cahnmann-Taylor and Siegesmund (2008), and Dónal O'Donoghue (2009) who advocate for educational research that more closely follows the imaginary and improvisational processes and practices of artists, poets, and musicians as compared with inquiry that is commonly associated with the logical-rational approaches in the sciences and social sciences. My premise is that the Exquisite Corpse folding of complex and contradictory narratives into and through each other offers significant possibilities for engaging in democratic discourse, understanding alterity, and respect for cultural differences and peculiarities.[4] Respect for alterity is possible, according to philosopher Emmanuel Levinas, by virtue of a nonreciprocal relationship with the other, where the self remains open and susceptible to difference, to not knowing, and to indeterminacy. Such "unknowable and unassimilable alterity" is possible insofar as the relationship with the other is only ever as strangers (Todd, 2001, p. 69).

In complementing my narrative about Chester's forklift, in what follows I briefly discuss the historical positioning of Exquisite Corpse in twentieth-century art, and I invoke artists' and scholars' research and creative works that correspond with the creative strategies proposed by the Exquisite Corpse process. In doing so, I address the following questions: What is Exquisite Corpse and how was it historically situated? How does it function visually and conceptually? How are subjectivity and otherness constituted by its incongruous discourse? How does its fragmented research and practice enable creative and political agency? And, how does its abstruse, heterogeneous criticality differ from the ideological discourses of academic, institutional, and corporate power?

Like Chester's forklift, the surrealists' Exquisite Corpse parlor game consisted of three or more individual sections, each rendered by a single player and joined together into a single, collaborative visual or written artwork. In the visual example of the game, a sheet of paper was folded horizontally into its sections (Figure 8.2) and assigned a vertical, corporeal order beginning with the head in the top section of the paper, the torso in its middle section, then the feet in the bottom section.[5] Important to preserving the chance element of the game, each section was made in secret, then folded and concealed under the previous sections until all were completed and the sheet was unfolded at the end of the game to reveal the juxtaposing of an Exquisite Corpse. For a sectional

Figure 8.2: Folded paper for Exquisite Corpse. Photograph courtesy Charles Garoian.

drawing to remain hidden, a player completed his or her part of the body out of sight from the other players, then continued its ending lines to the bottom edge of the section and just over the top edge of the next section to provide the next player clues as to where to start drawing their part of the body. While this collaborative procedure among the players seems constrained and regimented, any such limitations were dispelled when the adjoining and disjoining play between its sections were revealed at the unfolding of the sheet.

This oscillating movement between congruity and incongruity conjoins game theorist James Carse's (1986) differentiations of *finite* and *infinite* games, in which the prescribed structure and rules of the former are contrasted with the ambiguity, indeterminacy, and contingent improvisational structures of the latter. Given this to and fro movement of Exquisite Corpse, it is at its unfolding when the incongruities of the sections are revealed and when viewers are left with an interminable conundrum in fusing the disjunctions of its heterogeneous body; a monstrous body whose excessive figurations and reconfigurations resist normalization, homogenization, and what critical theorist Donna Haraway (1992) calls the hegemony of "artifactualism,"[6] within the singular frame of the paper sheet upon which it has been rendered.

The paradoxical and heterogeneous characteristics of Exquisite Corpse are evident in the 1938 playing of the game (Figure 8.3) by surrealists André Breton, Jacqueline Lamba, and Yves Tanguy.[7] The head section contains a large leaf with a caterpillar attached atop a bearded old man's head, like the adorned headdresses of military leaders in antiquity; a steam locomotive pulls a train of cars around the old man's right side, tunnels under his beard across his neck, and out the other side demarcating the area of his shoulders; while the juxtaposed beard, caterpillar, leaf, train, and its smoke seem incongruous, they have in common a biomorphic, serpentine configuration as compared with the geometric, machinic forms of the following sections.

In the torso section, what appears to be a machinist's or cabinet maker's industrial lathe stretches across what would be considered the man's chest area with the lathe's adjustment wheels and their extended rods stretching one to the left and the other to the right suggesting short, outstretched arms; the lathe is positioned at an angle on a teetering conical stand that rests on a round, drum-like form whose sides appear like pistons tightly contained in cylinders; in the foreground of the table a long pipe-like form extends at a slight angle but horizontally along the bottom fold of the paper and toward its outer edge.

In the third, the feet section, the pipe-like form in the previous section elbows downward at one end and into this section; together with a similar form nearby, and what appears to be a dangling counterweight at the opposite end, the apparatus suggests fittings among other components in an ambiguous hydraulic mechanism that is adjoined to the left hip of a workman's insulated underpants, leggings that also cover the feet, with suspenders that are strapped, buckled, and hooped adjacent to the section's fold like a garment hanging from a clothes line.

The effect of each individual section in relation to the composite is a collaged stacking of disparate images and ideas representing artifacts, detritus, and mechanical production

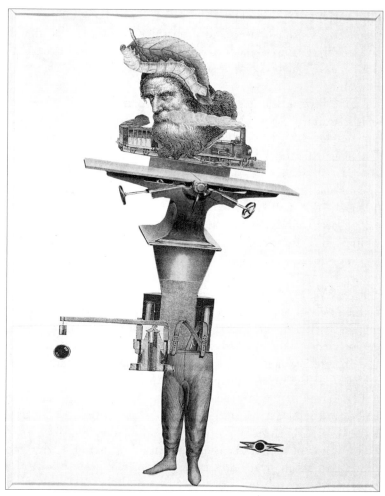

Figure 8.3: André Breton, Jacqueline Lamba, Yves Tanguy, *Cadavre exquis* [Exquisite Corpse] February 9, 1938. Collage on paper, 31.00 x 21.20 cm (unfolded 31.00 x 42.20 cm). Collection of National Galleries of Scotland. © 2010 Artists Rights Society (ARS), New York/ADAGP, Paris. © 2010 Estate of Yves Tanguy/Artists Rights Society (ARS), New York.

processes of industrial culture. When unfolded, the consolidation of Breton, Lamba, and Tanguy's three sections transforms into a whole yet disjunctive body, an anthropomorphic machine; a machine-man; a monstrous man-machine suggested by the image of the bearded old man's head and accompanying adornments in the top section, and supplemented by the placements and configurations of machine components in the other two sections; hence, the body is constituted as a mutable, indeterminate assemblage.[8]

Like Breton, Lamba, and Tanguy's assemblage, the adjoining words "exquisite" and "corpse" befit and confirm the incongruent folds of the game's process. According to the *Oxford English Dictionary* (OED), "exquisite" is defined as follows: "A. *adj*.1. Sought out, 'recherché'. a. Of an expedient, explanation, reason: Sought out, ingeniously devised, far-fetched. Of studies: Abstruse" (OED, 2011). Although the definition of corpse seems uncomplicated, specifically a dead body, its dormancy nevertheless serves as an important counterpoint to the differential possibilities suggested by exquisite. For example, two of the defining terms for exquisite, "*recherché*" and "abstruse," are pertinent to my argument in this chapter. While *recherché* is the French word for research, abstruse is defined as something concealed, hidden, or latent. Hence, searching, and searching again, and again … for knowledge that is latent yet incipient and emergent is at the heart of art research and practice that resists concrescence, and exemplifies the characteristic ambiguities and incompleteness of Exquisite Corpse.[9]

In terms of its corporeality, Exquisite Corpse affirms the embodiment of art research and practice as a processual, dialectical "algorhythm,"[10] which mutates between what is known and unknown, seen and unseen, familiar and strange, self and other, in fueling the body's imagination, improvisation, and creativity. Accordingly, art theorists Kochhar-Lindgren et al. (2009) use the neologism "algorhythm" to describe Exquisite Corpse as a process of art, theory, and pedagogy that "endlessly reinvents itself and reappears in a number of different contexts" (p. xviv). As such, the neologism corresponds with critical theorist Theodor Adorno's (1997) characterization of the dialectical movement of art as a "processual enactment of antagonisms (p. 176), and philosopher Brian Massumi's (2002) concept of art embodiment as a "processual rhythm of continuity and discontinuity" in and across contexts (p. 217). Exquisite Corpse similarly constitutes eccentric, ecstatic, and eclectic embodiment; an imminent dynamic of folding and unfolding, revealing and concealing knowledge that is capable of rupturing sedimented, normalizing ideologies and practices of hegemonic power; in doing so, its antinomies offer irreducible possibilities for the body's creative and political agency.[11]

Understanding that "exquisite" constitutes "research," its conjoining with "corpse" brings to mind the seeking of knowledge that is yet to be discovered and learned; and presumably an "exhumation" and "re-habitation" of ossified understandings; the transformation of socially and historically determined assumptions and ideologies; those that inscribe, choreograph, and regulate the body and the body politic. The restoration and renewal of lived experience that lays dormant within dead and frozen metaphors is possible within the diverse and dynamic, interstitial conditions, "the *bursting at the seams* of "Exquisite [*and*] Corpse [*and*]" (Sapier, 2009, p. 197), where cultural differences and peculiarities are contiguous and fluid; where labile understandings in-between private and public knowledge are exposed and enable examining and critiquing academic, institutional, and corporate structures; a differential space where originary lived experiences are restored, renewed, and the newness of lived experience sustained interminably.[12] Hence, in resisting intellectual closure and ideological sedimentations, Exquisite Corpse research and practice, "does not dismiss all knowledge, but rather activates it [differently] as a performance" (Sapier, 2009, p. 197).[13] In doing so, it serves as public pedagogy that exposes, examines, and critiques sedimented, ideological assumptions of the body and the body politic (Denzin, 2003, p. 9).

Concerned with the exhumation of immutable metaphors, my aim in this chapter is to revisit *cadavre exquis*, one of several free associative parlor games with which the surrealists' responded to Sigmund Freud's conception of dream cognition,[14] and to reconsider its mutable and indeterminate narrative as enabling the body's critical intervention within academic, institutional, and corporate culture. Within the context of modernist art, and the avant-garde's utopian ambitions, the disjunctive, mutable operations of Exquisite Corpse mirrored and mimicked the technological and production efficiencies of machine culture as evidenced by Breton, Lamba, and Tanguy's collaborative collage process. The dadaists' engineering of component fragments and parts of visual and material culture in collage, montage, and assemblage narratives, for example, is one parallel with industrial and mechanized construction, and the uncanny machinations of dreams, humor, and play in the mind as theorized and expounded by Freud and performed by the surrealists in games like the Exquisite Corpse, is another.

Art historian Susan Laxton (2009) describes the discrete yet significant differences between the disjunctive narratives of dada montage and surrealist Exquisite Corpse. She explains that the "tension of juxtaposition" of disparate fragments in montage represent "unambivalent 'difference,'" whereas that tension in Exquisite Corpse "is ameliorated by the way that drawing is regulated in the game, specifically by requiring each player to take up the contours of the image exactly where another player left off, effectively extending the previous contribution long enough to smooth the transition" (p. 32). In other words, while the fragments of montage remain disparate and disjunctive, the conjunctions of Exquisite Corpse oscillate between its disjunctive sections and its consolidated, figural structure, and in doing so they expose an interminable process of forming and becoming a figure.[15]

The radical procedure of Exquisite Corpse notwithstanding, the transgressive operations and contraventions of the surrealists' games were driven by a desire to break from and escape the codes and canons of historical art and culture. With progress as its imperative, the movement's dialectical critique of history fell short of its ambition to transform society. Relegated to the margins of art and culture by the procession of avant-gardism, the movement had little effect on "art's critical engagement with social praxis" as it had hoped for (Bürger, pp. 78–79; Laxton, 2009, p. 30). With minimal impact on society at large, its forceful critique remained bound to the art world as yet another ideological manifestation within the spectrum of modernist art, and its strategies and attempts at transforming social and historical regimes and ideologies of power were subsequently absorbed by the consumptive impulses and inducements of industrial capitalism in its endless thirst for novelty.[16]

Naive about the false consciousness of modernism, the differential critiques and strategies of the artistic avant-garde were easily co-opted by academic, institutional, and corporate systems of production and distribution in order to reinvent and expand their imperious positioning and power. Examples where the avant-garde's radical strategies have been appropriated by corporate capitalism are found in mass mediated advertisements that seduce and manufacture the body's desire for consumption by way of montage innuendos, parodies, and narratives on sex, health, and environmental issues. With consciousness raising as their purported aim, such spectacle entertainments and inducements deploy clever, fashionable juxtapositions of images and ideas whose interstitial contingencies are immediately claimed, tamed, and branded with corporate logos, and often endorsed by celebrities to ensure that consumers associate the advertisement's ingenuity and smartness with the commodities being advertised. In doing so, the impact of corporate capitalism on the body's creative and political agency is lost in the daze and dazzle of spectacle (Mirzoeff, 2002).

The profit motives of corporate capitalism are far reaching and have impacted institutions of higher education. Colleges and universities, for example, are experiencing rapid corporatization as the educational values of debt-burdened families are shifting from arts and liberal arts study toward academic disciplines that will ensure job security. Indeed, the high cost of tuition and accompanying expenses has resulted in a commodification of learning where students insist on high grades as an entitlement for merely showing up in class, and their helicopter-parents hover over them and their teachers to get the biggest bang for their tuition bucks. Political scientist Wendy Brown warns: "The danger [of liberal arts erosion] ... is that the public will give up the idea of educating people for democratic citizenship. Instead, all of public higher education will be essentially vocational in nature, oriented entirely around the market logic of job preparation ... [as such] universities will be expected to build human capital" (quoted in Glenn, 2010).

As capital, the body's desire for creative and political agency, which is constituted by indeterminate, individual, and differential processes like those of Exquisite Corpse and others in arts and liberal arts study, is usurped, rearticulated, and colonized as commodity fetishism by the spectacle of corporate culture.

Critical educator Paulo Freire (1998) opposes the wholeness and wholesomeness that educational capitalism offers: "It is in our incompleteness, of which we are aware, that education is grounded. ... Education does not make us educable. It is our awareness of being unfinished that makes us educable" (p. 58). Accordingly, the body's incompleteness, its "unfinished" awareness and desire for learning and creative agency, stands in stark contrast with the manufactured desire for and false promises of knowledge as power, which purport educational grounding and completeness by way of consumption rather than production. Like the proverbial emperor with new clothes, spectacle veils its control over the body by manufacturing a false sense of desire and agency (Debord, 1994, p. 23). By choreographing its choices and compulsion to consume through schooling and the mass mediated organs of newspapers, television, movies, magazines, advertising, and the Internet, the indifference of power toward the body continues to homogenize difference within the body politic.

Hence, my purpose in exhuming the spectacle of Exquisite Corpse from the confines of modernist art history is to reinhabit and reconstitute its originary abstruse research without underestimating, circumventing, or deserting the pitfalls of academic, institutional, and corporate power, but to ensure the "possibility of disarticulating their constitutive elements, with the aim of establishing a different power configuration" that challenges power's indifference toward the body's agency (Mouffe, 2010). It is my contention that situating the differential research and practice of art, like Exquisite Corpse, within regimes of power, be they classrooms, museums, or boardrooms, constitutes an interminable process of exposure, examination, and critique that counters ideological representations and sedimentations and facilitates latent power configurations that respect and allow for the differences and peculiarities of the body and the body politic.

Since its inception in the 1920s, visual artists have re-inhabited the dadaists' and surrealists' processes of radical juxtaposition in new and differing ways to disarticulate and reconfigure the sedimented and fetishized codes and practices of art and culture that stultify the body's creative and political agency. In the remaining portion of this chapter, I will describe and discuss two works of art as examples of how the generative research and practice of Exquisite Corpse has accrued since the surrealists. Before proceeding however, I want to elaborate on the process of collaboration, which is usually identified with the surrealists' renderings of Exquisite Corpse. My purpose in doing so is to extend and expand the understanding of collaboration to include the contextual shifts and folds of experience with which viewers interact with works of art. Hence, contrary to the assumption that defines viewers as disembodied spectators, their embodiment of an artwork's movements, affects, and sensations constitute them as collaborators, which is consistent with the dynamic relational engagement of Exquisite Corpse. An expansive understanding of collaboration

Figure 8.4: Joseph Kosuth (1945–). © ARS, NY. *One and Three Chairs,* 1965. Wooden folding chair, photographic copy of a chair, and photographic enlargement of a dictionary definition of a chair; chair 32 3/8" x 14 7/8" x 20 7/8z"; photo panel, 36" x 24 1/8"; text panel 24" x 24 1/8". Larry Aldrich Foundation Fund.Digital Image. © The Museum of Modern Art/Licensed by SCALA/Art Resource, The Museum of Modern Art, New York.

is a case in point in my discussion of the following works of art considering that solo artists created them.

In *One and Three Chairs*[17] (1965), conceptual artist Joseph Kosuth juxtaposed three representations of "chair" (Figure 8.4) to engage viewers' critical contemplation and participation. To the left of his installation, a large format photograph is pinned on a wall that contains an image of a life-sized wooden folding chair positioned on a white floor and against a white wall. The wall and floor in the photograph, it turns out, are those of the gallery where Kosuth has installed the actual folding chair positioned against the actual wall in the photograph, both of which are situated adjacent to a text panel tacked to the wall that contains the dictionary definition of chair; hence "one and three chairs." Kosuth has created a visual and conceptual conundrum with this installation, which exposes differences between actual and virtual representations of cultural artifacts, and differences between textual representations and those of images. Like Exquisite Corpse, it is at the "unfolding" of Kosuth's three representations of the "folding" chair where viewers are invited to intervene, collaborate, and respond with questions, and to explore, experiment, and improvise possible associations and understandings that challenge socially and historically constructed assumptions of art and culture. Functionality, for example, is one issue that viewers may reflect upon and question in their response to the installation's disjunctive mode of address. While chair is socially and historically understood as an artifact for the body's sitting comfort, the understanding of that function is disturbed, brought into question, and rendered mutable by virtue of its placement in an art exhibit where touching is prohibited by security guards. As such, the gallery context unfolds and raises additional questions about *One and Three Chairs.*

Although it might seem an exaggeration and eccentric to suggest that art galleries *are* chairs, considering that artworks are exhibited and essentialized in galleries suggests that that is where they "sit" or come to rest. According to philosopher Ludwig Wittgenstein's language-games,[18] a chair's significance would dependent on any number of contexts in which it would be placed. In other words, although we may assume that a chair

Figures 8.5. Joel Kyack, *Superclogger (public art initiative documentation photograph), 2010, Rush hour-210 East-Pasadena.* Courtesy of the artist and LA><ART, Los Angeles.

is only a chair based on its familiar use and meaning, its placement within an art installation represents a shift in context that throws its function and significance into question and attaches it with other, unexpected ones. Questions about language use, such as those raised by Kosuth's compelling chair installation *One and Three Chairs* correspond with the generative, folding-unfolding discourse of Exquisite Corpse research and practice.

While a folded structure is not readily apparent in artist Joel Kyack's *Superclogger: "Rush Hour–210 East-Pasadena"*[19] (2010), his live public artwork (Figure 8.5) during rush hour on a congested Los Angeles freeway does constitute movement across different contexts similar to Exquisite Corpse and Kosuth's *One and Three Chairs*. *Superclogger* consisted of puppet shows that were co-conceived with artist Peter Fuller and performed by Kyack from the tailgate of an ordinary white Mazda pickup truck with the rear hatch of its shell opened for viewing by commuters jammed in traffic. The show's cast consisted of "a group of funky, grimy, homemade Muppets, acting out short vignettes on themes that might speak to people stuck in traffic. Coping with uncertain conditions, for instance, or the state of being controlled" (Ulaby, 2010). Using FM broadcasting equipment like those found in drive-in theaters, Kyack transmitted the soundtracks of his puppet performances by way of radio waves to commuters' cars that were stalled bumper-to-bumper in traffic within 200 feet of his pickup.

Assuming puppet theater as a unifying, figural structure like Exquisite Corpse, the disjunctive folds of *Superclogger* are suggested by the pickup truck as performance stage complete with its tailgate proscenium; the highway an open air stage where commuter traffic is performed; and, cars, a lot of cars, stopping and starting, weaving and inching forward, controlled by the unpredictable ebb and flow of rush hour traffic constituting drivers' performances of driving as puppetry—a staging that is further controlled and regulated according to the script of state traffic laws.[20] ArtDaily.org, a Los Angeles–based Internet art newspaper, described the impact of Kyack's puppet performances on traffic madness as follows:

> *Superclogger* engages the traffic jam as a formal materialization of the principles of chaos, providing a direct experience with the evolving conditions that can effect a system and help to predict outcomes—in this instance, a person breaking [*sic*] a millisecond earlier than expected because of the puppet show would, over time, drastically change traffic patterns. Intervening in the commute experience of people driving behind the truck, *Superclogger* aims to *briefly halt* the progression of chaos by temporarily drawing the audience out of the commute experience and placing them within an intimate space of engagement that highlights their own individual presence within the broader structure of the traffic jam. (ArtDaily.org, 2010; emphasis added)

ArtDaily.org's characterization of *braking* cars affecting traffic patterns on the highway as a formal materialization of chaos[21] during the traffic jam corresponds with the disjunctive sectional folds of Exquisite Corpse, which *break with*, and extend our patterns of perception and thought and interconnect with others. Like Exquisite Corpse, the complex and contradictory research of *Superclogger* opened liminal, contingent spaces of experience where drivers' escalations of aggression over the chaos in which they were situated were delayed; in-between spaces where drivers were able to linger on the abstruse juxtapositions as the highway/performance unfolded and where they experienced its dynamic, intimate space of engagement. In doing so, the liveness of the performance transformed drivers' assumptions and expectations about sitting in their cars waiting for traffic to abate; about how a pickup truck constitutes a stage and the highway a theatre; and the use of their car radios speaker systems that receive the sounds and narratives of a live performance. In other words, *Superclogger* created a differential space where drivers were able to renew and restore their understanding of traffic from across multiple contexts of experience.[22]

Based on the unfolding of Exquisite Corpse research and practice in Breton, Lamba, and Tanguy's *Cadavre Exquis*, Kosuth's *One and Three Chairs*, Kyack's *Superclogger*, and including Chester's forklift, let us now consider each of these four works as folds in the Exquisite Corpse unfolding of this chapter. Although each work differs from the others, there exist *generative, figural correspondences* in-between their *generative, figural structures*, a folding-unfolding movement across the various bewildering contexts of Exquisite Corpse research. Such deterritorializing and reterritorializing machinations constitute the work of art as a body without organs (BwO) according to Deleuze and Guattari (1987); that is, a cultural body that resists sedimented *organ*izational assumptions, significations and representations through its dynamic movements, affects and sensations. Accordingly, "the BwO is not at all the opposite of the organs. The organs are not its enemies. The enemy is the organism [sedimented body of organs]" (p. 158).

Such resistance to concrescence (those dead and frozen metaphors mentioned previously) in-between and among the formations of Exquisite Corpse constitutes embodiment as a "plane of consistency" (p. 251), where disparate and disjunctive folds of experience temporarily consolidate, and where interminable affinities generate via multiple lines of flight across various unfolding contexts. Hence, in resisting sedimentation, or intellectual closure, the four aforementioned works enable figural rhythms and associations to emerge between and among them, as their plane of consistency is unfolded.

Accordingly, let us consider the disparate discontinuities of Chester's welded assemblage in processual rhythm with the continuities of its forklift form; *and* consider the discontinuities of Breton, Lamba, and Tanguy's machinic folds in processual rhythm with the continuities of its unfolded machine body; *and* consider the discontinuities in Kosuth's installation in processual rhythm with continuities that consolidate as *one* in three chairs; *and* consider the discontinuities of controlled movement during rush hour traffic in processual rhythm with the continuities that consolidate a formal materialization of highway chaos as puppetry through Kyack's pick-up truck performance ... *and, and,* then consider the continues and discontinuities of Chester's forklift assemblage in processual rhythm with the continues and discontinuities of Breton, Lamba, and Tanguy's *Cadavre Exquis* in processual rhythm with the continues and discontinuities of Kosuth's *One and Three Chairs* in processual rhythm with the continues and discontinuities of Kyach's *Supperclogger* ... and consider ... in processual rhythm with the continues and discontinuities of ... *and, and, and*. ...[23]

Hence, like *Superclogger*, the agonistic associative movements of Exquisite Corpse destabilize the gridlock of sedimented cultural organs that traffic and stultify our bodies' creative and political agency by unfolding and materializing a chaotic field of excess and possibility that Grosz (2008) ascribes to the emancipatory affects of art: "the generation of vibratory waves, rhythms, that traverse the body and make of the body a link with forces it cannot otherwise perceive and act upon" (p. 23). Therein lies the paradox of contemporary cultural life: While this *excessiveness*, the sensate body's becoming other through art, is frequently misunderstood and misrepresented as *frivolous* by academic, institutional and corporate organs of power, it is by virtue of its destabilizing frivolities—the very mis-understandings, mis-representations, and mis-firings of art research and practice like Exquisite Corpse—that our ways of seeing, understanding, and creating the world are transformed.

Notes

1. Rock musician Bruce Springsteen describing his song writing process for his 1978 album "Darkness on the Edge of Town" during an interview with actor Edward Norton in 2010.

2. Chester Alexanian (1924–1991), my father-in-law, owned and operated Chester Alexanian Trucking and Tractoring (CATT) beginning in the early 1950s until his death in 1991. He and his wife Ruby raised two daughters, Sherrie and Cindy, in the small agricultural community of Fowler, California, where they lived on 20 acres of land and Chester ran his business.

3. See Turner (1983, p. 234).

4. The Exquisite Corpse folding process of inquiry that is referred to in this chapter corresponds with the "braided metaphor" with which Sullivan (2005, pp. 103–109) theorizes the complex movements and interconnections that are enabled through visual arts research and practice.

5. Laxton (2009) writes that in the written version of Exquisite Corpse, subject/verb/object corresponded with the head/torso/feet structure of the visual version (p. 30).

6. Haraway (1992) characterizes "artifactualism" as postmodernism's reductive hyper-production, reproduction, replication, and globalization of denatured images and ideas that permeate, homogenize, and dominate the body's creative and political agency. The principle of artifactualism is that "the whole world is remade in the image of commodity production" (p. 297).

7. See a color reproduction of Cadavre Exquis [Exquisite Corpse], 1938, by Breton, Lamba, and Tanguy in the collection of the National Galleries of Scotland at http://www.nationalgalleries.org/collection/online_search/4:324/result/0/31332

8. Breton, Lamba, and Tanguy's machinic construction corresponds with Deleuze and Guattari's (1987) concept of assemblage—a gathering of disparate elements in a single context that resist concrescence and interpretation. In doing so, its affect is one of extension and expansion across multiple contexts, a rhizomatic "deterritorializing machine" that releases an interminable web of associations and understandings (pp. 4, 333).

9. Critical theorist Adorno (1997) characterizes artworks' resistance to intellectual closure, like Exquisite Corpse, as the antithetical procedure of montage: "Artworks … that negate meaning must also necessarily be disrupted in their unity; this is the function of montage, which disavows unity through the emerging disparateness of the parts at the same time that, as a principle of form, it reaffirms unity" (p. 154).

10. The neologism "algorhythm" plays on the word "algorithm," which the OED defines as "a step-by-step procedure for reaching a clinical decision

or diagnosis, often set out in the form of a flow chart, in which the answer to each question determines the next question to be asked" (OED, 2011).

11. Kochhar-Lindgren et al. (2009) argue that: "The Exquisite Corpse exem- plifies one manner in which difference is produced as a means of disrupting the normalizing of the hegemonic power of current cultural regime" (p. xxii).

12. The restoral and renewal capacities of Exquisite Corpse correspond with philosopher Michel de Certeau's (1988) differentiation of *spaces* and *places*. He describes the characteristics of space as contingent, performative, and differential, which oppose the stability and singularity of place (p. 117). Also, philosopher Henri Lefebvre (1991) characterizes the differences and peculiarities of differential space as resisting the abstract space of corporate capitalism (pp. 52–53).

13. Literary theorist Craig Sapier describes correspondences between the folds of Exquisite Corpse and Roland Barthes's *punctum* (1981).

14. See film theorist Anne M. Kern's (2009) characterization of surrealism's "crucial and consistent" relationship with Freud's theories (p. 4).

15. Following philosopher Gilles Deleuze's conception of the *figural* as the "abandonment of art as representation," cultural theorist Elizabeth Grosz (2008) writes: "The figural is the deformation of the sensational and the submission [of the] figurative to sensation. It is the development of art as an 'analogical language,' a non-representational 'language' of colors, forms, bodily shapes, screams" (p. 88).

16. Adorno (1997) describes the institutionalization and subsequent neutralization of the social impact of surrealist art as a "false afterlife" considering that it "began as a protest against the fetishization of art as an isolated realm, yet as art, which after all surrealism was, it was forced beyond the pure form of protest" (p. 229).

17. See a color reproduction of Kosuth's *One and Three Chairs* (1965) in the collection of the Museum of Modern Art at http://www.moma.org/collection/browse_results.php?criteria=O%3AAD%3AE%3A3228&page_number=1&template_id=1&sort_order=1

18. Similar to Wittgenstein's language-games, in which the significance of a word or object is dependent on the context in which it is found, and its use determines its meaning.

19. See a color reproduction of and listen to the National Public Radio story about Kyack's *Superclogger*, 2010 at http://www.npr.org/templates/story/story.php?storyId=129128690

20. Such a multiplicity corresponds with Deleuze and Guattari's (1987) analogy of the untying of *puppet strings* [author's emphasis] from the will of the artist-puppeteer, which in this case is Kyack, and extends as multiple lines of flight to form an expansive web of connections between and among other "puppet[s] in other dimensions connected to the first" (p. 8).

21. ArtDaily.org's use of "chaos" to describe *Superclogger's* materialization of form is the inverse of absolute order; rather what Grosz (2008) argues "as a plethora of orders, forms, wills—forces that cannot be distinguished or differentiated from each other, both matter and its conditions for being otherwise, both the actual and the virtual indistinguishably (p. 5).

22. For additional information about *Superclogger* see report on National Public Radio website at http://www.npr.org/templates/story/story.php?storyId=129128690

23. My use of the ellipsis [...] is to suggest an affinity between Exquisite Corpse and the rhizomatic alliances that Deleuze and Guattari (1987) characterize as having "no beginning or end." Contrary to the genealogical and onto-logical filiations of a tap root-tree that "imposes the verb 'to be'... the fabric of the rhizome is the conjunction, 'and ... and ... and ...'" (p. 25).

References

Adorno, T. W. (1997). *Aesthetic theory: Theory and history of literature.* G. Adorno & R. Tiedemann (Eds.). Minneapolis: University of Minnesota.

ArtDaily.org. (2010). Public art project presents various puppet shows to drivers caught in traffic. file:///Users/crg2/Desktop/Superclogger.webarchive (accessed July 12, 2010).

Barthes, R. (1981). *Camera lucida.* New York: Hill and Wang.

Bürger, P. (1984). *Theory of the avant-garde.* M. Shaw (Trans.). Minneapolis: University of Minnesota.

Cahnmann-Taylor, M., & Siegesmund, R. (2008). Challenges to the definition and acceptance of arts-based inquiry as research. In M. Cahnmann-Taylor & R. Siegesmund (Eds.), *Arts-based research in education: Foundations for practice*, pp. 1–2. New York: Routledge.

Carse, J. P. (1986). *Finite and infinite games.* New York: Ballantine Books.

Debord, G. (1994). *The society of the spectacle* (D. Nicholson-Smith, Trans.). New York: Zone Books.

De Certeau, M. (1988). *The practice of everyday life.* Berkeley: University of California Press.

Deleuze, G., & Guattari, F. (1987). *A thousand plateaus: Capitalism and schizophrenia.* B. Massumi (Trans.). Minneapolis: University of Minnesota.

Denzin, N. K. (2003). *Performance ethnography: Critical pedagogy and the politics of culture.* Thousand Oaks, CA: Sage.

Dewey, J. (1938). *Experience and education.* New York: Macmillan.

Freire, P. (1998). *Pedagogy of freedom: Ethics, democracy, and civic courage.* Lanham, MD: Rowman & Littlefield.

Glenn, D. (2010). Public higher education is "eroding from all sides" warn political scientists. *The Chronicle of Higher Education.* http://chronicle.com/article/Public-Higher-Education-Is/124292/ (accessed September 2, 2010).

Grosz, E. (2008). *Chaos, territory, art: Deleuze and the framing of the earth.* New York: Columbia University.

Haraway, D. (1992). The promises of monsters: A regenerative politics for inappropriate/d others. In L. Grossberg, C. Nelson, & P.A. Treichler (Eds.), *Cultural studies*, pp. 295–337. New York: Routledge.

Kern, A. M. (2009). From one exquisite corpse (in)to another. In K. Kochhar-Lindgren, D. Schneiderman, & T. Denlinger (Eds.), *The exquisite corpse: Chance and collaboration in Surrealism's parlor game*, pp. 3–28. Lincoln: University of Nebraska Press.

Kochhar-Lindgren, K., Schneiderman, D., & Denlinger, T. (2009). Introduction. In K. Kochhar-Lindgren, D. Schneiderman, & T. Denlinger (Eds.), *The exquisite corpse: Chance and collaboration in Surrealism's parlor game*, pp. xx–xxix. Lincoln: University of Nebraska Press.

Laxton, S. (2009). This is not a drawing. In K. Kochhar-Lindgren, D. Schneiderman, & T. Denlinger (Eds.), *The exquisite corpse: Chance and collaboration in Surrealism's parlor game*, pp. 29–48. Lincoln: University of Nebraska Press.

Lefebvre, H. (1991). *The production of space.* D. Nicholson-Smith (Trans.). Malden, MA: Blackwell.

Massumi, B. (2002). *Parables for the virtual: Movement, affect, sensation.* Durham, NC: Duke University.

Mirzoeff, N. (2002). *An introduction to visual culture.* London: Routledge.

Mouffe, C. (2010). The museum revisited. *Kostis Velonis.* http://kostisvelonis.blogspot.com/2010/06/museum-revisited.html (accessed January 16, 2011).

Oxford English Dictionary. 2011. http://www.oed.com/view/Entry/66815 (accessed January 15, 2011).

O'Donoghue, D. (2009). Are we asking the wrong questions in arts-based research? *Studies in Art Education: A Journal of Issues and Research in Art Education, 50*, 4, 352–367.

Sapier, C. (2009). Academia's exquiste corpse: An ethnography of the application process. In K. Kochhar-Lindgren, D. Schneiderman, & T. Denlinger (Eds.), *The exquisite corpse: Chance and collaboration in Surrealism's parlor game*, pp. 189–205. Lincoln: University of Nebraska Press.

Springsteen, B. (2010). Ed Norton interviews Bruce Springsteen on "Darkness." National Public Radio. http://www.npr.org/2010/11/12/131272103/ed-norton-interviews-bruce-springsteen-on-darkness (accessed November 15, 2010).

Sullivan, G. (2005). *Art practice as research: Inquiry in the visual arts.* Thousand Oaks, CA: Sage.

Todd, S. (2001). On not knowing the other, or learning from Levinas. *Philosophy of education archive.* http://ojs.ed.uiuc.edu/index.php/pes/issue/view/17 (accessed January 16, 2011) and http://ojs.ed.uiuc.edu/index.php/pes/article/viewFile/1871/582 (accessed January 16, 2011).

Turner, V.W. (1983). Body, brain, and culture. *Zygon, 18*, 3, pp. 221–245.

Ulaby, N. (2010). 'Superclogger': Free theater on L.A.'s freeways. National Public Radio. http://www.npr.org/templates/story/story.php?storyId=129128690 (accessed August 11, 2010).

Chapter 9

Cinderella Story
An Arts-Based and Narrative Research Project

James Haywood Rolling, Jr.

Rights and Responsibility

Perhaps the most crucial of all human rights is the right to signify self, to experience, affinities, aspirations, beliefs, and ideas. Without the liberty to mark oneself as a person who matters, to model one's personal experience to others without censorship, and to make special one's place in the world without assault, prohibition or desecration by those who rule or dominate, human agency is curtailed. Agency is conceived here not as the "freedom to do whatever the subject wills but rather freedom to constitute oneself in an unexpected manner—to decode and recode one's identity" (Stinson, 2004, p. 57).

The right to visibly decode and recode personal and social significance was on display in the great Harlem Renaissance literary and visual reinterpretation designated as "the New Negro," wherein the ridiculed, stereotyped, and degraded Negro body was reinterpreted as a document of strength and beauty, yet no less black (Locke, [1925] 1992). In addressing the theme of this volume, I will present arts practice both as the manifestation of a fundamental human right to represent one's lived experience and as a catalyst for the reclamation of interpretive and reinterpretive rights neglected.

Narrative Inquiry and the Politics of Reinterpretation

Cinderella Story (Rolling, 2010) employs a narrative methodology as a means to displace an oppressive bias against counter-stories to the kind of larger institutional grand narratives that are authorized solely to perpetuate the power of entrenched institutional systems to exert a self-sustaining order over their known world. Narrative inquiry is a kind of social research, "a collaborative method of telling stories, reflecting on stories, and (re)writing stories" (Leavy, 2009, p. 27). Narrative methodologies have been of great utility to arts-based researchers (Barone & Eisner, 2006; Leavy, 2009) as well as to critical, indigenous, and anti-oppressive researchers (Brown & Strega, 2005). It is research that seeks not to prove or disprove, but rather to create movement, to displace, to pull apart and allow for resettlement; it is research that seeks what is possible and made manifest when our taken-for-taxonomic certainties are intentionally shaken.

In contrast, the scientific method is most useful for addressing hypothesis-based questions—guesses about what will happen given a particular set of controlled variables and ultimately requiring experimentation to collect replicable data as evidence that the hypothesis is true. Social science researchers face major limitations carrying the success of the scientific method within the physical sciences over to social research since "persons are more difficult to understand, predict, and control than molecules" (Zeiger, n.d., para. 1). Narrative methodologies offer researchers another approach to educational research questions.

A resistance narrative is critical, indigenous or local, and anti-oppressive (Brown & Strega, 2005). In this chapter, I will tell the story of an identity crisis—public and private—ameliorated through the renegotiation of certain narratives and namings. This resistance is necessary because, as a historical scion, I have been ferociously, visually, named—Bad, Bad Leroy Brown, the brutal black buck; Topsy or Buckwheat, the untamed, unkempt watermelon-eating picanniny; Uncle Tom, the smiling, wide-eyed docile servant; Aunt Jemima, the obese, utterly contented, pitch-black maternal figure; Jezebel, the uninhibited whore, denizen of all sexual fantasies; Sambo, the lazy, inarticulate buffoon; Jim Crow or Zip Coon, the traveling darkie entertainers, song-and-dance minstrels; Peola, the quadroon, the self-hating mulatto, poisoned with the scourge of Negro blood and the selfishness of white social aspirations; Golliwog, the grotesque and alien rag doll, the antithesis of porcelain-skinned beauty. Within the conceptual hegemony of Western popular and visual cultural norms and ideals, African Americans have been consigned to inhabit ghettoized symbols of social stigma; so have other groups across the globe.

Except for Cinderella's paradigm of restoration, those who cannot occupy the center along with the normal, lacking the requisite politics or popularity or physiognomy or speech

Figure 9.1. First image from the 1865 version of *Cinderella* as she sits, steeped in stigma.

pattern—those who deviate, who are not safe or sensible, sedate or schoolable—are summarily stigmatized, labeled, and invalidated. But there is in the Cinderella story a template for addressing the conferral of invalidity (see Figure 9.1). In keeping with the story of fulfillment characterized by Cinderella, I seek a reorganizing self-image to address the problem of a spoiled identity (Goffman, 1963), both personal and public.[1] Self is the site of such research, and embodiments of the individual and collective, modern and postmodern selves are its data. Not the self in abstract, but in its living, breathing, reconstituting body or corpus. Deviations of self are always predicated on narrative norms and precedents. "Normalcy" or "normality" is a gilded fortress that attempts to permanently ensconce the unfortunate denizens outside the walls of acceptability in an oppositional system that "preserve(s) the irrational status quo" (Schafer, 1981, p. 41).

In the United States, we are told of something called the "American Dream," a version of the Cinderella story, purporting that everyone has the very same opportunity to rise from the ash heap. But that's not quite true—the evidence borne out by the cycle of poverty and the inheritance of wealth and status from one generation to the next simply does not support the assertion that everyone's life can be a fairy tale. It is more accurate to argue that there are those who discover the power of an extended reinterpretation. Fairy tales are not normal. The propaganda that power, fame, and fortune are always within reach in America is a tale of mythical proportions. But it isn't entirely useful. Reinterpretation, however, is normalizing; it levels the fields of play. We tend to be all over the map in any given day: we're good; we're bad; we are worthy; we are not worthy. But we make art of our lives when we extend a particular reinterpretation into a permanent reorganization of all that we know, possess, and wish to become.

It seems at first glance that the most familiar of the Western versions of the Cinderella fable does not offer an apt analogy for the life of a black man. But the Cinderella narrative—found among cultures as varied as China, the Eskimo peoples, France, Germany, Zuni Indians, ancient Egypt, and Xhosa Africans—is more than it seems to be because it began speaking to me, a black man, when I was still only a black boy. My desire was not to be transported from

Figure 9.2.
Breech baby.

rags to riches—that is not what the Cinderella ending was about.[3] My desire was to be transported from tragedy, from disaster and tribulation to reconciliation with a personal imaginary that might be considered normal, or at least allowing the possibility of tree-houses—a palliative for weak tree boughs, muffled lullabies, and the stigma of all who are survivors of breech births.

When I was still a child, I wasn't sure how I was supposed to feel whenever I was reminded that my mother was in labor with me for a full 12 hours as I attempted to enter the world butt-first (Figure 9.2). My mother always said the last three siblings entered the world easily; she still appears traumatized when recounting my birth. She has never had much to say about it actually. The firstborn of four, I always wondered at the awkward and nearly absent physical affection between my mother and me, very different than the constant and tender affection I saw poured out on my youngest brother. Perhaps the memory of the pain I must have caused her justifies an overextended period of detachment. In conversation, things are much better between us now; however, we still don't hug as much as I'd like. And I'm still uncomfortable when engaged in physical contact with most people, even family.

I grew up on Lincoln Place between Troy and Schenectady Avenues in the crowded borough of Brooklyn, New York. My neighborhood, Crown Heights, had no treehouses, but was topped with misshapen rooftops, full of tin hatchways, groping TV antennas, pigeon crap, and older kids doing improper things where no one could see.

My neighborhood was bone ugly. The corner of Troy Avenue with its overcrowded, dimly lit, and alarmingly overlarge apartment buildings was notorious for its drug trafficking, gunshots going off at night from the rooftops, and all manner of whispered incidents. When I was about 12 years old, a fair-skinned kid on my block named Kevin, with bronze-colored hair that looked to be the texture of cotton, was hanging out at the corner of Troy and Lincoln Place one night when he was shot through his handsome head. He died that night. He was only a little older than me. The word on the street was that it was a case of mistaken identity. We were all in high school at the time.

Right around the corner from my house in the other direction, at the intersection of Schenectady and Eastern Parkway, stood P.S. 167, an elementary school that was a testament to bygone years of architectural grandeur in certain neighborhoods in America with its castle-like appearance and oversized rooms, windows, and doorways. It is the school I would have attended if my parents weren't keenly aware that the quality of the education practiced within its high walls had fallen largely out of synch with the legacy of prowess in educational practice projected when standing before its monumental stone and brick edifice.

Still, a school it was—there was some obscure law we heard through the grapevine that police were enforcing that promised more severe penalties for illegal activities conducted within so many yards of any school. But the drug dealers in our neighborhood apparently knew that law very well and seemed to stay as far from the school as possible in their daily and nightly dealings, if only to keep the cops off their backs and make their illegal trade a little less hazardous. So the drug trafficking stayed on the Troy end of the block, and the schoolyard at the Schenectady end stayed relatively safe. With its bent-rimmed basketball courts and the chiseled exterior walls of the school and huge gated windows serving as makeshift obstacle courses in our daily handball and paddleball games, the schoolyard served as the largest playground for many of the kids in the surrounding neighborhood.

Playing in our schoolyard, we learned several things rather quickly: not to tear the skin from our knees by tripping and falling on the rough cement and shiny bits of broken bottles; avoid the odd corners that stank of old fermented urine; and avoid proximity with the large and shadowed stone staircases when congested with idling packs of jobless teenagers or haunted by homeless, faceless men roosting beneath old newspapers and cardboard boxes. It was impossible to live in these conditions, yet we lived and we played, and we navigated, and we stressed, and we hoped. I, in particular, always hoped for a life beyond the present ugliness, even if it was imagining that I lived in the artificial sunlight that lit the Brady Bunch home, a wall-to-wall-carpet and Formica-clad set produced for television by ABC.

The white parapets of P.S. 167 were remnants left behind in the flight of those Whites who fled Crown Heights when the demographics began to darken, except for a few like Dr. Schwartz, my mother's family doctor on Kosciusko Street of nearby Bedford-Stuyvesant ever since she was a little girl, and then the family doctor of her own children. I have unwanted memories of pants pulled down, his big graying ungloved hand brusquely placed on my bare scrotum, checking the old-fashioned way for any swelling that might signal the mumps at each increasingly infrequent visit. Old Dr. Schwartz stayed and practiced medicine in the changing neighborhood until he died. Crown Heights was slowly reconstituted as a low-income admixture of African Americans, Caribbean immigrants, Puerto Ricans, and black-garbed Orthodox Jews. As Crown Heights was abandoned to become a ghetto, the school building on my corner succumbed to the mediocrity of urban educational practices in America in spite of its impressive façade.

As a result, my parents made the decision to bus all four of their children to Sheepshead Bay—an overwhelmingly white neighborhood an hour away, near Brighton Beach and Coney Island—so we could receive the quality of education everyone desires for their children. A connection was drawn between my desire for yards with treehouses and this neighborhood in Brooklyn that was full of treehouses, yet wanted nothing much to do with those that looked like me. From first grade to eighth grade, I took a yellow school bus, or free public transportation on elevated subway rails, back and forth through fields of dreams.

Oh, the sights to be seen! If these were not quite the homes a Cinderella would aspire to, they certainly held all the magic of stage sets and theater and make-believe, these free-standing homes that did not share each other's walls, surrounded instead by front yards and back yards, two-car garages, and plastic swimming pools painted blue sitting on lawns that were the private playgrounds of children. Two-story Brady Bunch structures with pointed gables or vast flat overhangs, with parental trees hugging each dwelling place in high affectionate greenery; some with rope swings lashed to healthy boughs, some with treehouses swaddled in their branches.

How is it possible to have a treehouse if one doesn't have a proper tree, if one's backyard is covered over with cracked and crumbling cement, if one's front yard fits no more than a single ill-fitting hedge? Back in my part of Brooklyn, the one tree that grew in our backyard was there only because it had pushed its way past a corner of cement and no one had bothered to uproot it. We had attached a clothesline to this tree but that's about all we could do with it. It was one of those weed trees that grew in Brooklyn, the *Ailanthus Altissima*, not a great oak or a maple like those throughout Sheepshead Bay but an intrepid invader that had found a seam of inhospitable earth and bullied in its roots. An *Ailanthus Altissima* is equipped to survive a city's filth, shoot up fast, stink the air, and die young. Its weak branches were not a place for treehouses. Looking out from the kitchen window of our second-floor apartment, one could view the impropriety of this near useless tree, framed by an overly large apartment building jammed into the background across the junk-filled fissure between the Rolling family property and the rest of Crown Heights. Across the fence, beyond the broken and uneven surface of my backyard, the wall of that apartment building revealed portraits as still as I was in my clandestine surveillance through windows punched in brick. At other times, all that was visible were fleeting cinematic shadows through torn eggshell-colored shades and faded bed sheets hung in windows for an imperfect privacy.

Just like the city-sized neighborhood that allows it to breed without restraint—just like the Crown Heights section of Brooklyn desperate for any shade of green—the *Ailanthus Altissima* was an ugly outgrowth. And so was I. What tragedy can a little black boy know to confer upon him the awareness of his ugliness without having yet lived a full life? At first, it seems similar to the affliction of little Pecola Breedlove before she lost her mind, or her sense of shame, and acquired those piercing blue eyes to outstare the sun without ever blinking (Morrison, [1970] 1994). Simpler than adult tragedies, my tragedy was the affliction of bone ugliness, a curious affliction in that it first cut to the bone and then cleaved long to those bones, even though no one else gave a signal that they saw it. But unlike me, as described in Toni Morrison's *The Bluest Eye*, the Breedloves were born certain of their ugliness.

I was not born with the certainty of my affliction. That was fortunate for me, for in such cases there is little hope of restoration, lacking in the first place any sense of loss to once again be restored. On the contrary, I merely developed a flaw in my perception along the way, little more than a minor disaster. Therein was my first hope of restoration and my early awareness of the significance of Cinderella to black boys.

Even if other people kept quiet about my flaw—about the utter collapse of a favorable self-image and the aftermath of stigma—I know they could see it in my face. I avoided crossing glances only so that I wouldn't see it when others first noticed the flaw, when they noticed the breech in my façade.

※ ※ ※

When I was still a child, on sunny afternoons after school all the kids from surrounding blocks came to my block to play. A large portion of our square block was captured within the fenced schoolyard of P.S. 167. Even with just four basketball hoops, and no playground equipment, the air would fill with echoes cracking back and forth between the school's high white parapets and the red brick and stone houses on both sides of our narrow street, echoes encoded with the distortions of pounding rubber balls, the taps and scratches of shoe heels, the slapping of sneakers on the cement and asphalt, and the wild shouts of children.

Sometimes white chalk would appear and hopscotch boxes were quickly drawn on the neat squares of pavement in front of my Grandma's house. Grandma lived next door to us. Houses on our block were attached, sharing walls and the arguments that penetrate them. On a particular day, similar to other days, I watched as a small flat stone was tossed to bounce across the cement into a numbered box. I watched the one-foot, two-feet, one-foot hops from box to box to stop and balance on one small hopping foot, steadying oneself to drop a hand to pick up the stone. Some little girl I didn't know and whose face I don't remember came to sit beside me and asked me to look at her. We were sitting on one of Grandma's two wooden benches, just inside the front gate. Two steps down was the sidewalk and other kids. I ignored the little girl; my attention was elsewhere. I turned my body away from her gaze and avoided any physical contact with her on the bench. Why was she talking to me anyway? Didn't she see I didn't have anything I wanted to say?

"Look at me!" she said, tugging at my arm.

"Will you stop it!" I snapped back at her, jerking my arm away. Why was she bothering me? The skin underneath each of my eyebrows pulled toward the bridge of my nose and into a frown.

"Smile!" the little girl said slyly, smiling, trying to lure me into disarmament.

"Leave me alone!" I yelled. I tried to move away from the manipulation.

I may have grinned at that point. Perhaps I was embarrassed by the attention. A nervous grin perhaps. Grinning relaxes the frowns on faces. The girl clapped a hand over her mouth, all giggles. I asked what she was laughing so loud for. The kids playing hopscotch in front of us now had our attention as well. I can't remember the surrounding faces, just the noise and voices that seemed to stop. The little girl stood up, pointed at my face and declared, finger in my face, pointing, speaking out loud, "Look! He only has *one* dimple! See?! Look at his face!"

"No I don't," I said, dropping my eyes, my face, my voice. My head was down and I didn't want to see if anyone was looking. The attention made my face warm and I needed to move away fast.

"No I don't," I repeated, stiffly. My whole head seemed to glow brightly, very hot, drawing lots of attention. I was beneath windows, very near, on both sides of the street, windows cluttered with onlookers. I rushed through the painted iron gate, painted just enough to hide the unstripped layers beneath it, going quickly next door, up the staircase covered with old linoleum to "our house," to the second floor apartment my family

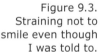

Figure 9.3. Straining not to smile even though I was told to.

lived in, down the slender hallway so dark after the bright outside, around a curve and a corner, into the bathroom, closing the door behind me. Locking the door with the frosted glass window. I didn't have to turn on the light to see. I waited until sight came. There was a light well in the center of the house, right beside the bathroom. My eyes adjusted to the murky sun working its way through the small window above and to the right of the toilet. I wanted the dimness. I wanted the coolness. I wanted the silence. I wanted the tile walls to barricade me in a small space of my own, away from the newly disinterested voices still curling toward my ears, back at play.

I sat on the edge of the sink. It was clean white porcelain. I had shorts on but the surface warmed quickly against my bare legs after the first biting contact. In front of the bathroom medicine cabinet mirror, above the sink, I stared long at my face. The house was quiet. Everyone else was outside.

Everyone else knew that you either have two dimples or no dimples at all. You could see that from all the illustrations and photographs in books and magazines. I saw what normal people looked like. I saw enough to be certain. In the soft, chubby skin of my left cheek was the only dimple I could manage. Although I strained or poked at my tiring, smiling facial muscles, the flesh of my right cheek remained undented. I poked and I strained. I made my facial muscles move very way I could think of. I stared at my flaw.

That was when I decided I would never let anyone else notice there was something very wrong with me. As best as I could help it, as much as I could keep anyone else from noticing, I would never let anyone else see my ugly smile (see Figure 9.3).

❋ ❋ ❋

My lopsided countenance and missing dimple thus became a synecdoche for all of my wrongness, all of my colored skin, all of my shyness, all of my unacceptability in neighborhoods with treehouses; when I hid my smile, I hid my ever after. With that, I fled the garden of childhood too early, not wanting to acquire immortality and the permanent etching of a spoiled self-image.

In earlier texts of the Cinderella fable, one of the labels attached by the stepmother and stepsisters upon she who would be Cinderella was "Cinderbreech," the equivalent of saying "Cinder-hind parts" or "Cinderbuttocks" as she crawled about to clean out the chimney debris. The name "Cinderella" itself makes no attempt to hide its owner's subjectivity to a starkly visual argument making mockery of her assignment to clean out the household cinders and ash. Where did she find the agency to manage a sullied self-image? If we assume that identity is subject to the discourses in which it is socially situated, and that discourses are, as is argued by Foucault ([1969] 1972), "practices that systematically form the objects of which they speak" (p. 4), how does the agent, as a subject—whether Cinderbreech, the marginalized African American, or unsmiling me—recode and reconstitute the manifest visuality of their subjectivity within the performance of public identity?

In my encounter with the little girl, I lost a visual argument. In evidence was my face—raw data in which a flaw was first perceived; as was implicit in the girl's public indictment, the claim could thus be entered that there was something wrong with me; this claim was warranted by the preponderance of faces in view without lopsided smiles—the faces of quizzical young bystanders in the flesh, as well as those reproduced in magazines, illustrations, and painted on plastic baby dolls. This visual argument was anchored in the background premise that beauty—or at the very least, normality—originates in the display of an evenly-hewn appearance. Seeing, after all, is believing. My drop-eyed counter-argument—that I *didn't* have only one dimple—was hopelessly lost on evidence of raw empirical data alone, as my bathroom mirror objectively corroborated.

Race, similarly, is also a visual argument. Race is used to justify casting the inference of inferiority on those who cannot occupy the center along with the normal, lacking as they do the requisite appearance or popularity or familiarity or speech patterns. In a consequence equal to the loss of my smile, the losers of the argument of race are cast into the breach as those who deviate, those who are signified as unsafe or insensible, not sedate enough or too unschoolable. Historically, the evidence of race has been the flesh, hair, and skull—raw data in which difference was first perceived. The raw data were implicit in the social indictment, eliciting the claim that there was something wrong with this speciation of humanity. The claim of racial inferiority is warranted by the proprieties of home, family, and the pursuit of private property; by faith in a god created in one's own image (and not in the image of Others); and by the voracious appetites of capital industry that forestalls the acceptance of dissimilar partners. Finally, the entire argument of race is anchored in the background premise that beauty—or at the very least, normality—originates in the display of homogeneity. Likeness, after all, is belonging.

In the modern Western version of the Cinderella narrative, Cinderbreech wins her visual argument against the assignment of ugliness quite handily, transcending the ash heap by *changing* the raw data, presenting a magical gown, a gorgeous horse-drawn coach, washed skin, and those brashly inflexible glass slippers. Alas, the first iteration of a new ending seemed destined for a troublesome birth as the clock's midnight stroke sent Cinderbreech tumbling backward to her "expected" appearance. But Cinderbreeches are translated over to Cinderella endings not by presenting alternative data sets alone; the warrant for the claim of ugliness must also be subverted and its background premises undermined.

The naming of Cinderbreech is warranted in the mind of her stepmother in that "the kindness of this pretty child … made her [own] daughters appear so odious" (Cinderella, n.d.), warranted by the desire to promulgate the appearance of her daughters as the ones nearest to polite society within her household; this warrant is subverted near the end of the Cinderella fable when the big-boned feet of those other daughters are unable to fit those inflexible glass slippers. Ah, the fault, dear sisters, lies not in your stepsister, but in yourselves that you are odious and unmarried to the prince; the reader of the narrative notes not only this subversion of the narrative of a lowly stepsister but also that each of the sisters has the opportunity to fit the slipper before Cinderbreech, tries to do so, but cannot. They are incapable of changing the raw data; they have no access to reinterpretation.

But the visual argument against our Cinderella is not only lost here. The background premise of the argument is fully undermined at the conclusion of this tale when Cinderbreech is rescued from the breach to marry the prince not because of her kindness or her prettiness, but rather because she fits an empty slipper, a signifier of unexpected possibility. From Cinderbreech to breech birth to Cinderella ending.

The inauguration of the performance of "The New Negro" throughout the Harlem Renaissance from the 1920s to the mid-1930s was an incomplete response to the visual argument of race, a worthy initial attempt at a changing of the raw data which did not go far enough to subvert the warrant for the persistent argument that we were, are, and have always been an ugly people. Failing to fully controvert the premises of the argument against us, "The New Negro" is easily co-opted as support of the claim of inferiority when presented as data that the exceptional Negro proves the rule that African Americans are generally inferior.

In the early twentieth century, most African Americans were disenfranchised enough to be rendered invisible in their contributions to society apart from being given a very visible platform by wealthy patrons, government work and welfare programs, or liberal-minded and philanthropic white society. "The New Negro" thus became yet another construct in the assembly of a modern Western conception of African American identity, the argument of which would not support the idea of a Cinderbreech insinuated as an exemplar of beauty—nor grant such a Negro a listing in the social register.

The visual representation of the African American body in Western visual culture, in commercial advertisement, paintings, and popular souvenir postcards, has been unique in the all-out effort of those who sought to define us as either less than fraternal, less than American, less than Christian, or less than statistically significant. African American identity was essentially reduced to a framing device for defining whiteness.

Defined in this way, black bodies became enclaves for the agency of Western hegemony; we became a part of the discourse of modernity, not entirely whole unless we were in service to the main storyline. Conversely, when we developed "ex-centric" approaches

(herising, 2005) to representation, reinterpretation, and research—
newly indigenous and idiosyncratic responses to the stereotyped
presentation of our identities—our responses entered the discourses
of public opinion and modern popular culture and began to reso-
nate there, changing some preconceptions. An ex-centric approach
to representation and reinterpretation allows for the displacement
of privileging ontological and epistemological assumptions about
the origin of new knowledge, moving the origins of new knowledge away from a central locus of validity and toward the margins
(Rolling, in press).

But in merely contradicting our presence as buffoons in visual
culture, yes, there was a rebirth—a renaissance—we were reenter-
ing the world butt-first. We succeeded only at getting some black
Americans seen in contradistinction to the accepted narratives of
the national discourse, but we did not succeed in changing the
discourse of modern identity itself. We went from Cinderbreech
to breech birth.

What pain our breech births must have caused the nation
whenever one of our "New Negroes" appeared in a nonsatiri-
cal suit and tie, or in a shiny-buttoned, starch-collared military
uniform, not looking that much different from a nigger at first,
until wrongly positioned connotations became sharply, blindingly
apparent. Breech babies were life-threatening obstructions to
social expectations. Threatening enough to erupt in a race riot or
the utter devastation of a town like Rosewood.[3] Painful enough
to marshal all available cloaked and hooded midwives to the birth
of a nation, Klansmen rushing in from nearby precincts to put
niggers in their place, to turn breech births around to their proper
position, to return them to the state of being a Cinderbreech.

And so we arrive at the crucial question: In the matter of
African American identity, how in the world does a breech
birth—a Cinderbreech and a Cinderella aborted—wind up as
Cinderella ending? John Henry Adams, Jr. writes of breech births
in America:

> Here is the real new Negro man. Tall, erect, commanding, with
> a face as strong and expressive as Angelo's Moses and yet every
> whit as pleasing and handsome as Rubens's favorite model. There
> is that penetrative eye about which Charles Lamb wrote with

such deep admiration, that broad forehead and firm chin. (Willis, 2000, p. 36)

Deborah Willis (2000) makes the point that "[t]he architects of the 'New Negro' doctrine could not, quite naturally, define the African-American experience through [the dominant culture caricatures], so there was a concerted effort to find the 'self' in visual images" (p. 36). But this new figurative self-image is not what was in view when I traveled in the summer of 2006 on a pilgrimage to see the legacy of this new agency, or its remainders, in the collections of the Hampton University Museum in Hampton, Virginia, and the Howard University Gallery of Art in Washington, DC. Rather, what I saw was unexpected.

In 2006, I won an internal grant as a new faculty member at The Pennsylvania State University to fund the completion of the research that began during my postgraduate studies in art education at Teachers College, Columbia University. Early in my studies, and ultimately in my dissertation, I began engaging in the discourse of African American identity in contemporary social history so as to make recognizable certain features that remained invisible to me—features I am still in the process of "figuring out" in scholarly word and in pencil sketch (Rolling, 2004). These are features that I believe serve to reposition African Americans in social, historical, and scholarly visual arguments just as radically as was Cinderella's allegorical movement from the ash heap of obscurity to redeemed prominence and acclaim.

My initial goal was to travel to various historically black colleges and universities to sketch and draw works and artifacts from their art collections, as well as to record written and sketched impressions of the people and places I interacted with along the way in autobiographical and testimonial fashion. If there was any physical evidence of the definitive "New Negro," were they not sure to be found in these collections of art by "New Negroes" as they were becoming new? When did we find the agency to cross the threshold to a new ending? When did "black" forever become "beautiful?"

As I roamed through the Hampton University Museum with sketchbook in hand, I was stopped in mid-step by a work by the artist Felrath Hines, entirely in black and white and full of geometrics. Hines was a member of Spiral, a group of about fifteen or so New York City–based artists of African American descent including Romare Bearden, Hale Woodruff, Charles Alston, Norman Lewis, and Richard Mayhew. Formed in 1963, the year of my breech birth, Spiral sought to explore race, identity, art, and the possible roles they might play in the Civil Rights movement in the era when Blacks would first be heralded in the United States as beautiful. A website relates the following exchange[4]:

> Spiral member Norman Lewis framed the question: "Is there a Negro Image?" To which group member Felrath Hines responded, "There is no Negro Image in the twentieth century—in the 1960s. There are only prevailing ideas that influence everyone all over the world, to which the Negro has been, and is, contributing. Each person paints out of the life he lives."

Several works by these artists were on display at the Hampton University Museum, such as Richard Mayhew's gorgeous *September*, a landscape painting. I was also struck by the work of Dr. Samella S. Lewis, including a painting called *Waterboy*, completed when she was a student at Hampton Institute and yet here they were, still here, in the museum's collection. And I was absolutely astounded by a series of serigraph, or silkscreen, prints by Jacob Lawrence titled *Hiroshima*, featuring the manipulation a single color palette of about four colors into eight wholly distinct color worlds and narrative episodes.

So where was the "New Negro"? The answer: It's just one figure in the storyline, one that has already been reinterpreted. Whereas the "New Negro" remains a historical artifact, largely definitive in its initial introduction, the effort to draw from and paint out of the life one lives, out of localized conceptions of beauty and identity, has proven to be an inherently *emergent* exercise. "Black [as] beautiful" reinterprets African American identity a thousand instances a day, introducing an identity ever in flux into the visual culture and the lexicon of modernity, a root structure as rhizomatically complex as the variations of color socially agreed as constituting the spectrum of black identity. It is all there in the response of Felrath Hines to Norman Lewis— the agent, in this case the artist, makes manifest and recodes his or her identity with each new work, each new attempt at what once before was merely a possibility. Each new exercise initiates a Cinderella ending born of the previous iteration of identity. The Cinderbreech, the marginalized African American, or unsmiling me—we are each undone in the act of rewriting precedents towards the possibility of new endings. The glass slipper is there for the wearing, a postmodernism, simultaneously measured to fit us in our present state of being, and to fit an imagined station of becoming.

Can identity be created from the narrative reinterpretation of identity? Yes. This chapter is offered as evidence. This is a reinterpretive research agenda that continues to search for hybridities in the mass culture: images and (re)presentations revealing archaeologies of identity that are at once ambiguous and anomalous; deceivers and trickplayers; shape-shifters; situation-inventors; messengers and imitators of the cultural hegemony; bricoleurs of the sacred and the lewd (Hynes & Doty, 1993). The act of locating the nucleus of new knowledge within the marginal story and the act of then insinuating such a story within a work of educational research is simultaneously a political act (hooks, 1990) and a subversive act (Gooding-Brown, 2000), one that attends to the "transformative potential of the margin" (herising, 2005, p. 144). Telling the marginalized story, the invisible story, the heretofore unspoken, suppressed or silenced story, is a borderland space in research (Anzaldúa, 1988). These unearthed hybridities are self-representations that might mean one thing within the "normalized" borders of dominant culture America while at the same time an altogether different thing to those living in African American communities. They are the self-representations that allowed us to teach ourselves new names in full view of those who needed us to remain ensconced in a singular ugliness. Images, songs, and words can be set to work as hybrid signs—simultaneously present and becoming—and set into place to serve any marginalized individual or group.

In summation, I am not a "New Negro." I am postmodernity in the flesh, a collaborative and transgressive reinterpretation. I am both made and unmade; I respond and thus, remake. Here, at the end of this chapter, treehouses now sprout from ghetto rooftops around the globe. The African American reinterpretation also represents the reinterpretation of your own identity crisis. And there is enough agency available to us all for yet another Cinderella ending in the making.

Notes

Acknowledgment: The investigations related in this chapter were partially supported by a 2006 grant from the Africana Research Center at The Pennsylvania State University, University Park.

1. I am referring here to the title of Erving Goffman's classic sociological study published in the year of my breech birth (1963).

2. See Cook (1975) and Gough (1990). Both texts caution against misinterpreting the Cinderella narrative as merely a story of rags to riches.

3. Information about the 1923 massacre of African Americans in Rosewood, Florida, and the destruction of this entire community was accessed September 23, 2008, at http://en.wikipedia.org/wiki/Rosewood_massacre

4. Accessed September 23, 2008, from a resource for teachers on the life of artist Romare Bearden at http://www.nga.gov/education/classroom/bearden/lead1.shtm

References

Anzaldúa, G. (1988). Bridges, drawbridge, sandbar, or island. In M. Blasius & S. Phelan (Eds.), *We are everywhere: A historical sourcebook of gay and lesbian politics* (pp. 712–722). New York: Routledge.

Barone, T., & Eisner, E. (2006). Arts-based educational research. In J. L. Green, G. Camilli, & P. B. Elmore (Eds.), *Handbook of complimentary methods in education research* (pp. 95–110). Mahwah, NJ: Lawrence Erlbaum.

Brown, L., & Strega, S. (Eds.). (2005). *Research as resistance: Critical, indigenous, & anti-oppressive approaches.* Toronto: Canadian Scholars' Press.

Cinderella. (n.d.). New York: J. Wrigley. http://www.usm.edu/english/fairy-tales/cinderella/cind2.html (Accessed January 15, 2011).

Cook, E. (1975). *The ordinary and the fabulous: An introduction to myths, legends and fairy tales for teachers and storytellers.* London: Cambridge University Press.

Foucault, M. ([1969] 1972). *The archaeology of knowledge and the discourse on language,* trans. Alan M. Sheridan-Smith. New York: Pantheon.

Goffman, E. (1963). *Stigma: Notes on the management of a spoiled identity.* New York: Simon & Schuster, Inc.

Gooding-Brown, J. (2000). Conversations about art: A disruptive model of interpretation. *Studies in Art Education, 42,* 1, 36–50.

Gough, J. (1990). Rivalry, rejection, and recovery: Variations of the Cinderella story. *Children's Literature in Education, 21,* 2, 99–107.

herising, F. (2005). Interrupting positions: Critical thresholds and queer pro/ positions. In L. Brown & S. Strega (Eds.), *Research as resistance: Critical, indigenous, & anti-oppressive approaches* (pp. 127–151). Toronto: Canadian Scholars' Press.

hooks, b. (1960). *Yearning: Race, gender, and cultural politics.* New York: Routledge.

Hynes, W. J., & Doty, W. G. (Eds.). (1993). *Mythical trickster figures: Contours, contexts, and criticisms.* Tuscaloosa: The University of Alabama Press.

Leavy, P. (2009). *Method meets arts: Arts-based research practices.* New York: The Guilford Press.

Locke, A. (Ed.). ([1925] 1992). *The new Negro.* New York: Touchstone.

Morrison, T. ([1970] 1994). *The bluest eye.* New York: Vintage

Nelson, M. A. (1972). *A comparative anthology of children's literature.* New York: Holt, Rinehart & Winston.

Rolling, J. H. (2004). Figuring myself out: Certainty, injury, and the poststruc- turalist repositioning of bodies of identity. *Journal of Aesthetic Education, 38,* 4, 46–58.

Rolling, J. H. (2010). *Cinderella story: A scholarly sketchbook about race, identity, Barack Obama, the human spirit, and other stuff that matters.* Lanham, MD: AltaMira.

Rolling, J. H. (in press). Circumventing the imposed ceiling: Art education as resistance narrative. *Qualitative Inquiry. 17,* 1, xxx–xxx.

Schafer, R. (1981). Narration in the psychoanalytic dialogue. In W. J. T. Mitchell (Ed.), *On narrative* (pp. 25–49). Chicago: University of Chicago Press.

Stinson, D. W. (2004). African American male students and achievement in school mathematics: A critical postmodern analysis of agency. Unpublished doctoral dissertation. Georgia State University, Atlanta.

Willis, D. (2000). *Reflections in black: A history of black photographers, 1840 to the present.* New York: W. W. Norton & Co.

Yolen, J. (1977). America's Cinderella. *Children's Literature in Education, 8,* 1, 21–29.

Zeiger, P. (n.d.). *Scientific method in the social sciences.* http://www.sdp.org/sdp/ spirit/SocSci.htm (accessed January 15, 2011).

Chapter 10

Intimacy, Empathy, Activism

A Performative Engagement
with Children's Wartime Art

Elyse Pineau

In the fall of 2003, a traveling exhibit of children's drawings enti-tled *They Still Draw Pictures: Children's Art in Wartime from the Spanish Civil War to Kosovo* (Geist & Carroll, 2002) was brought to my campus through the collective action of a "living archive" of Spanish Civil War experts and a local coalition of historians, pro-gressives, and peace activists. The traveling exhibit was comprised of seventy-two framed drawings curated from a larger collection of over 600 children's wartime drawings held in the Southworth Spanish Civil War archives of the Mandeville Special Collections Library at the University of California, San Diego (UCSD). Most of the drawings date from the Spanish Civil War (1936–1939), although in recent years additional artwork has been collected from warzones and refugee camps in Sierra Leone, Sri Lanka, Gaza, Iraq, Afghanistan, Kosovo, and the Sudan.[1] Given the age and fragility of the original Spanish artifacts, however, none of those drawings have been available to public view since their limited cir-culation in 1938 when they were used to publicize the plight of the children and raise funds for evacuations and other assistance.

The exhibit of *They Still Draw Pictures*[2] was curated and subse-quently published by historians Anthony Geist and Peter Carroll and sponsored by the Abraham Lincoln Brigade Archives (ALBA), "a non-profit national organization devoted to the preservation and dissemination of the history of the North American role in the Spanish Civil War (1936-1939 and its aftermath" (ALBA, 2011, para. 4). In his framing chapter, Geist acknowledges the concentric circles of expertise and influence that ultimately shepherded the project, but he is careful to anchor its impetus in the power of the drawings themselves and the visceral memory of his first encounter with them. Opening the document case during a routine tour of the UCSD library holdings, he recalls: "I was stunned. The pictures spoke to me with a vibrancy and emotional power that spanned the more than sixty years that had lapsed since they were drawn" (Geist & Carroll, 2002, p. 10). Enlisting the support of the collection's archivist, the resources of ALBA, and the collaboration of fellow ALBA board member, Peter Carroll, they began the arduous task of sifting through the "artistic remains" of 600 children. Struck by the painful similarities between the Spanish children's drawings and those spanning the later twentieth century, Geist and Carroll instructed that several contemporary drawings be hung periodically throughout the exhibit, below those of the Spanish children. With this sporadic visual juxtaposition, Geist reasoned, they hoped to highlight "both the specificity of a particular historical circumstance and the universality of a child's response to the conditions of war and displacement" (p. 11).

In a similar spirit, I want to ground my examination of children's wartime art in the vibrant emotional power of my first encounter with the Spanish drawings and my embodied engagement with one drawing in particular. I want to hold in generative tension, the specificity of this particular drawing and the universality of children's wartime trauma across generational, geographic, and geopolitical contexts. In making explicit the network of activists and public intellectuals (Giroux, 1988) whose work shielded and shepherded the children's drawings for four generations, I acknowledge that my reading of this singular drawing is itself a social, historical convergence of many efforts, alliances, and perspectives. Finally, in deploying performative autoethnography as both an interpretive and a textual method, I want to advocate for performance as a means of creating intimacy, developing empathy and spurring activism in response to global crises such as these. I turn, then, to the particulars of the Spanish Civil War, the origins of the children's drawings, and the spectrum of allies whose cultural work in the service of those children brought their drawings to my doorstep.

A Historical Context and a Living Archive

The Spanish Civil War raged from 1936 to 1939, when Franco's forces, aided by Nazi Germany and fascist Italy, circled Madrid, driving out the Republican government and forcing over 600,000 Spanish citizens into exile. The Spanish war is historically significant for many reasons, not least because it marked the genesis of modern mechanized warfare directed systematically at a civilian population. Germany tested out its new warplanes and aerial tactics in a macabre rehearsal for its WWII *blitzkrieg* by repeatedly strafing working-class neighborhoods, markets, hospitals, schools, museums, and libraries. Cities suffered waves of aerial bombing, forcing massive emergency evacuations and creating a constant dread of "death from a distance," which has come to characterize modern war technologies and the civilian casualties they leave in their wake.

For their safety, an estimated 200,000 Spanish children were evacuated from the cities into the countryside in eastern Spain still under Republic control, or over the border into France. The Republic set up children's colonies, called *colonias infantiles* in abandoned country estates, schools, and other public buildings where the children were fed, educated, and cared for during the war. It was at the *colonias* that international teams of teachers and social workers initiated what is believed to be the first systematic use of art therapy with the child refugees. The children were given whatever art materials could be bought or scavenged and encouraged to draw their experiences, memories, and hopes for reuniting with their families in a peaceful, post-war Spain. Through the collective efforts of the Spanish Board of Education, the Carnegie Institute of Spain, and The Spanish Child Welfare Association of the American Friends Service Committee (Quakers), almost 3,000 of the drawings were collected and about 100 of them toured the eastern United States in 1938.

In his Editor's Note to the original 1938 exhibit of *They Still Draw Pictures*, Joseph Weissberger presents the drawings as "autobiographical pages of unkept diaries," rendered in crayon, ink, pencil, and watercolor by children aged 8 to 14. Despite the children's lack of tools or training, Weissberger lauds the remarkable skill and sophistication in their drawings, particularly in the intricate, accurate documentation of warplane models and insignia. The documentary realism of the warplanes is complicated by the consistently exaggerated scale of the planes in relation to the human figures in the frame. In his Foreword to the 1938 exhibit catalog, Aldous Huxley argues that the pervasive role the airplanes play in the children's imaginations marks them as the paradigmatic signifiers of a new generation of warfare and war victims. His prophetic description is worth quoting at length:

> To the little boys and girls of Spain, the symbol of contemporary civilization is the military plane—the plane that, when cities have anti-aircraft defenses, flies high and drops its load of fire and high explosives indiscriminately from the clouds; the plane that, when there is no defense, swoops low and turns its machine-guns on the panic-stricken men, women and children in the streets. For hundreds of thousands of children in Spain, as for millions of other children, the plane, with its bombs and its machine guns, is the thing that, in the world we live in and helped to make, is significant and important above all others. This is the dreadful fact to which the drawings in our collection bear unmistakable witness. (para 7)

The exhibit was very successful in generating American sympathy for the Spanish children, and the catalog went through three printings with all funds directly funneled back to the Friends' relief efforts.

"Then the artworks just disappeared," says Geist (Geist & Carroll, 2002, p. 11). Many were sold in 1939 to raise funds, and some eventually turned up in private collections or were donated to public libraries. Currently, in addition to the 609 drawings in the UCSD Mandeville Special Collections, Harvard University holds another seventeen Spanish drawings; the American Friends Service Committee owns twenty, and 153 are held in the Avery

Museum at Columbia University. Angela Giral, former director of the Avery collection and herself a child refugee of the Spanish war, uses the collection's website to issue an open invitation to other child refugees and artists:

> I, too, was evacuated from the war zone about the same time that these drawings were made in the children's colonies. ... Some of these children never saw their parents again, others went back to Spain at the end of the war, some went into exile, like myself, and grew up in far away lands. My hope is that many are still alive and willing to add some pages to these incomplete autobiographies, bringing them up to date. (para. 1)

There are no records of what happened to most of these children after the war, but using the signatures and *colonias'* locations on many of the drawings, Geist has been able to contact ten of the original artists. An interview with one of them is included in his book (Geist & Carroll, 2002).

Enter the story of the Abraham Lincoln Brigade and their living archive. During the war, approximately 40,000 volunteers from fifty-two countries formed the international brigades to fight alongside the Republic against Franco. The American volunteers who served in combat, medical, transportation, and social service capacities came to be known collectively as the Abraham Lincoln Brigade. Sam Sills, who produced and co-directed the documentary film, *The Good Fight: The Abraham Lincoln Brigade in the Spanish Civil War* (Buckner & Sills, 1984), notes that "the Lincolns" were a exceptionally diverse unit, drawing men and women from all walks of life who were committed to resisting fascism and the human atrocities being committed against the Spanish people. "Notwithstanding its exclusion from American textbooks," Sills argues elsewhere (2007), "the Abraham Lincoln Brigade commands attention as a unique example of prescient, radical, and selfless action in the cause of international freedom (para. 8). Following the war, the brigade veterans continued to aid refugees and to participate in various progressive political actions and peace work. Their "living archive" was conceptualized as an international network of scholars, artists, veterans, and cultural workers committed to preserving and disseminating information about the war and the brigade volunteers. According to the ALBA website:

> In 1979, recognizing the vital importance of their radical history, and the need to collect and preserve writings, letters, photographs, oral histories and artifacts that would preserve that history, the Veterans of the Abraham Lincoln Brigades formed their "living Archive" (ALBA) ... and began to take over the commemorative performances, helping to produce these key events, telling, re-telling and contextualizing the veterans' stories. (2011, para. 3)

The preservation and circulation of the Spanish children's drawings is testament to the need and efficacy of the archive as both an artifactual and a performative entity. ALBA's network of international and interdisciplinary cultural workers exemplifies, for me, the spirit of critical collective action within and around the academy.

Local Contact

"Remembering is an act of citizenship," Michael Batinski (2005, p. 17) argues in his review of Peter Glazer's *Radical Nostalgia: Spanish Civil War Commemoration in America* (2005). Resisting the conservative lull common to war memorials and reenactments, Batinski argues that nostalgia can serve progressive agendas the degree to which its historicizing gesture is grounded in the contemporary moment and aimed toward transformation of the future. "Radical nostalgia becomes a political act situated in the present and focused on a just future. Commemorative performance evokes such political yearnings and sustains a sense of community among political activists" (p. 17). *They Still Draw Pictures* presented just such an opportunity for radical memory and progressive solidarity. As chair of the History Department and himself a longtime member of ALBA, Batinski was the point person responsible for bringing the exhibit to campus. He wanted to use the drawings to spark reflection on the ongoing global crisis of war-torn children and to challenge academics' responsibility in the face of it. He proposed a series of interdisciplinary panels and presentations to run concurrently with the exhibit that could facilitate a campus-wide dialog on the historical, aesthetic, and psychosocial significance of the drawings and the stories they told of trauma and resilience.

Initially, I was puzzled by Michael's invitation to contribute to the series and concerned that my untutored interpretations of the drawings would have little scholarly merit. Unlike my colleagues, I had little prior awareness of the Spanish Civil War, and none of the Abraham Lincoln Brigade and its cultural archive. I am not an art historian; I could not contextualize the drawings within the visual culture of the Spanish war, or the documentary photography, or the propagandist iconography of that time. While the art that I make may have therapeutic results, I have no formal training in art therapy or child development, and my eye is not sensitive to the psychodynamics of children's self-portraiture. Outside of a ready curiosity and an ideological predisposition to engage the children's work as meaningful cultural artifacts, I protested that I had no disciplinary expertise to contribute to the series. The provocative ambiguity of Michael's response to my hesitation echoes for me to this day: "From the perspective of your discipline," he told me, "speak as the spirit moves you."

As an autoethnographic performance poet in communication studies, my work centers on personal narrative, methodologies of embodiment, and poetic-performative textualities. I am interested in the ways that people story their lives in artful ways and what can be learned from engaging these narratives somatically through an articulate performing body. In this disciplinary context, I understand performance epistemically and I use it methodologically to engage the experiences of others in *a systematic process of corporeal intimacy leading to critical insight and social action.* The perspectives I bring to any interpretive encounter reflect an interdisciplinary landscape too broad to chart here, but I can mark a set of commitments that guide and ground my work and that formed the methodological core of my engagement with the drawings. I proceed in the spirit of Pelias's (2004) "methodology of the heart" that takes seriously the nested relational contexts in which our work unfolds and the primacy of emotional responsiveness to the subjects we study. I work primarily in the autoethnographic tradition articulated by Spry as a political praxis constituted through a "performative-I co-presence" (2006) and grounded in "an ethic of aesthetic epistemology ... an ethic grounded in the dialogic engagement between craft and emotion, between form and production, between technique and experience, between life and art" (Spry, 2009, p. 159). Like Spry, I situate embodied experience at the core of my methodological process and I rely on autoethnographic narrative to render the somatic landscape of my engagement and the questions that emerged in the course of it. Regarding the children's drawings, I take my interpretative task to be what Holman Jones (2005) terms "a critical ekphrasis," or a poetic meditation on others' creative acts designed to reframe and refract the sites/cites where lives intersect and bodies coalesce (p. 766). I use performative writing (Pollock, 1998) to textualize my engagement with the exhibit because I want to evoke the somatic dialog that unfolded between my performing body and the "bodies of experience" that the children rendered in their drawings. I believe that only a poetic register can capture the transfiguring insights a body experiences, methodologically. And finally, I contextualize this essay as just one small "act of activism" (Madison, 2010) within a global network of cultural workers whose groundwork made possible the creation and preservation of the children's drawings in the first place.

It is from this disciplinary stance, then, that the spirit moves me to craft a story. It is a story about attending to one child's drawing—just *one child* and *one drawing* out of a hundred in the exhibit—but attending to it closely and corporeally and writing to embody on the page, as artfully as I can, what I discovered through that encounter. This is a tale about witnessing, about *bearing witness* to a story by Miguel Ercano Garcia, age 12, drawing from an "unidentified locale" during the Spanish Civil War.[3] It is, ultimately, a story about maintaining a "disciplined perspective" when the spirit moves you to the edge of an interpretive cliff and demands a leap of faith. For me, this was the only response I could ethically make when I encountered, one day, drawings by a group of small children nailed up on the wall, each with a story to tell.

Figure 10.1. *Drawing* by Miguel Ercano Garcia, age 12

A Moving Encounter[4]

Standing stark and isolated on a barren cliff, the tree in the draw-ing by Miguel Ercano Garcia, age 12, bears witness to a drama of human cruelty that is eerily archetypal in its familiarity.[5] Who has not seen or heard echoes of this image in the gritty folklore that accompanies war: A captive man watches as a soldier on horseback charges at a woman flinging herself from the edge of a cliff (see Figure 10.1).

I first encountered Miguel's drawing when I requested an evening alone and after hours in the gallery before the exhibit opened on campus. I wanted to get acquainted with the collec-tion on my own terms—in performance terms, if you will—by turning the empty gallery into a rehearsal space where I could be physically and emotionally receptive to the ways the draw-ings might speak to me, the ways they might move my body in relation to them. Most of the drawings had been hung, but a few still rested on the floor, their standard black frames leaning in stark relief against the white walls, a conspicuous gap overhead marking absence: the absent picture, the absent child. The draw-ings had been arranged into narrative categories: pastoral images of "Before" contrasted sharply with those of "Displacement" and "War" before finding a measure of comfort in "Life in the Colonies" and the final projections of "Peace." Moving through the gallery in the order suggested, the visual rhythm of black lines on white walls became a signifying reminder of the endless repeatability of war and its consequences. As Geist and Carroll intended, I was shocked at the uncanny similarities between the Spanish drawings and the contemporary ones mounted beneath them. The strategy of interspersal was a rhetorical masterstroke; it foregrounded the Spanish children's narrative agency while communicating the relentless subtext of war's brutal repeatability.

Alone in that silent, dimly lit gallery, I felt as if all the world's war-ravaged children were pressing their noses flat up against glass-paned window frames that could barely contain their stories of loss and longing, of homelessness, and of hope. Occasionally, when the angle of light and body aligned, I would glimpse my own face reflected in the glass, "larger than life" and enveloping the small figures in the frame. These sudden superimpositions created an unsettling indeterminacy of art and witness fused together in the act of attending. The overblown scale of my reflection dwarfing the framed scene served as a striking visual analogy of the asymmetry between the war-ravaged and the warmongers. A child's drawing is "the soul's message," Robert Coles advises in his Foreword to the exhibit: "the point is for us to be shown something by certain boys and girls who become our teachers: thereby we are broadened and deepened responsively in our minds and hearts "(2002, p. 9). Wall upon wall, the souls of these long-ago children stared out at me from their glass houses with wide and unflinching eyes. In the presence of such stories as these standing in for the bodies of children who could not, and apparently still cannot, claim agency or the world's attention in any other way—I was shocked and shamed into silence. And in humble silence I began to move slowly about the rooms of the gallery: pausing in the center to feel the panorama of the bombing raids in the "War" wing; stepping close, face to face with the anguish of exile in "Displacement'; reaching out to lay fingertip to frame in the *colonias*, to breathe out a name—"Carmen Sierra, age 12; Faustina Guadano, age 8; Teresa Vazquez, age 13; Alejandro

Chilian, age 11; Rafael Barber, age 10; Felix Fernandez, age 12; Margarita Garcia, age 10." In the charged hush of the gallery, my body moving into the performative attitude of receptive stillness and physical immersion that marks the epistemic readiness of the performing body. … I understood that the most potent and primary task of the responsible witness is committing *to hear and to hold* each one of these stories. Without flinching.

Yet even as I moved from picture to picture overwhelmed by their cumulative force, one particular drawing by Miguel Ercano Garcia, age 12, followed me like a shadow, like a ghost haunting my footsteps, calling out to me, just over my shoulder. And although it was just one drawing out of the hundred in the exhibit that night, Miguel's was the drawing that called me by name. It is the drawing that haunted me, the one that haunts me still. And so I did precisely what I do in my rehearsal hall or my classroom when I need to attend deeply and critically to what is playing out before me. Positioning myself just a body's length away from the wall, I hunkered down on my haunches on the floor of that empty gallery. And I gave Miguel Ercano Garcia's drawing my undivided attention.

A Performative Reading[5]

Instantaneously, I find myself cast into the heart of this drama from the precise geographic vantage point of the invisible witness (see Figure 10.2). Crouched in the low right-hand corner, just outside of the picture's frame, Miguel Ercano Garcia and I stare up … and up … (what feels impossibly high) up the face of a cliff where a soldier charges and a woman makes her leap. From this vantage point, the story unfolds chronologically, but right to left, against the grain of the usual read as if the passage of time were at war with itself in the drawing. A faceless man is caught and bound to a tree by—a rope? a whip?—too small to see clearly from this distance. The foot soldier who has bound him is bent double by the effort, his body caught somewhere between reaching out and pulling back, holding taut against his captive's struggle. In the center of the drawing, a soldier on horseback, a stormtrooper with insignia like crossed lightning, charges down

Figure 10.2.
Elongated view
of drawing.

on a woman poised at the cliff's edge. Two arms lifted, reaching out and beyond the edge of the cliff, the woman has just left the earth in a leap of faith, I imagine, that crashing down on the rocks below is a better fate than remaining to weather the approaching Storm. In the low left-hand corner of the drawing, just on the horizon of sea and sky, the sun sits. Whether it is setting or rising I cannot say, nor need to, I think, for "time" seems a paradox this drawing arrests in its freeze-frame of charging and leaping.

Sitting here at the edge of the frame, gazing intently up at the drawing, it is not difficult for me to imagine what my students might say or to recall what some colleagues have asked: Is this a true story? How can a child's drawing offer empirical evidence of the event depicted? Is this a reliable and representative example of the 600 drawings in the collection? What instructions were given to prompt such an image and what records remain of the art therapy protocols, or the media propaganda of the time, or the collective folklore of wartime that may be the generative force and the real source behind the image drawn?

I'll grant that these are legitimate questions for many whose disciplinary stance is different than my own, perhaps more numeric than narrative. But as these are not the questions staring me in the face as I sit and gaze upward through a child's eyes, I cannot fathom why they would ask them! Why is a story *outside* of the story the one they are drawn to, the one they can see? Why be so quick on our academic feet when this is a time for sitting still, a time for looking and for listening? But as I am a teacher accustomed to the literalism of students, and as I am an academic familiar with the cynicism of colleagues, and as I am an artist who chooses to see differently, and as I am a performer trained to look through another's eyes, and ultimately, as I am a public intellectual whose work is to recognize the "teaching moment," I like to imagine that I would swallow my impatience and simply remind them that in the absence of Miguel Ercano Garcia, age 12, all we have is his story. All that we have is an invitation to look and to listen to a story that survived, to a story revived 60 years later, now nailed to a wall awaiting a witness. And sometimes, when you're invited to a story, it can be wise to just take a leap of faith and see where it leads you.

And then I imagine that is exactly what we do.

A Performative Rendering

Can you see this man by the tree?" I might ask, standing up and stepping into the image, bending double and reaching out with one arm like a whip, reaching out as if armed with a whip that can bind a man to a tree. Can you feel, can you see the force that it takes to snake out a whip and encircle a body? Can you see, can you feel how taut a rope need be to hold a man motionless? Can you feel, do you see the price of such binding? The way that it bends a body double? How it bears down with a weight that can

Figure 10.3. Detail of man and tree.

cripple? Attend to this. Attend to the way roping and whipping and binding can bend a body double, can cripple the binder until one wonders if a body could ever again stand upright, could ever recover, could ever be other than one who has thrown his weight to bind up another. Look in the eyes of the man who is bound to the tree. This man without motion, volition to do other than stand still and witness. One eye wide, the other downcast, this captive man is forced to witness the motion of others: the one who is binding, the one who is charging, the one who is leaping. With a half-sketched face and no active place in the drama unfolding, this one-eyed everyman is fixed to a tree while time rushes by on the pounding of hoofs (see Figure 10.3).

And the stormtrooper, so straight and controlled, is mounted high on his charger. Yet the stiff, upright body seems to rein in the horse even as they rush toward the edge where a woman is choosing her death with defiance. The horse's double, sketched as a faint, diminutive palimpsest of itself, appears just ahead of the main figure, replicated in intricate and accurate detail down to the reins and insignia. And this is no mistake by the artist! This drawing is too careful, too meticulous to feature an error, as if in corrective afterthought, the artist had simply drawn the figure over and neglected to cover his tracks (see Figure 10.4). I like to imagine that Manuel Ercano Garcia, age 12, was careful and

Figure 10.4. Detail of stormtrooper.

meticulous when he erased and retraced his antagonist's mount. I like to imagine that this young boy was using his drawing to steal back time, to reach out and rein in the inevitable, to arrest the charge of death and to stop a horse dead in its tracks. And I know that this child understands, in some way I can only imagine, that death can diminish; that death makes us hollow when we are the charger, when we are death's harbinger, charging a woman about to leap from a cliff.

But what I imagine can wait, for there is more to this story ahead and it begs my attention. Stepping forward, I arrive at the heart of the drawing, face to face with the defining tragedy of the story: A woman flings herself from a cliff while a boy watches, a

Figure 10.5. Detail of woman at cliff's edge

boy no older than 12, who now must bear witness (Figure 10.5).

Small wonder I pause here, poised at the edge of the drawing. Am I willing to step into this frame, this sliver of time Miguel has framed at the height of her leap? Dare I place my body alongside of this image and take it on faith that his drawing has something to teach me about death, about the gravitational pull of war and the leaps of faith we force children to take in the face of it. But ethic engagement demands unflinching commitment and performance commands the unflinching body, so I surrender to Miguel's story. I step up and into the pose of the leaping woman, raising my arms and reaching out and away in precisely the angle and attitude of the sky-bound figure. And instantaneously I experience an epiphany—like a lightning bolt of embodied insight—that I could not foresee from a distance because it cannot be grasped in abstraction. With arms raised and palms tips lifted, body arched and head high, eyes fixed on the far horizon, I *can feel* that the woman is not falling, but *flying*. In the second before gravity hits, her body is lifted and held by the updraft of her fierce intention, her courage to meet death on her own terms. From falling to flying, our mutual bodies are reconfigured by this simple adjustment in our line of vision. And for an imagined instant together, the woman and I reach up and away from the cliff until our bodies break free against the clear sky.

This is the moment the child has chosen.

This is the heartbeat of time he has captured.

This is the story he tells to live on, the story he *lives on* for the rest of his life.

As he was her witness, he is the one who must story her flight.

And story he does, this 12-year-old witness. Falling faint and ghostly down the face of the cliff, three ghostly figures juxtapose the flyer-in-flight. In the generative space between real and imagined, Miguel Ercano Garcia has drawn three palimpsest women, their contours grown so faint over time one need peer closely to see them. The first is bent double from the weight of her body descending, her head curving inward like a diver tucking the body before plummeting down to the sea. The second has grown larger and more clearly defined, her face aligned parallel to the rocks that await her. The third has turned outward (see Figure 10.6).

Figure 10.6. Detail of palimpsest face.

With commanding equanimity, this face—the single largest image in the drawing—looks out at the witness: the boy who is watching; the artist who's drawing; the witness attending; the body performing; the researcher writing; the reader imagining. Together we witness, across time and space, an image of death and defiance held in animating equipoise, and seen through the art of a child who lived on.

Coda: Palimpsest Bodies

I would like to imagine that Miguel Ercano Garcia grew to a ripe old age, that he saw peace return to his homeland, and that the ghosts of the civil war ceased to haunt him. I want to believe that he will be among the adult survivors of the *colonias* whom ALBA, or some other living archive of scholars and activists, find and commemorate. I hope that, ever after, when Miguel saw a man bent double with effort, or a mounted horseman on a chessboard, or a cliff diver raising his arms, or a tree on a barren hill, or the spray of water against rock, or the sun sitting on sea—I would like to believe that when these palimpsests of memory came haunting (and we can be sure that they did, ever after), he could raise up his arms and remember how to fly while he fell. And this thought gives me comfort; this thought gives me courage to bear witness in turn, by turning attention to a world where children draw pictures like this in the aftermath of wars that strike them.

I would hope that when strangers meet Miguel—and the hundreds of other children whose drawings survive—they are struck just as I was by the death-defying leaps of these artful memories. Perhaps they'll pay attention if they know how to look, if they can look through the eyes of a child who whose art may be his only remains. And I would like to imagine that, for the space of this essay, I have helped you do just that.

Notes

1. Portions of the UCSD collection and the Avery collection of 153 Spanish drawings at Columbia University are accessible through the museums' websites. Site-specific, digitized collections from contemporary warzones are increasingly common, as networks of researchers, social service workers and peace activists continue to work with and for the children of war.

2. The title is an homage to the 1938 exhibit of drawings with a catalog introduction by Aldous Huxley; the 2002 collection features a Foreword by Robert Coles.

3. Miguel Ercano Garcia is not among the children located by Anthony Geist as part of his ongoing preservation of *colonias* materials and narratives. It is not known if the boy survived the war, nor at which of the colonies he resided at the time of this drawing.

4. An early version of this performance piece appeared in the ALBA publication, *The Volunteer* in 2004.

5. Permission to reproduce this image was granted November 24, 2010, by the Mandeville Special Collections Library, UCSD. All subsequent images are close-ups of this drawing.

References

Abraham Lincoln Brigade Archives (ALBA) (2011). History of the VALB and ALBA. http://www.alba-valb.org/history/history-of-alba (accessed January 18, 2011).

Batinski, M. (2005). Remembering the VALB. *The Volunteer: Journal of the Veterans of the Abraham Lincoln Brigade, 27*, 4, 17.

Buckner, N., Dore, M. & Sills, S. (Producers/Directors). (1984). *The good fight: The Abraham Lincoln Brigade in the Spanish Civil War.* Motion picture. New York: First Run Features and Kino International.

Coles, R. (2002). Foreword: Children's art in wartime. In A. T. Geist & P. N. Carroll (Eds.), *They still draw pictures: Children's art in wartime from the Spanish Civil War to Kosovo* (pp. 6–11). Urbana: University of Illinois Press.

Garcia, M. E. (ca. 1936–1939). *Drawing*. [colored pencil]. Southworth Spanish Civil War Collection, (plate 10). Mandeville Special Collections Library, University of California, San Diego.

Geist, A. T. & Carroll, P. N. (2002). *They still draw pictures: Children's art in wartime from the Spanish Civil War to Kosovo*. Urbana: University of Illinois Press.

Giroux, H. A. (1988). *Teachers as intellectuals: Toward a critical pedagogy of learning*. New York: Bergin and Garvey.

Glazer, P. (2005). *Radical nostalgia: Spanish Civil War commemoration in America*. Rochester, IL: University of Rochester Press.

Holman Jones, S. (2005). Autoethnography: making the personal political. In N. K. Denzin & Y. S. Lincoln (Eds.), *The Sage handbook of qualitative research* (2nd ed., pp. 763–792). Thousand Oaks, CA: Sage.

Huxley, A. (1938). Introduction. In *They still draw pictures*. New York: The Spanish Child Welfare Association of America for the American Friends Service Committee. (Re-issued by Oxford University Press, 1939.) http://orpheus.ucsd.edu/speccoll/tsdp/frame.html (accessed December 12, 2010).

Madison, D. S. (2010). *Acts of activism: Human rights as radical performance*. Cambridge: Cambridge University Press.

Pelias, R J. (2004). *A methodology of the heart: Evoking academic and daily life*. Walnut Creek, CA: AltaMira.

Pollock, D. (1998). Performative writing. In P. Phelan & J. and Lane (Eds.), *The ends of performance* (pp. 73–101). New York: New York University Press.

Sills, S. (2007). *The Abraham Lincoln Brigade of the Spanish Civil War*. http://www.writing.upenn.edu/~afilreis/88/abe-brigade.html (accessed December 10, 2010).

Spry, T. (2006). A "performative-I" copresence: Embodying the ethnographic turn in performance and the performative turn in ethnography. *Text and Performance Quarterly*, *26*, 4, 339–346.

Spry, T. (2009). Some ethical considerations in preparing students for performative autoethnography. In N. K. Denzin & M. D. Giardina (Eds.), *Qualitative inquiry and human rights* (pp. 158–170). Walnut Creek, CA: Left Coast.

Weissberger, J. A. (1938). Editor's note. *They still draw pictures*. New York: The Spanish Child Welfare Association of America for the American Friends Service Committee. (Re-issued by Oxford University Press, 1939.) http://orpheus.ucsd.edu/speccoll/tsdp/frame.html (accessed December 12, 2010).

Chapter 11

Fathers, Sons, and Protest at the School of the Americas

Countering Hegemonic Narratives of Masculine Might and Militarism

Tami L. Spry

This essay, written in 2006, is a collage of narratives from the men in my life as they respond to questions of masculinity and the military. The collage includes excerpts from interviews with my husband, my son, and the letter that accompanied my father's Bronze Star in 1946; my father died in 2003. The interviews were conducted when my husband of 27 years, Barry, was 52; he is a veteran of the Marines during the Viet Nam war years. Our son Zeb was 16. The inspiration of this essay came from my husband and son attending the protest at the School of the Americas (SOA) for 8 straight years. The SOA is a military installation that, among other things, trains U.S. and South American military in "information extraction."

Citation for the Bronze Star Medal from the Office of the Commanding General United States Army, Western Pacific, 26 January 1946:

> Technician Fifth Grade KIRK W. SPRY, 36586930, Infantry, United State Army. For heroic achievement at Zamboanga, Mindanao, Philippines, from 10 March to 12 March 1945, in connection with military operations against the enemy.

My dad was a decorated WWII soldier in the Army. My uncle was a drill sergeant in the Marines. My brother worked on Navy helicopters in the Atlantic. My husband was in the Marines during Viet Nam. My nephew was in the Navy 4 years. My son has turned 16, is an outspoken leftist political radical, but still by his own admission, finds himself sometimes seduced by the mountain-climbing Internet-surfing jet-flying muscle bound "high and tights" flashing across any number and manner of screens. The tail of these images wagging the dog of masculinity. And my son is 16.

Zeb

> The commercials make it look like a valuable, a valuable learning experience that'll turn you tough as nails. The commercials show guys doin, you know, cool technical stuff and this and that and they show them jumping out of helicopters, jumping over walls and stuff. And you know, with rock music in the background, [which] makes it look more tough and quote unquote masculine.

❧ ❧ ❧

I interviewed my son, Zeb, and my husband Barry for this essay. Asking them about manhood and the military was a little like listening through a door, not because the conversation was secret, but because manhood and its entanglements with representations of the military are a kind of knowing that they share apart from me as surely as if I were in another room. Though we are a tight family unit, cultural perceptions of masculinity are sometimes like a homeland security system constructed within our safe and warm family borders with and without our complicity. The gendered borders between us are geopolitical, written on our bodies in the lead of pencils and bullets.

In December 2006, the Republican National Committee released a new web video, writes Joan Vennochi of the *Boston Globe*: "It features a white flag of surrender and the theme: 'Our country is at war. Our soldiers are watching, and our enemies are too. Democrats: Retreat and Defeat is not an option.'" The video highlights critical comments about the Iraq war made by Howard Dean, John Kerry, and Barbara Boxer.

"In essence, for the GOP," writes Vennochi, "'staying the course' is a measure of strength and masculinity. Democrats who question administration policy regularly find their manhood under attack."

But I think things might be changing a bit what with eight generals speaking out against the secretary of state.

Zeb

I said to a couple of kids at school, I don't really like the military. And one of them said, "Well if it wasn't for the military you wouldn't have your freedom," which is a bunch of BS because the reason we have our quote unquote freedom is because of the Revolutionary War and the Revolutionary War wasn't military, that was militia. Those guys gathered up the only guns they had, which wasn't from the military, and they they just did what they had to. It was a revolution. "It wasn't "the military." So, yeah, there's that.

※　　※　　※

Bronze Star

As the driver of a Landing Vehicle Tracked in an Amphibian Tracktor Battalion, technician Fifth Grade SPRY participated in the initial assault on Zamboanga, Mindanao. Following the landing, he drove his vehicle along the beach toward the city in order to mark the position of the Infantry front lines for Naval gunfire supporting the advance upon the enemy.

Barry

Both my older brothers were in the Air Force during the Viet Nam war. I kind of took [my older brother] Micky's advice on most things up to that time, but he was away of course. And my dad was not around. And the reason was, to go in the service, ah, was a way to get the GI bill and go to college. But the GI bill now isn't what is used to be.

※　　※　　※

My Dad was given the Purple Heart and two Bronze Stars in WWII. He was with Special Forces. He seldom to never talked about his time in the military. My recollections of his war stories are disjointed because he would start to break down during the telling. I would become so shocked and concerned about his tears that it was hard for me to listen even while I hung on every word. Moreover, he would tell the stories only to my brother and, later, to my husband, but never directly to me. I heard the stories only if I happened to be there.

Bronze Star

After enemy machine gun fire had pinned down the Infantry troops and again halted the advance, he maneuvered the tractor into a position to give supporting fire which enabled the attack to continue once more. Without regard for his own welfare, he dismounted from the vehicle and assisted in placing two wounded, helpless Infantrymen in it despite the heavy machine gunfire, and returned them to the rear area for medical aid.

Barry

I went down and talked to the Air Force recruiter sometime in my senior year. And all the recruiters were all in the same building and the offices were side by side. But the Marine posters really stood out. It showed these guys leaping over the logs and they got these high and tight hair cuts and they're carrying guns and they have a look on their face like their not takin' any bullshit. I saw that as very tough and I thought, "Well they could make me into a Marine." And without a dad at home and anybody to tell me that it was OK for me to be who I was. ... I had a lot of self-esteem problems and I thought, "Hey going into the Marines would be a good idea."

☙ ☙ ☙

Zeb

Kids that have the military stickers on the back of their cars feel like they have to join the military to be a man, they want to learn how to fight and shoot a gun and kill someone. Probably cuz their dad didn't really ever talk to them about being a man. And the stereotype is being a man is a tough killing machine, I assume.

❀ ❀ ❀

Michael Kimmel (2004) writes about the ways in which fear operates in dominant representations of masculinity. He argues that men are ashamed to be afraid.

Joan Vennocchi of the *Globe* writes: "Charles Knight of the Commonwealth Institute, a public research center in Cambridge, has spent time analyzing what he calls the 'toughness discourse' in American politics, especially after 9/11. When it comes to national security, he says, 'tough' means 'using violence as a priority tool for international relations.'"

"Backed into a corner," continues Vennocchi, "by conservatives who equate 'liberal' with unmanly and weak, Democrats are buying into their opponent's definition, that violence solves every dispute."

Zeb

Another thing is video games, and I love video games, and some really dumb kid, say he's interested in video games, he may want to join the military because he figures it's the same as video game. But of course, it's completely different because you'd actually have to see someone die and see you're friends die in real life rather than virtually in the game.

❀ ❀ ❀

Barry

I thought it would make me a man. If I became a Marine, there would be no doubt that I was a man. I needed a rite of passage. I think that's one thing the military does for boys, because we're talking about boys here, we're not talking about men.

For me, there is no such thing as, "today I did this and now I'm a man." I think it's ah, a matter of years of thoughtful introspection over many years that makes you think like "OK, yeay, I'm a man now." And I think a lot of that has to do with being a good father, being a good husband, being a good person, and knowing the game. Cus, this is a game that we're talkin about here, this is a big game this military thing. the leaping over logs and the propaganda to make you think, "Oh, yeay, I want to do that!"

※ ※ ※

Dad used to wake screaming into the night from his dreams of WWII. He couldn't watch anything on TV that in any way resembled Mindanao Philippines or her people. The TV would seem to catch him in its grip. Helpless to turn away, he would weep. Hard.

In an exceptionally rare time, he told of a mission where he and twenty-five other men had captured close to seventy-five combatants. After believing that they had disarmed the enemy, Dad and his group relaxed to have a smoke. Suddenly, from the middle of the prisoner's group, a hand grenade was lobbed into the middle of dad's group. At this point in the telling, Dad's voice would break, "There were only a few of us left alive. We had to take them out; we had to take them out." They sprayed the seventy-five men with their machine guns. None were left alive.

Craig Gingrich-Philbrook (1997) writes of personal narrative, "The story comes, after the accident, to identify the body."

Barry

> I wanted Zeb to be around strong men who work for peace. And in [my work against] the School of the Americas, I feel like I'm doing so much more good than I did in any of my 4 years as s Marine. I feel like I'm doing something good for myself, for my family, country, people in the world. And I'm glad to have Zeb as a part of that. And I hope he looks back on this and carries on something, it doesn't have to be the same thing but anything that makes him feel good about being a man. It's something he and I share.

※ ※ ※

To be or not to be all that you can be seems to be the question. We went to see *Hamlet* at the Guthrie last month. And while Zeb enjoyed what I thought was an overly energetic and anxious Hamlet, he also liked the guns. The play was set in Europe's WWI. I am not upset that he likes the guns. I become worried about what the guns are attached to symbolically. I become worried that the guns are viewed as an "absolute" symbol of power and powerful communication. It is almost impossible to counter this narrative. And yet, my son did find a way.

Zeb

I think being involved in the SOA makes a guy a better man cuz ah, someone, someone scared is immediately gonna ah, take the easy action of just, you know, fight. But someone whose not scared is gonna step up to someone who has the guns and say, "Stop. I have no gun, you know, but I have a voice and I think you should stop killing and stop causing war and murder, you know, world-wide murder." The guys with the guns are hiding behind their guns. The gun is their voice, you know, the soldiers of SOA their gun is their voice and their crotch is their voice because there's rape. That may sound kind of weird, but it's true. But these other guys at the protest, they have more things to say rather than ah, the gun blast you know. They talk about why it's wrong.

❀　　❀　　❀

Barry

I never know what Zeb's going to say when he does say it. But this last time on the trip to the School of the Americas protest he, ah, everyone wanted to hear him speak about his arrest experience. He was nearly arrested. And he spoke about his adventure and how he felt about it, and I was very proud of him. I felt like for Zeb that was kind of a rite of passage. He went through something that could have been bad and he handled it very well.

❀　　❀　　❀

Bronze Star

By his initiative, and courageous devotion to duty, technician Fifth Grade SPRY contributed to the successful completion of an important mission on Mindanao and averted the possible loss of two comrades' lives.

—Citation to accompany General Orders No. 50
Headquarters United States Army forces
Western Pacific, dated 26 January 1946

References

Gingrich-Philbrook, C. (1997). Refreshment. *Text and Performance Quarterly*, 17, 4, 352–360.

Kimmel, M. (2004). Globalization and its mal(e)contents: The gendered moral and political economy of terrorism. In M. Kimmel, J. R. Hearn, & R. W. Connell (Eds.), *Handbook of studies on men and masculinity* (pp. 414–431). Thousand Oaks, CA: Sage.

Vennochi, J. (2006). Common ground remains key. *Boston Globe*, December 7. http://www.boston.com/news/globe/editorial_opinion/oped/articles/2006/12/07/common_ground_remains_key/ (accessed January 15, 2011).

Chapter 12

Learning to Remember the Things We've Learned to Forget

Endarkened Feminisms and the Sacred Nature of Research

Cynthia B. Dillard

(Nana Mansa II of Mpeasem, Ghana)

The Question of Memory

I can remember the day as if it were yesterday. ... Ma Vic, with whom I stayed during my time in the village, was not only my dear friend, but my guide in the maze of the market. She had her favorite sellers: the woman from whom she bought baskets of plump red tomatoes; another woman her plantain, another yam; still another, her spices and food staples. And as a regular customer, her loyalty was rewarded with the expected "dash" of a few extra onions or an additional handful of rice. As Vic very confidently maneuvered her way through the market, I warily negotiated the open sewers, the sharp corners of the metal roofs, and the young market women who, without a stall, carried their store—big trays of fish or mango or other goods—on their heads. So my eyes faced downward most of the time, tenuously watching every step. My observations of the market were primarily at the places where we stopped to make a purchase, the places where my eyes could focus on what was around me and not on my feet.

We stopped at the plantain woman's stall. "My sister!" the woman exclaimed, greeting Vic with the enthusiasm of someone who knows she's going to make a big sale. "You are welcome," she said to me, the customary greeting in Ghana when you haven't seen someone for a while. Her smile was warm, seeming to remember my presence on previous visits to her stall. Exchanging more small talk in Twi, Vic and the woman began their search for the biggest and the best plantains in the pile. And that's when our eyes met. About 70 years old, this woman (possibly the aunt or mother of the seller) was sitting in the shadows of the stall. She stared at me, a clear combination of curiosity and suspicion in her eyes, yellowed with age. She looked me up and down. I smiled at her, very uncomfortable with her unwavering gaze. As Vic and the seller were finishing their transaction, the old woman reached over and touched Vic's arm, her face now absolutely perplexed, nodding in my direction: "What *is* she (me)? Is she a white woman?" I nearly fell over, a rush of emotions running through me, from absolute horror to disgust to disbelief to sadness. Vic giggled and explained to the woman (who had still not quit staring at me) that I was not a white woman but a black American.

That evening in my researcher's journal (and through confused, angry, and sad tears that could've filled a river), I wondered aloud as I wrote: "How could she see *me* as a white woman?" "Couldn't she see the African woman I could see in myself?" "Didn't she know what had happened to millions of Africans who'd been forcibly taken from the shores of Ghana and other West African countries?" "Where did she think we had gone?" "Had she never imagined that some of us would return?" "How can this sister/ mother see me this way?" On reflection, what frightened me most about her question was that, at that very moment, I couldn't answer it myself:

> What had been the rather solid taken-for-granted nature of my African American identity—an identity that I'd used to make sense of myself—melted down like butter on a hot summer's day in that moment in Ghana. Something very rich that I loved dearly had become useless fat on the sidewalk, no help whatsoever in explaining and understanding what she saw, or who I was. But I know there is wisdom in her question or it wouldn't have come to teach me a lesson. If I'm to "be" a researcher in this space, I will have to struggle with the butter on the sidewalk,

the shifting ground of African identity through Ghanaian eyes. Neither here nor there (Ghana or the US), neither African nor American, neither recognizably Black nor white. Maybe it's not either/or: Maybe it's both/and? Somehow, it feels like it's beyond these dualities. They seem too simple. Regardless, it hurts to do this work. (Journal, 1/22/98)

And this pain stayed with me until the following week, when market day came again:

Today is market day again. Honestly, I'm dreading it. But I don't think there's an acceptable excuse not to go and help. ... As we approached the plantain seller's stall, my stomach churned and my nerves were shattered, afraid of what "insult" (however innocent) would come from the old lady. Vic, oblivious to my inner turmoil, again greeted the plantain woman and went about her business. But before I could properly greet the seller, I glanced to my right and caught the eye—and the smile—of the old lady. "Morning Black American lady! How are you?" she says happily, clearly concentrating hard to speak to me in her heavily accented English. I replied in my equally faltering Twi: "Me ho ye," ("I'm fine.") And she reached over and grabbed my wrist. "Black American. Yea." (Journal, 1/29/98)

This story is from my book *On Spiritual Strivings* (Dillard, 2006a). In the book, I sought to examine the ways that centering spirituality in an academic life transforms its very foundations, creating the site for spiritual healing and service to the world. And I chose to begin this talk with that story because it is still on my mind and in my heart, gnawing in the pit of my gut. "*What is she?* Is she a white woman? A black American—yea!" Both the question and the way the old lady asked it threw my entire sense of who I was into confusion. Yet, in retrospect, it is in the answer to that question that I have come to better understand my self, my life's purpose and a new direction for my work.

What I would like to do in this chapter is to try to reflexively read and remember this story and so many others created and lived by black women everywhere, to make visible the spiritual, cultural, and ritual memories that are necessary to appreciate the complex and contested spaces and places of black women's lives in our fullness. What I am also suggesting here is that you too must travel with me/with us in this journey, in the same engaged process of re-membering and seeing what Busia (1989) calls our "icons of significance" as well. This is our re-search *together*, in community, the goal being to develop a better sense of reading the Diaspora, of truly being able to see Africa's children at home and in the New World. And although this may seem like a very private and singular her/story of travel, journey, awakening, and cultural memory, it might also be read/considered as a metaphor of the history/herstory of African people as we traverse and settle, move, and create homeplace in the New World and Africa as well.

These memories are about the concrete aspects of our lives, where meaning—within our memories—"becomes what we can read and what we can no longer or could never read about ourselves and our lives" (Busia, p. 198). Busia goes on to say: "This act of reading becomes an exercise in identifications—to recognize life experiences and historic transformations that point the way toward a celebration, a coming together attainable only through an understanding and acceptance of the demands of the past, which are transformed into a gift of the future" (p. 198).

And as researchers, we will read and hear differently, and at varying depths, depending on our ability to read productively, to read the signs along the way.

Central to my thinking about the meanings of culture and race in research and other decolonizing projects is an often unnamed element of identity, one that is inherent in the acts of research and teaching. And both are *deeply embedded in the act of memory and of re-membering*. Often in research by scholars of color and others, we see that racial/cultural memory is at least part of what is raised up in our on-going quest to be "seen" and "heard" and "unlimited" in the myriad ways we approach our questions, our scholarship (see Alexander, 2005; Coloma, 2008; Daza, 2008; Strong-Wilson, 2008; Subedi, 2008; and Subreendeth, 2008 for examples). In common, memory can be thought of as a thing, person, or event that brings to mind and heart a past experience—and with it, the ability to "re"-member, to recall and think of *again*. The *American Heritage Dictionary* (2000) goes so far as to say that to remember is "to bear in mind, as deserving a gift or reward" (p. 597). And the very intimate nature of research narratives like the story from Ghana suggests that memory is also about an *awakening*, an opening to the spirit of something that has, until that moment, been asleep within us.

For many researchers of color, embracing an ethic that opens to spirit is fundamental to the nature of learning, teaching, and by extension, research. We seem to inherently recognize that such spaces and acts—and our memories and ways of being with/in them—are always and in all ways also political, cultural, situated, embodied, spiritual: They are alive and present within us. However, all too often, we have been seduced into forgetting (or have chosen to do so), given the weight and power of our memories and the often radical act of re-membering in our present lives and work, that is remembering as a decolonizing project. And if we assume, as I do, that the knowledge, wisdom, and ways of our ancestors are a central and present part of everything that has existed, is existing, and will exist in the future, then teaching and research must also undertake an often unnamed, unrecognized, unarticulated, and forgotten task that is important for individuals who yearn to understand ways of being and knowing that have been marginalized in the world and in formal education. Simply put, *we must learn to re-member the things that we've learned to forget.* Whether through wandering into unfamiliar/always familiar contexts, making conscious choices to use/not use languages and cultural wisdom, or strategically choosing to cover or uncover, in returning to and re-membering, an awakening in research and teaching is possible and powerful. And there are several lessons we must learn to remember, to answer the question asked by the old lady: *What is she?* The first lesson we must recognize and remember is embedded in this very story, a lesson that many African-ascendent people already know:

> Being scattered in diaspora is an act of dispossession from our past, from our original homeland, from our languages and from each other. We must re-member, "to see again the fragments that make up the whole, not as isolated individual and even redundant fragments, but as part of a creative and sustaining whole." (Busia, 1989, p. 197)

So part of the old lady's questions is about remembering as an act of piece-gathering. But the bigger part of this lesson is about seeing ourselves in the gaze of another and not looking away, but looking deeper. It is fundamentally to answer the question: Who are we in relation to others—and staying long enough to find out.

A Memory in Time: Praisesong for the Queen Mother[1]

You woke me this morning
And I became part of Your divine plan
Chosen on this day
To be among the living.
You dressed me in a purple kaba[2]
And I became the color of royalty,
Traveling to the village in a dirty old van
That felt like my royal carriage,
The curtains drawn for the privacy
Of the new Queen Mother.
You introduced "Professor Cynthia Dillard"
To the Chiefs of the kingdom,
And I became my own desire
To know as I am known,
You honored my family name
On the front of the community center and preschool,
And I became my parents, their parents, parents, parents,
Those who, by virtue of the Blackness of Africa
Were considered by some
Not to be fully human,
But whose depth of humanity shone like the sun in this moment.
You brought my sister-mothers to bathe me in the soothing waters of life,
And I once again became the child of all my mothers
Marion Lucille Cook Dillard
Wanda Amaker Williams

Florence Mary Miller
Nana Mansa, the first,
And those unknown to me.
You wrapped me in the swath of traditional kente,
And I became the weavers of that cloth,
The men who learned from their fathers and their fathers'
fathers,
An art so special that had taken months and months
Of skill, patience, and love in its creation.
You sat me on my Queen's stool
And I became Nana Mansa II, Nkosua Ohemaa[3]
The spirit of Nana Mansa, the first, now residing
not in my head,
But in the stool,
She speaks centuries of cultural memories
directly to my heart, as an African American,
"I had many children, but you are the only one who has
returned."
You lovingly dress me in beads old and new,
Adorning my fingers with gold rings, my Queen's chain
around my neck,
And I became the precious riches and treasures of the
Universe
Now and then.
You fanned me with cloth and palms and bare hands,
And I became the wind
Carrying Your voice:
"Don't be afraid, Nana.
Trust me.
You have all that you need.
I will show you what you already know."
You poured libation
And called me into the sacred ritual of remembering,

And I became my own full circle as a researcher,
A searcher again, honoring the knowledge of
Who and what is here and there
Of what's been and is to be,
Inseparable realities, united by Your gift of breath,
A committed teacher and student of my own becoming.
You drummed and we danced
And with each beat,
I became the rhythms of my passed on ancestors,
Who gathered with us on that day
Brothers and sisters of the village, the community, the
diaspora,
A holy encounter indeed!
You gave food to feed the whole village,
And I became my own full belly,
And the too often empty bellies of the village children and
families,
For that moment, we were all satisfied.
Full.
Happy.
Joyful in Your bounty.
You've blessed me with life,
A chance to manifest extraordinary works
Through You.
By becoming all of myself
I can live not into the smallness of the world's expectations
But into the greatness of the true names
You've given to me.

Praisesongs are traditional types of poems, sung in various places all over the continent of Africa. They are ceremonial and social poems, recited or sung in public at celebrations such as outdoorings (in Ghana, a christening or naming ceremony) or anniverseries or funerals. Embracing the history, legends, and traditions of a community of people, praisesongs can be used to celebrate triumph over adversity, bravery and courage, both in life and death. They can also mark social transition, upward movement culturally, socially, or spiritually. While the meditation above is a praisesong to my ascent as a queen mother in Ghana, here's the question: How might our memories, our encounters and representations of those, act as praisesongs in the world? As we teach, conduct research, and examine and create texts—whether the research narrative, the lesson plan, the interview transcript, the representational text in publication—our sense of who we are, our identity, our very selves and spirits are seen/understood/recognized/grounded in our past: They make sense to us based on something that has happened (in memory) versus simply as a present moment or a future not yet come. I am arguing here that it is from our memories that we can recognize and answer the question: "Who am I?" and collectively "Who are we?" This isn't just about being able to recognize times past on a calendar or datebook. This is fundamentally to see that our known and unknown and yet-to-be-known lives as human being are deeply imbued with meaning that is based in our memory. Booth (2006) suggests that to answer the question of who we are, we have to go deep into the well of memory:

> to draw a boundary between group members and others; to provide a basis for collective action; and to call attention to life-in-common, a shared history and future. ... All of these involve claims about identity across time and change, and about identity and responsibility as well. ... Statement[s] of identity turn out to involve a strong *temporal* dimension. (p. 3; emphasis added)

This is also fundamental to an African cosmology, one that is based on understanding one's place, space, and purpose in time through recognition of a common destiny: I am because we are. And for those of us who think and feel ourselves into our scholarship through frameworks and paradigms that are African in nature and that just "*feels* right" to us[4] (Lorde, 1984, p. 37; emphasis added), we also recognize that we cannot feel or engage our scholarship without seeing that, as singer Dianne Reeves (1999) suggests in her song "Testify": "God and time are synonymous/ and in time God reveals all things/Be still/Stand in love/and pay attention." Within African spaces, time is not thought of in the abstract, but in relation to Spirit. Time is what has happened here, what continues to happen here, and the honoring of "the relationships that linger [here]" (Bargna, 2000, p. 25). This is one of the major ways that African cosmology challenges Western conceptions of time, space, and location: It is circular, based in past, present, and future as intricate connective, and collective webs of meaning making:

You honored my family name

On the front of the community center and preschool,

And I became my parents, their parents, parents, parents,

Those who, by virtue of the Blackness of Africa

Were considered by some

Not to be fully human…

That brings us to the second lesson: Our memories are based in a sense of connective and collective time, from which we both re-cognize our identities and from which we can trans-form those identities.

For example, any research of the African American might need to explicitly acknowledge the importance of the transatlantic slave trade and the Middle Passage as relevant experiences in the collective memory of African-ascendent personhood. The Middle Passage was the forced enslavement and forced journey of millions of Africans from Africa to the New World. Spaces associated with this trade in human beings—the slave dungeons that dot the western coast of Africa, the routes and rivers that were used for the inland walk to the coastal forts and dungeons, sites in the United States that commemorate the places where enslaved African people resisted and created new homes, new communities—are ripe with memory and with meaning for African-ascendent peoples who *chose* to remember, who *choose* to make pilgrimage to these spaces to feel, see, and better understand the place of such memories in the formations of our identities, our personhood.[5]

And although the events of the Middle Passage and slavery in the New World are now centuries old (and often unrecognized in the memories of many both on the continent of Africa and in the Diaspora), for those who choose to remember, these engagements have the profound ability to transform us, to bring us back to places (both literally and spiritually) that we hear in the praiseong: *"I had many children, but you were the one who returned."* How do we see these recognitions in our scholarship? *"Everything* about the placing of the questions of research is important here, as our lives and those of the participants we study are full of 'icons of significance'" (Busia, 1989, p. 201; emphasis in the original). With every question we ask, don't ask, answer, don't answer, it is crucial for us to recognize and remember that our participants are being forced to ask central questions of their lives as well. As we are "studying" literacy practices, or teacher education or the ways that African American culture shapes mathematics instruction, what does it really mean to say: "Tell me about yourself." Where is the place of racial/cultural memory of the Middle Passage there, both for the researched and the researcher? This is key, as so many "study" with/in/about African-ascendent communities. How do we—or might we—re-cognize the child you are observing as an *African* American, as connected to and collectively a part of the circle of African time? How is our entire enterprise shaped by the lack of memory of an event so very traumatic that it forever changed the very time, space, and spirit of humanity, that there would be no African American without it?

Irwin-Zarecka (1994) states that "personal relevance of the traumatic memory and not personal witness to the trauma [is what] defines community" (p. 49). But the power and relevance of the memory endures. It matters. An African cosmology requires that we see and better understand this persistence across time (it's enduringness, as described by Booth, 2006), as its presence describes one of the ways that the African community is bounded and has borders and cultural understandings that bind and define its members. Such boundedness within community when conscious and connected transforms one's identity such that the question "Who am I?" is no longer a total and bewildering mystery for African Americans and others in Diaspora. It may become, as we see in my praisesong imbued with meaning and with response-ability, both at the core of claims to membership from an endarkened feminist epistemology (see Dillard, 2000; Dillard & Bell, 2011; Dillard & Okpalaoka, in press). It is the time where we find ourselves a part of something bigger than what we already are.

One of the many ways that African feminist scholars working from/through endarkened frameworks are re-membering, or putting back together notions of time that honor and lift up "the relationships that linger there," is to attempt to ask a different set of questions, starting first with ourselves. These are the echoes that you heard in the praisesong, an interrogation of the ways that memory is always already there. It is the way that the sacred also shapes memory and is inseparable in memory. Within the temporal and physical movement that Africans in Diaspora have undergone, it is also what gives the memory shape within Western epistemological frameworks, including frameworks of feminism.[6] It is embedded in the ways that a researcher like myself can re-member, put it back together again:

By becoming all of myself

I can live not into the smallness of the world's expectations

But into the greatness of the true names

You've given to me.

What is needed are models of inquiry that truly honor the complexities of memories. Of indigenous and the "modern" time, experienced not just in our minds, but in our bodies and spirits as well. Frameworks that approach research as sacred practice, worthy of reverence. A way of thinking and feeling and doing research that honors the fluidity of time and space, of the material world and the spiritual one. Mostly, as we point out in recent work located in the slave dungeons in Ghana (Dillard & Bell, 2011), we need a way to inquire that acknowledges both the joy and pain of location/dislocation and the transformation of both in our stories: African women are not stories of a singular self, but are stories of *we*, collective stories deeply embedded in African women's wisdom and indigenous knowledges. In his discussion of the Middle Passage, Tom Feelings (1995) further and eloquently states:

I began to see how important the telling of this particular story could be for Africans all over the world, many who consciously or unconsciously share this race memory, this painful experience of the Middle Passage. ... But if this part of history could be told in such a way that those chains of the past ... could, in the telling, become spiritual links that willingly bind us together now and into the future, then that painful Middle Passage could become, ironically, a positive connecting line to all of us, whether living inside or outside the continent of Africa. (p. ii)

Formed as a question, what do such memories mean for the teacher/scholar of color (and conscience), and how might we more explicitly and systematically engage them, re-member what we have forgotten as a way toward healing not just ourselves but those with whom we teach and research? Turning back to Feelings (1995) above, he suggests first that such memories, from a spiritual framework, have the potential to connect those on the continent of Africa to those in the Diaspora, the result of the traumatic acts of the trans-Atlantic slave trade. This is a central characteristic of racial/cultural memories for all who live with/in Diaspora. So, first, *these are memories acknowledge an ever present thread between the Diaspora and the continent, a heritage "homeplace."*

It is not accidental that many scholars of color take up the exploration and research into/about connections to or with/in some version of an ancestral, heritage, or cultural homeplace and that our representations—in art, in inquiry, in personhood and identity—represent those cultural spaces and places. Second, *racial/cultural memories are intimate*: They are memories that, good or bad, make you ache with desire "to find the marriage of meaning and matter in our lives, in the world" (Mountain Dreamer, 2005, p. 42). I believe this may be true for Whites and others who have not carried or been politically or culturally marked or "racialized"—and it is worthy of being explored by all researchers, regardless of race. Such intimacy is inextricably linked to racial and cultural identities; that is, memories are part and parcel of the meanings of identity, of the meaning of who we are and how we are in the world. Husband (2007), in his work on African American male teacher identity, suggests that cultural memories are those memories of experiences and/or events related to collective and or individual racial/cultural identity "that are either too significant to easily forget or so salient that one strives to forget" (p. 10). He goes on to describe the fundamental nature and character of racial/cultural memories:

> In the case of the former, cultural memories can be thought of as memories of events as racial/cultural beings that are/were so remarkable that we consider them to be defining moments in our life histories. … Pertaining to the latter, race/cultural memories are those related to our racial/cultural identities that are so potent [often painful] that we tend to suppress [them] in order to function as human beings. (p. 10)

What we see here is that the intimate nature of racial/cultural memories and their work in identity creation is inseparable from what it means to be vulnerable in our work, from reaching down inside of one's self and across toward others to places that may "break your heart" (Behar, 1996)—but, like many courageous researchers, choosing to go there anyhow.

That brings us to the final part of a definition of racial/cultural memories: *They are memories that change our ways of being (ontology) and knowing (epistemology) in what we call the present.* They are inspirational, breathing new life into the work of teaching, research, and living. They are the roots we must first grow in order to have our leaves. They are memories that *transform* us, a place within and without that feeds our ability to engage new metaphors and practices in our work (Dillard, 2000).

The Claim of Memory

Here's lesson #3:

While remembering is about claiming, it is also about being claimed in a space of recognition that has "[held] your people to this earth" (McElroy, 1997, p. 2; emphasis added).

It's been lights off (no electricity) since about 7 pm. Around 7:30 pm, the seamstress arrives with my dresses. They are both really beautiful. But so was what happened with the purple kaba. The seamstress asked me to go and try it on so she could make any adjustments that might be needed. Given my experience with the old lady in the market, I was a little leery about what she might say once I put the dress on. I carefully tied my head wrap and tentatively came out of the side room. "Mmmmmm," she exclaimed, looking at me in my kaba, clearly in admiration. "Who tied it for you?' she said, pointing to my head wrap. "I did it," I said, realizing that I had done so in a manner that surprised her. "Turn around," she said sternly. And as her hand brushed down the back side of my body, I knew that, like the brothers earlier in the day, she too recognized [another] one of the many carry-overs of African womanhood that could not be oppressed or suppressed, even through the violence of the slave trade: The African woman's ass [as she wears the slit skirt]. She turned to Vic: "She **is** an African woman." So, however weak were our identifications of these links between us, as African women, they were clear and apparent to her and to me in that moment. And her look of recognition is one I will never, ever forget. (Journal, 1/22/98)

Irwin-Zarecka (1994) speaks brilliantly of how people make sense of the past, particularly relevant to this discussion of memories and personhood of African people. That is that, in a wholly racialized society, our collective memories are less about an intellectual "truth" about what we are referencing, what we are working to construct, what we desire to put back together again. That is spiritual and sacred work, the "rules" of which will be different for different groups of people. Mostly, these memories bear weight on the experiences being remembered for these different groups shape our claims to "mine," "theirs," "ours." I'm arguing here that this memory-work is critical for marginalized peoples, to be able to see ourselves more clearly in order to see how we are mutually recognized, mutually remembered, mutually mediated. Such memories are reference to the place that holds us to this Earth, the ways we are because we have been. And as researchers, while our claims to knowing are always subjective,

> it is the definition shared by people we study that matters. In many cases there is a rather radical difference between the observer's and the participants realities. ... But whether the past as

we understand it and the part as understood by our subjects are closer or further apart, we ought to consider both in our analysis. Our baseline is a needed standard for critical judgment and their baseline is what informs remembrance [and hence, the answers]. (Irwin-Zarecka, 1994, p. 19)

In many ways, this positions the qualitative researcher as a narrator and creator of memory, both her and his own and the collective memory of, the hearts and soul of humanity, in all its variations. However, for the black or endarkened feminist researcher, whose work is often deliberately situated in indigenous spaces and places, and focused on knowledge and cultural production, this is not simply the narration of a story: It is the *deliberate* work of engaging and *preserving* these stories, both of the "thing" itself and our engagements and experiences with it. But mostly, it is also our *duty*—our responsibility—to *remember*: We are those who can bear witness to our African "past," diasporic "present," and future as a full circle: That is, after all, what it means to be in community, to be in the spirit collectively. Let it be so.

Notes

1. Becoming a Queen Mother is part of a collection of meditations from an unpublished manuscript entitled Living Africa: A Book of Meditations. This is also in honor of Paule Marshall's *Praisesong for the Widow* (1984), a book that has had a profound influence on my thoughts on the endarkened nature of memory.

2. Kaba is a style of dress worn by Ghanaian women made from batik/wax print cloth. It consists of a fitted top, often embellished with very elaborate necklines, sleeves, and waist and a form-fitting skirt with a slit and a head wrap.

3. Queen Mother of Development

4. See Dillard (2006b) for a full discussion of paradigms and endarkened feminist thought.

5. For further explorations of these memories, see Dillard & Bell (2011). See also Dillard .(2008).

6. See Dillard & Okpalaoka (in press) for an in-depth look at the sacred and the spiritual in endarkened transnational feminist praxis and research.

References

Alexander, M. J. (2005). *Pedagogies of crossing: Meditations of feminism, sexual politics, memory, and the sacred*. Durham, NC: Duke University Press.

American Heritage Dictionary of the English Language. (2000). Boston: Delta Books.

Bargna, I. (2000). *African art*. Milan, Italy: Jaca Books.

Behar, R. (1996). *The vulnerable observer: Anthropology that breaks your heart*. Boston: Beacon.

Booth, W. J. (2006). *Communities of memory: On witness, identity, and justice*. Ithaca, NY: Cornell University Press.

Busia, A. (1989). What is your nation? Reconnecting Africa and her diaspora through Paule Marshall's *Praisesong for the widow*. In C. Wall (Ed.), *Changing our own words: Essays on criticism, theory, and writing by black women* (pp. 116–129). New Bruswick, NJ: Rutgers University Press.

Coloma, R. (2008). Border crossing subjectivities and research: Through the prism of feminists of color. *Race, Ethnicity and Education, 11*, 1, 11–28.

Daza, S. (2008). Decolonizing researcher authenticity. *Race, Ethnicity and Education, 11*, 1, 71–86.

Dillard, C.B. (2000). The substance of things hoped for, the evidence of things not seen: Examining an endarkened feminist epistemology in educational research and leadership. *International Journal of Qualitative Studies in Education, 13*, 6, 661–681.

Dillard, C. B. (2000). The substance of things hoped for, the evidence of things not seen: Examining an endarkened feminist epistemology in educational research and leadership. *International Journal of Qualitative Studies in Education, 13*, 6, 661–681.

Dillard, C. B. (2006a). *On spiritual strivings: Transforming an African American woman's academic life*. Albany: State University of New York Press.

Dillard, C. B. (2006b). When the music changes, so should the dance: Cultural and spiritual considerations in paradigm "proliferation." *International Journal of Qualitative Studies in Education, 19*, 1, 59–76.

Dillard, C. B. (2008). When the ground is black, the ground is fertile: Exploring endarkened feminist epistemology and healing methodologies of the spirit. In N. K. Denzin, Y. S. Lincoln, & L. Tuhiwai-Smith (Eds.), *Handbook of critical and indigenous methodologies* (pp. 277–292). Thousand Oaks, CA: Sage.

Dillard, C. B., & Bell, C. (2011). Endarkened feminism and sacred praxis: Troubling (auto)ethnography through critical engagements with African indigenous knowledges. In G. Dei (Ed.), *Indigenous philosophies and critical education* (pp. 337–349). New York: Peter Lang.

Dillard, C. B., & Okpalaoka, C. L. (in press). The sacred and spirtual nature of endarkened transnational feminist praxis in qualitative research. In N. K. Denzin & Y. S. Lincoln (Eds.), *Handbook of qualitative research* (4th ed.). Thousand Oaks, CA: Sage.

Feelings, T. (1995). *The middle passage.* New York: Dial Books.

Husband, T. (2007). Always black, always male: Race/cultural recollections and the qualitative researcher. Unpublished paper presented at The Congress of Qualitative Inquiry, May 3–6, University of Illinois, Champaign-Urbana.

Irwin-Zarecka, I. (1994). *Frames of remembrance: The dynamics of collective memory.* New Brunswick, NJ: Transaction Publishers.

Lorde, A. (1984). *Sister outsider: Essays and speeches by Audre Lorde.* Freedom, CA: The Crossing Press.

Marshall, P. (1984). *Praisesong for the widow.* New York: Dutton.

McElroy, C. J. (1997). *A long way from St. Louie: Travel memoirs.* Minneapolis: Coffee House Press.

Mountain Dreamer, O. (2005). *What we ache for: Creativity and the unfolding of the soul.* San Francisco: Harper Collins.

Reeves, D. (singer). (1999). Testify (audio recording). On album "Bridges." New York: Blue Note Records.

Strong-Wilson, T. (2008). *Bringing memory forward: Storied remembrance in social justice education with teachers.* New York: Peter Lang.

Subedi, B. (2008). Contesting racialization: Asian immigrant teachers' critiques and claims of teacher authenticity. *Race, Ethnicity and Education, 11,* 1, 57–70.

Chapter 13

Globalizing the Rural

The Use of Qualitative Research for New Rural Problems in the Age of Globalism

Isamu Ito

Globalization has had a deep impact on every part of the world. In general, it seems to have had a destructive effect on agriculture and has led to a fundamental transformation of rural communities. In addition, a few peculiar problems have arisen in highly industrialized countries like Japan. Rural researchers call them the "new" (or "post-productivist") rural problems to contrast them with the old (but still existing) ones that have centered on agricultural production.[1]

New refers to the following situations. While Japan's agriculture and rural society are on the verge of collapse, there is, strangely, an increasing interest in or concern with agriculture and rural life among city people. Moreover, policy makers and administrators are taking measures to promote this interest, and various media discuss rural life favorably to encourage this boom and to put rurality in a good light. Rural people have responded to this rise in interest in various ways. Some have gone along with it; others gone against it or gone their own way. As a result, competition has arisen about the social representations and the meanings of the rural.

How can we make the best use of qualitative research to address these new rural problems? In this chapter, I reflect about this question and then turn to my own qualitative research project on this topic.

Agriculture and Rural Society on the Verge of Collapse

Japan's agriculture and rural society are on the verge of collapse, although many older farmers still work hard to provide us with food and a few members of the younger generation have returned to farming. Since the 1960s, the status of agriculture and rural society have been declining along with industrialization. Globalization, specifically the trade liberalization of agricultural products in the 1990s (through the agreements on agriculture at the GATT [General Agreement on Tariffs and Trade] Uruguay Round and the foundation of the World Trade Organization [WTO]), has accelerated this decline. As a result, the production of agricultural products has decreased dramatically, and now the Gross Agricultural Output accounts for only 1% of gross domestic product. Accordingly, the food self-sufficiency rate has fallen to 40%, the lowest level in the world. Thus, Japan has become more dependent on imported foods from the United States, China, Australia, and other countries.

Along with this change, the population of farming and farm households has decreased and aged. In 2007, there were only 7.64 million farm households, 6% of the total population. Moreover, in 2009, there were just 2.90 million people engaged in farming, and 61% of them are over 65 years of age. Farmers have worked hard, but their income from farming has been too low for them to make a living at it. So they had to turn to off-farm jobs to make additional money. Nowadays, in most Japanese farm families, the younger members engage in off-farm jobs while the elderly engage in farming to hold onto their ancestral farmland. Because of this marked decrease in the farming population and farm households, farmers and their families are in the minority even in rural areas. Japanese farm families have managed to continue to live in their hometowns. However, in rural areas, especially in mountainous regions, many villages are disappearing and farmlands are increasingly being adandoned.[2]

Boom in Agriculture and Rural Life

Although these crises have become increasingly serious, strangely there seems to be an increasing interest in agriculture and rural life among city people. Last year, my wife and I drove to Kyoto to visit my daughter. On the way, in the countryside of Shiga prefecture, we came across an advertising billboard: "Rural Life on Sale!" What does that mean? It was an advertisement by a real estate agent who sells vacation houses with farming plots, where you can spend weekends farming in the countryside or settle there permanently. Presently, there are many real estate companies that sell these kinds of vacation houses throughout Japan. Here, you can see the frank expression of a commodification of rural space as well as enthusiasm for rural life among city people.

Indeed, there is a boom in agriculture and rural life among city people of every generation.[3] Let me describe a few examples. Figure 13.1(1) is a monthly magazine that is a guide to rural life for city people, and Figure 13.1(2) is another magazine featuring *teinen-kino*, which means the return to farming at the age of retirement. Figure 13.1(3) is the web page of a TV program, *Dash-Mura*, which is very popular among the younger generation.

(1) (2) (3)

Figure 13.1. (1) Monthly magazine *Inaka-Gurashi no Hon* [Guide to Rural Life], September 2009. (2) Monthly magazine *Gendai Nogyo* [Contemporary Farming] featuring farming after retirement, May 2006. (3) Web page of *Dash-Mura* (http://www.ntv.co.jp/dash/village/index.html).

In this program, the famous pop music band Tokio performs on their rural lives in a fictional village called Dash-Mura. The clever production of this program gives viewers a pseudo-experience of life in the countryside. Rural sociologist Motoki Akitsu (2007) analyzed this program to point out that we can see the desires of city people for rural life in Tokio's performances.

Interpreting the Boom

What makes city people so eager for agriculture and rural life? To paraphrase the discussions among Japanese scholars, based on empirical studies and some qualitative ones, we can point out the following interconnecting contexts.

First, a growing number of city people feel a lot of stress and alienation in their very competitive business life, school life, and social life, so they seek a kind of healing or peace of mind in farming and the green landscape.

Second, the more they depend on imported foods, the more anxiety they feel about the safety and security of food. Such anxiety makes city people seek safer domestic products and sometimes motivates them to farm for themselves.

Third, there seems to be nostalgia for the recent past among middle-aged and older people. Specifically in the 1950s and the 1960s (i.e., just before Japan's rapid economic growth), farming and rural life were familiar experiences for most people. A great number of current urban residents migrated from all over the Japanese countryside during the past 50 years. So, aspects of rural life are easily associated with memories of their home (see Tokuno, 2007).

Nostalgia often brings idealization. Let me describe two examples. Figure 13.2(1) is an advertisement of a collection of photographs of rural life in the 1950s and the 1960s (Sudo, 2004–2008). The catchphrase says, "We were poor, but we had good faces, dreams, and pride." What a frank idealization it is! It conceals a lot of suffering and troubles behind the pictures. Such an idealized and romanticized past seems to attract the younger generation who do not have any real experience in the preindustrial period. To borrow the phrase of anthropologist Jennifer Robertson, this can be seen as "nostalgia for nostalgia" (1988, p.

(1)   **(2)**

Figure 13.2. (1) Advertisement of *Shashin Monogatari Showa no Kurashi* (Sudo, 2004–2008). (2) Cover of *Japan Country Living* (Kato & Kimura, 2004).

495). A romanticized past also attracts foreigners. Figure 13.2(2) is a collection of beautiful photographs of very traditional rural living, houses, crafts, foods, and landscapes (Kato & Kimura, 2004). The author came from the United States, married a Japanese man, and stayed in Tokyo for 40 years. She wrote, "This is the journey to my home in my mind, and I'm determined to keep all of the old and beautiful things in these pictures before they disappear." A very sincere but very backward-looking gaze, isn't it? Yet this seems to be typical among urban residents.

Fourth, globalization brings uniformity or standardization, while it also seems to heighten the desire for one's own ethnic and cultural identity. And, as is often the case, people seek to find the archetypal image of Japan in preindustrial rurality: *Furuki Yoki Nihon* (the good old Japan). Some folklorists explain this kind of mentality and the situations involved with it in terms of *folklorism*, which means the invention of folklore or a decontextualized folklore (see Iwamoto, 2006; Nihon-Minzoku-Gakkai, 2003).

Policy and Media Promote the Boom

New agricultural policies promote this boom. The trade liberalization of agricultural products had a destructive impact on Japan's agriculture in the 1990s. As a reaction, the Japanese government made a big shift in agricultural policy. The concept of the "multifunctionality" of agriculture, which emphasizes the various roles of agriculture other than food production such as land conservation, water resources conservation, environmental conservation, creation of a beautiful landscape, and cultural inheritance, was introduced as a logical way to protect domestic agriculture in the negotiations on agriculture in the WTO.

Accordingly, the new policies have been applied to conserve the environment, the landscape, traditions, the culture, and the lifestyle in rural areas. For example, "green tourism" (tourism in which tourists stay with local people who live in the countryside and participate in farming or village activities) has been encouraged by the Ministry of Agriculture as a measure to revitalize the rural economy to preserve rural society. Some regions benefit from more tourists than others. In any case, the new policies encourage city people to be more interested in the countryside to further the boom and the commodification of rural life. And, as mentioned above, various media, including the Internet, take up the countryside in a favorable way to promote the boom and to dress up rurality.

Cultural Turn and Qualitative Research

Competition of Representations and Meanings

As a result of these developments, various social representations and meanings about rurality have appeared and compete with each other. This competition occurs relatively independently of the actual activities and crises of agriculture and rural life mentioned above. Roughly speaking, in this competition the urban side (urban residents, policy, and the mass media) has gained great advantage in exercising a powerful effect on the way Japan's agriculture and rural society are defined. The countryside, so to speak, is being captured by the outsider's gaze. For example, agricultural policies define agricultural production, and the expectations of "green tourists" direct the rural landscape and the behaviors of rural residents.

I don't think that this situation is in itself undesirable or harmful, because the growing interest and concern about the countryside can play important roles in reaffirming the values of farming and rural life. However, the languages of the urban side are so policy centered and consumer centered that they diverge from the actual contexts of farming, rural living, and the communities. They may romanticize the rural rather than empower rural people. The most serious issue is that the voices from the countryside are less expressed and less heard. Nevertheless, various efforts to speak out have been made (see, e.g., Kishi, 2009; Tenmyo & Sato, 2010; Une, 2005; Yamazaki, 2004), and we can see new magazines, books, and websites of farmers and rural residents (see

Figure 13.3. Various books and magazines published by farmers (Kakei & Shirato, 2009; Kishi, 2009; Tenmyo & Sato, 2010; Une, 2005; Utano, 2002; Yamazaki, 2004; *Agrizm,* September 2009, http://www. agrizm.jp/).

Figure 13.3). They (natives, newcomers, farmers, non-farmers, younger people, older people, women, men, and so on) respond to the urban side in various ways. Some go along with it, and others go against it or go their own way. But their voices are too quiet compared with the voices on the urban side. That is why I am conducting interviews with rural people.

Cultural Turn in Rural Studies

There are numerous opportunities for qualitative researchers to approach this problematique. In fact, recently scholars of the younger generation in Japanese rural studies have launched several kinds of qualitative research under the name of the "cultural turn," inspired by the work of scholars in Europe, Oceania, and North America.[4]

Some scholars study the representations or images of rurality among ordinary people in cities and in the countryside (see, e.g., Makino, 2008; Takahashi & Nakagawa, 2002), or their representations in popular culture (see, e.g., Ichinomiya, 2008). Others are engaged in discourse analyses of farmers' discourse practices, politics on food, and agricultural policies (see, e.g., Ikegami et al., 2008; Nakamura, 2008; Tokugawa, 1998), and another group focuses on "rural others" (e.g., rural women and newcomers) (see, e.g., Akitsu et al., 2007). It is my hope that various kinds of qualitative research flourish in Japanese rural studies.

My Project

Interviews on the Values of Farming and Rural Life

I wish to participate in the competition of social meanings of rurality through my own qualitative research project. That is, I want to conduct an inquiry aimed at reaffirming the values of farming and rural life from the standpoint of rural people,[5] while understanding and critiquing the representations and meanings of the rural among city people. In the final section, I will outline my ongoing project. This project explores how rural people value their farming and rural lives, specifically by analyzing their vocabulary, rhetoric, and logic, and studies the relationships between these values and the experiences of farming, family life, community life, and the media in the biographies of rural people.[6]

I am conducting semistructured interviews to collect the narratives of various types of rural people (mainly through individual interviews but sometimes through group ones), while also utilizing other narratives from books, magazines, and websites written, spoken, or run by rural people. I have adopted the interview as the main method precisely because we can have a dialog with interviewees to not only ask questions, but also to discuss the issues mentioned above. As for the methodological stance, I adopt a dialogic approach.[7] In the interpretation of narratives, I utilize the legacy of Japanese rural sociology, folklore, and history.

I selected interviewees using snowball sampling (starting with my friends and their network, which led to strangers). The criteria of selection are that interviewees should be positive in their farming or rural activities and that various types of rural residents (old, young, men, women, natives, newcomers, farmers, non-farmers, and so on) should be included. Through a series of questions (about twenty questions subcategorized from several points of view), I ask the interviewees how they value their farming and rural life and how they relate those values to their biographical experiences.

Standpoint of Living

As the inquiry is still ongoing, I cannot state anything conclusively, but I have learned much from the dialogs. Here are several provisional findings.

First, I have realized one thing that I felt for a long time but never asked directly. That is, most rural residents unanimously say they wish to lead their lives in the country as long as possible by somehow earning a living through farming and other jobs. This modest but earnest wish seems to be central to their values. They are ready to do anything they can to live in their native place or second home for a long time. Therefore, they would develop friendly relationships with people on the urban side, and they would even flatter city people and accommodate themselves to the language of policy or the market if it were somewhat beneficial to their life in the country. Japanese rural sociologists and folklorists have emphasized this stance and called it "the standpoint of living."[8] On this point, I have renewed my appreciation of the legacy of Japan's rural studies.

Rural residents would use flattery if necessary, but they do not want to fall under the control of the outsiders. So they seem to attempt the strategy of welcoming the new, urban, or outside factors while maintaining some autonomy. Some interviewees explained their viewpoints regarding this strategy.

Hyakusho **and** *Senzo*

Second, some old terms have new meanings in the narratives. These seem to be expressed sometimes self-consciously, and sometimes unconsciously. Here are two examples. One is *hyakusho* (farmer), and another is *senzo* (ancestor).

Hyakusho is a very old term. It originally meant "common people" or "farmer" and had no discriminatory connotation, but in the modern period it has often implied being poor, vulgar, ignorant, or outdated. Furthermore, it has been regarded as a politically incorrect term in the mass media, in education, and in official use, except as a self-descriptive expression. Recently, however, not a few farmers have begun to use this term self-consciously to show their pride in their work, their way of life, and their self-image (see Une, 2005). Among my interviewees, several farmers gave me name cards that declare their title as *hyakusho* or *donbyakuho* (mere farmer). As they have become farmers after pursuing careers in other jobs, they seem to be more aware of the significance of their farming in contrast with their former jobs. For them, farming is not just an occupation or a way of earning money but a way of life and a way of relating with other humans and nature. The politically correct term to signify a farmer in Japanese is *nomin* or *nogyosya*, but it does not convey the real sense of these farmers. The term is used only in formal settings. So they dare to use this old but potentially rich term. I cannot point out all their nuanced narratives on this term with my English, but surely we are witnessing an emergence of new values or revaluations of farming with the renewed old term. I will explore their variations and contexts in detail.

Senzo (ancestor) is similarly a very old term with many traditional meanings. It has been regarded as the most important key to the traditional Japanese family system, their faith, worship, custom, and so on. Although some fundamental changes have happened to rural families, we still often hear narratives around this term, especially among elderly native residents. Seemingly, their narratives express an old-fashioned conservative idea. In fact, for example, an expression of *senzo-daidai-no-tochi* (ancestral farmland) usually means that the farmland belongs to the patriarchal family and that it should be maintained and passed on from a father to his son, the heir. If that is the case, it is understandable that those who advocate a modern family and modern farming regard such an idea not as desirable but as an obstacle to remove.

However, when I interviewed Mr. and Mrs. Nagata, they explained to me, in their narrative, a very elegant usage of *senzo* that seemed to imply a way of thinking beyond the mere traditional one. That is, they think that farming and farmland should be maintained and taken over from generation to generation, but they do not insist on the traditional succession by the stem family or by close relatives. They welcome newcomers from cities and teach and assist them in their resettlement. So, in the context of their narrative, the term "ancestral" implies a sense of common ownership over generations. This is both a traditional and a trans-traditional sense, which may have a universal significance for the future of agriculture and rural society. I recently discovered it when I read the transcript repeatedly. I will visit this couple to discuss this point after I return home. My inquiry is obviously just in progress, but I feel it has great promise.

Notes

Acknowledgment

An earlier version of this paper was presented as a keynote address to the Sixth International Congress of Qualitative Inquiry, University of Illinois at Urbana-Champaign, May 27, 2010. I thank Norman Denzin for giving me this opportunity. I also thank the audience for their sympathetic feedback and insightful comments on my address. This work was supported by the Japan Society for the Promotion of Science KAKENHI (21530494). All of the figures were reproduced by kind permission of the publishers concerned.

1. I very much owe my understanding of this problematique in Japan to the discussions of the Japanese Association for Rural Studies (see Nihon-Sonraku-Kenkyu-Gakkai, 2005; Tachikawa, 2005).

2. Rural sociologist Akira Ono has invented the term *genkai shuraku* (village on the verge of collapse) to point out the harsh conditions of rural people's lives and of the communities in mountainous areas (Ono, 2005).

3. The opinion poll conducted by the Cabinet Office in 2005 (opinion poll on the exchange between city and rural districts) reveals that 38% of urban residents want to spend weekends in the countryside and that 20% want to permanently settle there.

4. On the cultural turn in Western rural studies, see Cloke et al. (2006), and see Akitsu (2007) on the turn in Japanese rural studies.

5. This project is intended to take over some of the tasks tackled by the works of Hosoya et al. (1993) and Soda and Ohara (1994).

6. On the setting of an agenda of qualitative inquiry, I have received valuable suggestions from Norman Denzin, especially his proposal of "interactionist-based cultural studies" and "interpretive interactionism" (Denzin, 1992, 2001).

7. As to the methodological stance on qualitative interviewing, Japanese sociologist Atsushi Sakurai has proposed the concept of "dialogical constructionism" (Sakurai, 2002), with which I sympathize. I also sympathize with the concept of "Inter-Views" by Steiner Kvale (Kvale, 1996).

8. Seeing things and events from the standpoint of rural people's lives has been emphasized in Japanese rural studies since the beginning (see Hosoya, 1998; Torigoe, 2002).

References

Agrizm (September 2009). Quarterly magazine. http://www.agrizm.jp/ (accessed February 12, 2011).

Akitsu, M. (2007). Karuchuraru-tan suru inaka (Cultural turn in Japanese rural studies). In K. Noda (Ed.), *Seibutsushigen mondai to sekai* (*Problems of bio resources and the world*) (pp. 147–177). Kyoto: Kyoto University Press.

Akitsu, M., Fujii, W., Shibuya, M., Oishi, K., & Kashio, T. (2007). *Noson jenda* (*Rural gender*). Kyoto: Showado.

Cloke, P., Marsden, T., & Mooney, P. (Eds.). (2006). *Handbook of rural studies*. London: Sage.

Denzin, N. K. (1992). *Symbolic interactionism and cultural studies: The politics of interpretation*. Cambridge, MA: Blackwell Publishers.

Denzin, N. K. (2001). *Interpretive interactionism* (2nd ed.). Thousand Oaks, CA: Sage.

Hosoya, T. (1998). *Gendai to Nihon noson-shakaigaku* (*Modern times and Japanese rural sociology*). Sendai: Tohoku University Press.

Hosoya, T., Kobayashi, K., Nakajima, N., Akiba, S., & Ito, I. (1993). *Nomin seikatsu ni okeru ko to shudan* (*Collectivity and individuality in contemporary farmers' lives*). Tokyo: Ochanomizu-Shobo.

Ichinomiya, M. (2008). Popyura-karucha ni okeru nogyo noson hyosho to sono henka (An analysis of the representation of agriculture and rural space in popular culture and its change). *Sonraku-Shakai Kenkyu, 29,* 1, 13–24.

Ikegami, K., Iwasaki, M., Harayama, K., & Fujihara, T. (2008). *Shoku no kyo-dotai* (*Toward solidarity through eating*). Kyoto: Nakanishiya.

Iwamoto, M. (2006). Toshi-dokei to fokurorisumu (Yearning for the urban and folklorism). In M. Shintani. & M. Iwamoto (Eds.), *Toshi to furusato* (*City and hometown*) (pp. 1–34). Tokyo: Yoshikawa-Kobunkan.

Kakei, J., & Shirato, Y. (2009). *Hyakusho Nyumon* (*Introduction to the way of farmers' living*). Tokyo: Shinsensha.

Kato, A. S., & Kimura, S. (2004). *Japan country living.* Tokyo: Charles E. Tuttle Publishing.

Kishi, Y. (Ed.). (2009). *No ni hito ari kokorozashi ari* (*Interviewing active farm-ers*). Tokyo: Soshinsha.

Kvale, S. (1996). *Inter views: An introduction to qualitative interview research.* Thousand Oaks, CA: Sage.

Makino, S. (2008). Hyosho to shiteno sizen to seikatsu-kankyo to shiteno sizen (Nature as representation and nature as an environment of living). *Ningen-Kagaku Kenkyu-Nenpo, 2,* 1, 67–83.

Nakamura, M. (2008). Nogyo-taiken eno manazashi to shokuiku no seidoka (Gaze upon agricultural experiences and the policy formation process of *Shokuiku*). *Sonraku-Shakai Kenkyu, 28*, 1, 38–49.

Nihon-Minzoku-Gakkai (Eds.). (2003). Special Issue: Folklorism. *Nihon Minzokugaku, 236*, 1, 1–188.

Nihon-Sonraku-Kenkyu-Gakkai (Eds.). (2005). Special Issue: Shohi sareru noson (Consumed rurality). *Sonraku Shakai Kenkyu, 41*, 1, 7–200.

Ono, A. (2005). *Sanson kankyo-shakaigaku josetsu (Introduction to the environmental sociology of communities in mountainous areas)*. Tokyo: Ochanomizu-shobo.

Robertson, J. (1988). *Furusato* Japan: The culture and politics of nostalgia. *International Journal of Politics, Culture, and Society, 1*, 4, 494–518.

Sakurai, A. (2002). *Intabyu no shakaigaku: Raifu sutori no kikikata (Sociology of interviewing: How to listen to life stories)*. Tokyo: Serika-shobo.

Soda, O., & Ohara, K. (Eds.). (1994). *Gendai Nihon no nogyo-kan (Outlooks on agriculture in contemporary Japan)*. Tokyo: Fumin-kyokai.

Sudo, I. (2004–2008). *Shashin-monogatari Showa no kurashi (Photo stories of life during the Showa period)*. Tokyo: Nobunkyo.

Tachikawa, M. (2005). Posuto-seisanshugi eno iko to noson ni taisuru manazashi no henyo (Postproductivist transition of rural Japan and transformation of its social representation). *Nenpo Sonraku-Shakai Kenkyu, 41*, 1, 7–40.

Takahashi, M., & Nakagawa, S. (2002). Hitobito no motsu noson-zo no tokucho (People's images of rurality). *Noson-Keikaku Gakkaishi, 21*, 2, 143–152.

Tenmyo, N., & Sato, J. (2010). *Tenshin! Riaru noka (Becoming a new farmer)*. Niigata: Niigata-nippo-jigyosha.

Tokugawa, N. (1998). Jiyuka to Inasaku-noka no ronri oyobi imi-sekai (Farmers' decisions and universe of discourse in an age of "struggle for existence"). *Sonraku-Shakai Kenkyu, 8*, 1, 22–33.

Tokuno, S. (2007). *Mura no shiawase machi no shiawase (Happiness in the countryside and happiness in the city)*. Tokyo: NHK Publishing.

Torigoe, H. (2002). *Yanagita minzokugaku no firosofi (Philosophy of Yanagita Kunio's folkore)*, Tokyo: University of Tokyo Press.

Une, Y. (2005). *Kokumin no tameno hyakushogaku (Study of farmers for the people)*. Tokyo: Ienohikari-kyokai.

Utano, K. (2002). *Inaka-Gurashi no Ronri (The logic of rural life)*. Fukuoka: Ashi-shobo.

Yamazaki, Y. (2004). *Inaka no hiroin ga jidai wo kaeru (Heroines in the countryside open a new epoch)*. Tokyo: Ienohikari-kyokai.

Index

About the Authors

Norman K. Denzin is Distinguished Professor of Communications, College of Communications Scholar, and Research Professor of Communications, Sociology, and the Humanities at the University of Illinois, Urbana-Champaign. One of the world's foremost authorities on qualitative research and cultural criticism, Denzin is the author or editor of more than two dozen books, including *Performance Ethnography, Reading Race, Interpretive Ethnography, Images of Postmodern Society, The Recovering Alcoholic, The Alcoholic Self,* and *Flags in the Window.* Most recently, he has completed two-thirds of a trilogy on the American West, *Searching for Yellowstone* (Left Coast, 2008) and *Custer on Canvas* (Left Coast, 2011). He is the editor of the landmark *Handbook of Qualitative Research* (1st, 2nd, 3rd, and 4th editions, Sage, with Yvonna S. Lincoln), and coeditor of the *Handbook of Critical & Indigenous Methodologies* (2008, Sage, with Yvonna S. Lincoln and Linda Tuhiwai Smith). With Michael D. Giardina, he is coeditor of *Contesting Empire/Globalizing Dissent: Cultural Studies after 9/11* (Paradigm, 2006), and a series of books on qualitative inquiry published by Left Coast Press, Inc.: *Qualitative Inquiry and the Conservative Challenge: Confronting Methodological Fundamentalism* (2006), *Ethical Futures in Qualitative Research: Decolonizing the Politics of Knowledge* (2007), *Qualitative Inquiry and the Politics of Evidence* (2008), *Qualitative Research and Social Justice* (2009), and *Qualitative Research and Human Rights* (2010). He is also the editor of the journal *Qualitative Inquiry* (with Yvonna S. Lincoln), founding editor of *Cultural Studies/Critical Methodologies* and *International Review of Qualitative Research,*

editor of *Studies in Symbolic Interaction*, and *Cultural Critique* series editor for Peter Lang Publishing. He is the founding president of the International Association for Qualitative Inquiry and director of the International Congress of Qualitative Inquiry.

Michael D. Giardina is an assistant professor in the College of Education at Florida State University. He is the author or editor of a dozen books, including most recently *Sport, Spectacle, and NASCAR Nation: Consumerism and the Cultural Politics of Neoliberalism* (PalgraveMacmillan, in press; with Joshua I. Newman) and *Sporting Pedagogies: Performing Culture & Identity in the Global Arena* (Peter Lang, 2005), which received the 2006 Most Outstanding Book award from the North American Society for the Sociology of Sport. In addition to a series of books edited with Norman K. Denzin on qualitative inquiry and interpretive research, Giardina is the editor of *Youth Culture & Sport: Identity, Power, and Politics* (Routledge, 2007; with Michele K. Donnelly) and *Globalizing Cultural Studies: Methodological Interventions in Theory, Method, and Policy* (Peter Lang, 2007; with Cameron McCarthy, Aisha Durham, Laura Engel, Alice Filmer, and Miguel Malagreca). His work has appeared in scholarly journals such as *Qualitative Inquiry, Cultural Studies/Critical Methodologies, American Behavioral Scientist, Policy Futures in Education*, and *Journal of Sport & Social Issues*. He is associate editor of the *Sociology of Sport Journal*, a member of the editorial board of *Cultural Studies/Critical Methodologies*, and the associate director of the International Congress of Qualitative Inquiry. With Joshua I. Newman, he is completing a book titled *The Health of Neoliberalism: Physical Culture and the Bio-Politics of Everyday Life*.

Contributors

Svend Brinkmann is a professor of psychology at Aalborg University, Denmark, where he is codirector of the Center for Qualitative Research. He is the author of many books, including *John Dewey—En introduktion* (*John Dewey: An Introduction*) (Copenhagen, Hans Reitzels Forlag, 2006), and P*syken: Mellem synapser og samfund* (*Psyche: Between Synapses and Society*) (Aarhus University Press, 2009), and editor of such books as *InterViews: Learning the Craft of Qualitative Research Interviewing* (Sage, 2008; with Steiner Kvale).

Gaile S. Cannella is the Velma E. Schmidt Endowed Chair of Early Childhood Studies and professor of teacher education and administration at the University of North Texas. She is the editor (with Marianne Bloch) of the *International Critical Childhood Policy Studies Journal* and the author and editor of multiple publications, including the following books: *Deconstructing Early Childhood Education: Social Justice and Revolution* (Peter Lang, 1997), *Kidworld: Childhood Studies, Global Perspectives, and Education; Childhood and Post-Colonization: Power, Education, and Contemporary Practice* (Routledge, 2004; with Radhika Viruru), *Embracing Identities in Early Childhood Education: Diversities and Possibilities* (Teacher's College Press, 2001; with Susan Grieshaber), and *Childhoods: A Handbook* (Peter Lang, 2010; with Lourdes Dias Soto).

Judith Davidson is associate professor of education at the University of Massachusetts-Lowell, where she teaches courses in qualitative research and action research.

Kathleen deMarrais is professor of lifelong education, administration, and policy at the University of Georgia. From 1999 to 2004, she was the coordinator of the Qualitative Inquiry Program, and from 2004 to 2009 she served as associate dean for academic programs in the College of Education at UGA. She has published numerous articles and book chapters, as well as books such as *Foundations for Research: Methods of Inquiry in Education and the*

Social Sciences (with Stephen D. Lapan; Routledge, 2003), *Life at the Margins: Profiles of Diverse Adults* (with Mary Beth Bingman, David Hemphill, and Juliet Merrifield; Teacher's College Press, 1997), and *Inside Stories: Qualitative Research Reflections* (Routledge, 1998)

Cynthia B. Dillard is professor of multicultural education in the School of Teaching and Learning at The Ohio State University. Her major research interests include critical multicultural education, spirituality in teaching and learning, epistemological concerns in research, and African/African America feminist studies. Most recently, her research has focused on Ghana, West Africa, where she established a preschool and was enstooled as Nana Mansa II, Queen Mother of Development, in the village of Mpeasem, Ghana, West Africa. She is the author of *On Spiritual Strivings: Transforming an African American Woman's Life* (SUNY Press, 2007).

Silvana diGregorio is a sociologist who founded SdG Associates in 1996 after 20 years in academia. She consults and runs training courses in a variety of software packages supporting qualitative analysis in the United Kingdom, Europe, and the United States.

Charles R. Garoian is director of the School of Visual Arts and professor of art education at Penn State University. He is the author of *Spectacle Pedagogy: Art Politics, and Visual Culture* (SUNY Press, 2008; with Yvonne M. Gaudelius) and *Performing Pedagogy: Towards an Art of Politics* (SUNY Press, 1999). His scholarly articles can be found in *Leonardo, The Art Journal, The Journal of Aesthetic Education, Journal of Visual Arts Research, Journal of Social Theory in Art Education, Journal of Multicultural and Cross-Cultural Research in Art Education, Studies in Art Education, Teacher Education Quarterly*, and *School Arts Magazine*.

Uwe Flick is professor of qualitative research at the Alice Salomon University of Applied Sciences in Berlin, Germany. He is the author most recently of *An Introduction to Qualitative Research* (4th ed., Sage, 2009), *Qualitative Research in Psychology*

(Sage, 2009), *Managing Quality in Qualitative Research* (Sage, 2008), and *Designing Qualitative Research* (Sage, 2008). Dr. Flick has also been a visiting scholar at various universities, including the London School of Economics, Cambridge University, École des Hautes Études en Sciences Sociales, Paris, and Massey University, New Zealand.

Kenneth R. Howe is professor in the educational foundations, policy, and practice program area and director of the Education and the Public Interest Center at the University of Colorado at Boulder. Professor Howe specializes in education policy, professional ethics, and philosophy of education. He has conducted research on a variety of topics, ranging from the quantitative/qualitative debate to a philosophical examination of constructivism to a defense of multicultural education. His current research is focused on education policy analysis, particularly school choice. His books include the *Ethics of Special Education* (Teachers College Press, 1992; with Ofelia Miramontes), *Understanding Equal Education: Social Justice, Democracy and Schooling, Values in Evaluation and Social Research* (Sage, 1999; with Ernest House), and *Closing Methodological Divides: Toward Democratic Educational Research* (Springer, 2003).

Isamu Ito is a professor of sociology in the Department of Regional Policy at the University of Fukui, Japan. He is the author of *Social Psychology of Social Interaction* (Hokuju Publishing, 2002) and translator (Japanese) of *The Sage Dictionary of Qualitative Inquiry* (2009) and the *Sage Handbook of Qualitative Research* (2006), among numerous texts.

Michelle Salazar Perez is an assistant professor in the Department of Curriculum and Instruction at Southern Illinois University, Carbondale. She has worked in Houston as the coordinator of Texas A&M University's student teaching program, Learning to Teach in Inner City Schools, and as an Arizona State University graduate assistant for the Navajo Early Childhood Education Partnership. Her dissertation research in New Orleans uses black feminist thought and other marginalized feminist, postmodern, and poststructural philosophies to reveal structures of power that have impacted access to public education for young children, especially those who are of color and/or poor. This philosophical lens also allows for community-based activism to be part of her overall research.

Elyse L. Pineau is associate professor in the Department of Speech Communications at Southern Illinois University, Carbondale. Dr. Pineau has been published in numerous professional journals, including *Text and Performance Quarterly*, *Qualitative Inquiry*, and *Liminalities: A Journal of Performance Studies*. She has also written, directed and adapted many performances, most recently, "The Penelopiad," an adaptation of the novel by Margaret Atwood.

Judith Preissle is Distinguished Aderhold Professor of Lifelong Education, Administration, and Policy at the University of Georgia and a Fellow of the American Educational Research Association. She is the author or editor of numerous books, including *The Handbook of Qualitative Research in Education* (with Margaret D. LeCompte and Wendy L. Millroy, Academic Press, 1992) and *Educating Immigrant Students in the 21st Century: What Educators Need to Know* (with Zue Lan Rong, Corwin Press, 2008).

James Haywood Rolling, Jr., is chair of art education and a dual associate professor in art education and teaching and leadership at Syracuse University. He is the author of *Cinderella Story: A Scholarly Sketchbook about Race, Identity, Barack Obama, the Human Spirit, and Other Stuff that Matters* (AltiMira Press, 2010). In 2006, he was awarded the Narrative and Research Special Interest Group (SIG) Outstanding Dissertation Award from the American Education Research Association (AERA) for his doctoral dissertation, "Un-naming the Story: The Poststructuralist Repositioning of African-American Identity in Western Visual Culture." His work has also appeared in journals such as *Qualitative Inquiry*, *Studies in Art Education*, *Journal of Aesthetic Education*, *Journal of Curriculum Studies*, and the *Journal of Curriculum & Pedagogy*.

Tami L. Spry is professor of communication studies at St. Cloud State University, where she teaches courses in performance studies and communication theory. Dr. Spry performs her autobiographical and autoethnographic work around the country, focusing on issues of gender violence, mental illness, race relationships, shamanic healing, and loss. She is currently working on a book, *Paper and Skin: Writing and the Performing the Autoethnographic Life*. Her publications appear in journals such as *Text and Performance Quarterly*, *Qualitative Inquiry*, and *Women and Language* as well as chapters in various anthologies.

Elizabeth Adams St. Pierre is professor and graduate coordinator of language and literacy education at the University of Georgia. Her work has appeared in a range of scholarly journals, including *International Review of Qualitative Research*, *Educational Researcher*, *Qualitative Inquiry*, *Journal of Contemporary Ethnography*, and *International Journal of Qualitative Studies in Education*. She is also the editor of *Working the Ruins: Feminist Postructural Theory and Methods in Education* (with Wanda Pillow, Routledge, 2000).